9/14(5)

FEB 2 1 2013

WITHDRAWN

UNDAUNTED

UNDA
★★★

UNTED

★★★

The Real Story of America's Servicewomen in Today's Military

TANYA BIANK

NAL
CALIBER

NAL CALIBER
Published by New American Library, a division of
Penguin Group (USA) Inc., 375 Hudson Street,
New York, New York 10014, USA
Penguin Group (Canada), 90 Eglinton Avenue East, Suite 700, Toronto,
Ontario M4P 2Y3, Canada (a division of Pearson Penguin Canada Inc.)
Penguin Books Ltd., 80 Strand, London WC2R 0RL, England
Penguin Ireland, 25 St. Stephen's Green, Dublin 2,
Ireland (a division of Penguin Books Ltd.)
Penguin Group (Australia), 250 Camberwell Road, Camberwell, Victoria 3124,
Australia (a division of Pearson Australia Group Pty. Ltd.)
Penguin Books India Pvt. Ltd., 11 Community Centre, Panchsheel Park,
New Delhi - 110 017, India
Penguin Group (NZ), 67 Apollo Drive, Rosedale, Auckland 0632,
New Zealand (a division of Pearson New Zealand Ltd.)
Penguin Books (South Africa) (Pty.) Ltd., 24 Sturdee Avenue,
Rosebank, Johannesburg 2196, South Africa

Penguin Books Ltd., Registered Offices:
80 Strand, London WC2R 0RL, England

First published by NAL Caliber, an imprint of New American Library,
a division of Penguin Group (USA) Inc.

First Printing, February 2013
10 9 8 7 6 5 4 3 2 1

LIBRARY OF CONGRESS CATALOGING-IN-PUBLICATION DATA:
    Biank, Tanya.
    Undaunted: the real story of America's servicewomen in today's military/Tanya Biank.
        p.   cm.
    Includes index.
    ISBN 978-0-451-23922-8
    1. United States—Armed Forces—Women—Biography.   2. Women in combat—United States.
    3. United States—Armed Forces—Military life.   I. Title.
    UB418.W65B53 2013
    355.0092'52—dc23   2012031014

Set in Adobe Garamond
Designed by Spring Hoteling

Printed in the United States of America

PUBLISHER'S NOTE
While the author has made every effort to provide accurate telephone numbers, Internet addresses,
and other contact information at the time of publication, neither the publisher nor the author
assumes any responsibility for errors, or for changes that occur after publication. Further, publisher
does not have any control over and does not assume any responsibility for author or third-party
Web sites or their content.

For my sister,
Colonel Maria A. Biank
United States Army

"All that I am, I will not deny."

—Joan of Arc

"And though she be little, she is fierce."

—*A Midsummer Night's Dream*, William Shakespeare

CONTENTS

PART II: DOUBLE TIME

PART III: IN THE TRENCHES

PART IV: DECISION POINT

UNDAUNTED

INTRODUCTION

★ Lieutenant Candice Frost and I first met on a scorching late-summer afternoon twelve years ago at Fort Bragg, North Carolina. I was a military reporter at the time for the local paper, the *Fayetteville Observer*, and was writing a story about servicewomen in the 82nd Airborne Division, an almost all-male unit whose mission is to parachute behind enemy lines, seize airfields, stake out ground, and pave the way for follow-on forces. At that time only 3 percent of the division's 15,000 paratroopers were women.

I came on post to interview the lieutenant because she was breaking new ground in the Army. For the first time in its history, the 82nd, an elite fighting force, had a female soldier assigned to an infantry regiment: Candice had recently been named as the assistant intelligence officer for the 505th Parachute Infantry Regiment—the only woman in the 4,000-member brigade.

As I sat across from Candice in a shaded office, the thin twenty-four-year-old redhead, two years out of West Point, sat up straight with an earnest look on her rosy-cheeked face, like a precocious student onstage about to win the spelling bee. It was evident that Candice had things to accomplish and dragons to slay, and she'd have no time for knuckleheads who got in her way.

"What if the unit jumps into combat but doesn't take you with them?" I asked.

"If you put me in this slot," Candice said, looking at me intensely with her blue eyes, "I'm going to war." It was easier for me to imagine Candice at my door selling Girl Scout cookies than with a helmet on her head, but her looks were clearly deceiving.

"Hell hath no fury if they don't send me," she continued. "They had enough faith to put me here. I am willing and able."

I scribbled in my notebook and continued my questioning. "What about soldiers who don't think you should be in an infantry unit?"

"The guys that have the biggest mouths, I say, come on, let's run." Candice was a marathoner, and being a good runner in the 82nd was as important as being a good shooter. "That's the great equalizer."

After we said our good-byes, I realized I hadn't expected her bluntness. But in a division where the male ego was as high as the operational tempo, I figured that attitude would serve her well.

On the last Sunday of August, on the front page of the *Observer*, the story ran with a headshot photo of Candice, her face covered in camouflage paint, lying prone and aiming an M4 at the camera, and when Candice arrived at work Monday morning, someone had cut out and taped her picture to the door of her office and everywhere else in the unit. She took the attention, however it was intended, in stride.

A few weeks later Candice got married to a fellow officer, an infantry lieutenant named Will O'Brien. Two days after her first wedding anniversary, planes hijacked by terrorists struck the Twin Towers and the Pentagon. The next decade put the American military on an unprecedented path of war service.

Candice and I would not talk again until ten years later. I was looking for the right mix of subjects for a book I wanted to write about women in the military. A mutual military friend referred me to a Major Candice O'Brien, now a mother of two getting ready to deploy for her second tour to Afghanistan.

"I think you interviewed me a long time ago at Fort Bragg for a story about women in the 82nd," Candice said when I contacted her. "Do you remember?"

How could I forget?

Candice is just one of many women whose service in the military has made a lasting impression on me. In the course of reporting, I've seen them in action, while sharing a tent in the Middle East, on board a boat in the South China Sea, along the DMZ in Korea, and on the side of a steep jungle mountain in Vietnam. We've shared stories, as well as granola bars and toilet paper.

More recently, as an Army wife living on military posts, I've gotten to know servicewomen off duty as neighbors, wives, mothers, and volunteers. I've sat beside them in church pews, on playground swings, at memorial services, and formal military balls. Over the last twenty-two years, I've had the privilege of pinning on my sister Maria's rank, as she rose from lieutenant to colonel, and I've been fortunate to have her as a neighbor at three duty stations, including our current one, where she is a brigade commander at Fort Eustis, Virginia.

I've come to recognize the issues these women face—professional and private, large and small, sad and funny—and I've admired their commitment and courage.

The purpose of this book is to give a full picture of military women, from the junior ranks to the highest echelons. Juggling marriage, motherhood, and the military may not be dramatic, compared to war service; and grappling with less tangible concerns about femininity, gender roles, and discriminatory labels may seem trivial when held up against true physical dangers. But even for women who choose a warrior profession, these are challenges that may affect serious decisions and have life-changing consequences. They are also the issues most servicewomen deal with daily and often out of public view. It is important, therefore, to shed light on these women's personal lives, including their behind-the-scenes struggles and insecurities. These are the things that give new meaning to their courage on and off the battlefield.

To be sure, servicewomen have long confronted problems of hazing, trying to belong to an old-boys' club, sexual harassment, dating, marriage problems, pregnancy, separation from children, questions about life goals, career trajectories, and self-worth. But today the context for all this is very different. The women are part of a military that little resembles the armed forces of the past.

Though women had been employed in the armed services since the

Revolutionary War, they could not exceed 2 percent of the active-duty force and couldn't be promoted beyond the ranks of lieutenant colonel or commander until Congress changed the law in 1967. Throughout the 1980s, half the jobs in the military excluded women. Then, in 1994, the Department of Defense did away with its direct-combat-risk rule and replaced it with a women's assignment policy. That policy said: "Service members are eligible to be assigned to all positions for which they are qualified, except that women shall be excluded from assignments to units below the brigade level whose primary mission is to engage in direct combat on the ground."

Because the soldier's workplace is the battlefield, in many ways Washington's "combat ban" remained the final frontier on employment gender discrimination. Yet the military has a history of effecting social change by employing women and giving them opportunities they would not have found elsewhere. That hasn't happened without controversy. In the nineties, as public debate raged over women and combat, senior female officers and congresswomen like Pat Schroeder of the House Armed Services Committee argued for across-the-board equality, while male military leaders and a number of lawmakers opposed such changes. The argument to keep women out of combat units centered on a number of issues: lack of strength, endurance, and temperament; lack of mixed-gender accommodations; a disruption to unit cohesion; and a distraction to fighting capability. Lawmakers were also concerned about the treatment of captured female soldiers and pilots and how it would play out on the evening news.

Events over the last decade essentially made many of these points moot.

In February 2012, after a year of reviews ordered by Congress, the Pentagon changed the policy to allow women to be "officially" assigned to combat battalions. It was like finally giving a team jersey to a player who had been hitting home runs on the field for years. In essence, the revision was catching up to the reality on the ground in Iraq and Afghanistan, where women were already serving in the battalions as intelligence and signal officers through a policy loophole that "attached" them to the units.

Today there are 194,000 women serving on active duty—14.5 percent of 1.4 million troops—plus 80,000 in the Reserves and 65,000 in the National Guard. There are 1.8 million female veterans in the United States. Since 9/11 more than 250,000 women have deployed to Iraq and Afghanistan, making them 11 percent of the fighting force. Many have served overseas multiple times, leaving today's generation of servicewomen with more war service than either their fathers or grandfathers.

In a great irony, female troops are often needed in near-frontline situations in Muslim countries, where they can defuse culturally tense interactions that involve local women. But this—and the fact that they serve as truck drivers, as medics, and as military police—has also placed them close to combat or other wartime dangers. More than 145 women have died in Iraq and Afghanistan, and more than 860 have been wounded.

Yet you can't measure the lives of military women through statistics. The military is not just a job but a way of life. It has always been a place of paradox, most evident by its curious mix of traditional men and unconventional women drawn to its ranks. The women who see the military as an attractive career are constantly pressed to prove themselves in a profession outside society's norms for women. They believe they can protect, defend, fight, and lead, despite conventional wisdom.

In *Undaunted* I explore in depth the lives of four active-duty servicewomen, all of whom are leaders and professional standouts, over a crucial few years of their careers that take them from beginnings and hard work to choices, changes, and growth. It is not easy to achieve a dream in the military. Servicewomen come to their profession on different paths. Their experiences at Marine boot camp, airborne school, West Point or a military college like Norwich University, and advanced study at places like the School of Advanced Military Studies are critical components in developing their doctrinal, technical, and tactical expertise, which is key to professional development, and, ultimately, valuable in combat. Those settings, as well as posts in the United States and abroad, are an important aspect of these women's stories.

It was vital to me to show these servicewomen as full human beings, beyond caricature. Their stories, which include their personal and professional relationships, are mostly told through their eyes. In a few cases, some minor characters' names have been changed. My intent is for the reader to walk away with an intimate understanding and appreciation of who these women are and what it takes to succeed as a woman in today's military.

And who are they?

•**The General: Brigadier General Angela Salinas** is a feisty, five-foot-tall, fifty-four-year-old Marine with a firm handshake and more than thirty years of service. She is the Marine Corps' first Hispanic female general. She battles naysayers and disinformation as a commander at an all-male institution while finding her identity as a general and fitting in at the apex.

It was important to me to have one of the main subjects of this book be a seasoned military woman with decades of service who got her start in a military that little resembles the one she serves in today. I found that and so much more in General Salinas.

•**The Platoon Leader: Second Lieutenant Bergan Flannigan** is a twenty-two-year-old, baby-faced introvert and newly minted officer who wanted to go to airborne school though she'd never been on an airplane. After playing Army for four years at a military college in Vermont, she finds herself leading troops on the front lines in Afghanistan, serving in the same military police company as her husband.

I first heard about Lieutenant Flannigan and her dramatic story through back channels. She had been a platoon leader in the battalion that my friend's husband commanded at Fort Stewart, Georgia. I'd been told she was "tough" and not to expect much in the way of conversation. That turned out to be true. But I liked the idea of telling a platoon leader's story in combat, and over time she got used to me and my endless questions. The military police have an incredibly dangerous worldwide mission, and Lieutenant Flannigan and her soldiers were in the thick of it on a daily basis in Afghanistan. I start her story much earlier, however, far from the hell of Afghanistan, in an idyllic spot in the mountains of Vermont at Norwich University; showing Lieutenant Flannigan's life as a cadet underscores the innocence of her early years and gives context and depth to her leadership responsibilities in a war zone.

•**The Drill Instructor: Sergeant Amy Stokley** is a "diva in boots." The twenty-five-year-old has a martial arts black belt and earned a combat action ribbon in Iraq. She readies her voice for the day by screaming above her car stereo on the way to work at Parris Island. She loves to make recruits cry and does so while wearing false eyelashes, acrylic French-tipped nails, and lipstick. Spending 140 hours each week with her recruits, she has little time for a personal life and is resigned to being married to the corps.

The first time I called Sergeant Stokley, she spoke in a husky whisper. I could barely understand her.

"Do you have a cold?"

"No, ma'am," she said. "I've been yelling all day."

And so our relationship began.

When I arrived at Parris Island to do research, I realized she wasn't kidding. Marine Corps drill instructors are a breed of their own, female drill instructors even more so, and I wanted one of the best. Sergeant Stokley had worked her way up from truck driver to drill instructor, and her story follows her path to the most revered position in the Marine Corps. Who was the woman beneath the Smokey Bear hat? I was set to find out.

•**The Iron Major: Major Candice O'Brien** is the woman I interviewed a dozen years ago. A brainy thirty-three-year-old redhead who can outthink her fellow officers in the plans room and outrun them on the track, she is a hard-charging overachiever. But she was unprepared for what turns out to be combat on the home front. When she deploys to NATO headquarters in Afghanistan, she leaves behind two young children and a troubled marriage.

I was attracted to Major O'Brien's story because she represented so many mothers in dual military marriages. How did she keep all the balls in the air? Can a military woman really have it all? During the writing of this book, her story unfolded in real time in ways neither of us could have predicted when she left for Afghanistan.

Their stories also counteract the perception that military women are cookie-cutter alike. I couldn't help but be intrigued by their contradictions. General Salinas is tiny in stature, yet she founded and was the captain of her college's women's basketball team. Lieutenant Flannigan is a hard-charger, yet she loves her stuffed animals and took her favorites on deployment. Sergeant Stokley loved to "blast" her recruits, and she always made sure she looked damn good doing it. Major O'Brien could brief General

Petraeus on counternarcotics in Afghanistan, but she was also captivated by the simple beauty of a sunflower outside the base perimeter.

The more I learned about these women, the more I wanted to know.

The positions these women hold bring them public praise but also private challenges and, for some, extraordinary scrutiny. Their stories, on American soil and abroad, are riveting in themselves. But even more, these four military women are emblematic of the issues facing so many U.S. servicewomen today, from marriage and motherhood to career trajectories and life goals. The subjects of this book are unforgettable individuals, but they represent far more than themselves.

Their stories, broadly chronological, cover a five-year period, from 2006 to 2011, a time frame that marks a historic presidential election, an economic downturn, budget cuts, a military stretched by deployments to two war zones, and a U.S. public weary of war. During these years, phrases such as "sectarian violence," "suicide bombers," "the surge," "IEDs," "exit strategy," "al-Qaeda," "the Taliban," and "airstrikes" have become a familiar part of our vocabulary, etched in the minds of Americans.

Against this complex and challenging backdrop, the four main subjects of varying ages, ranks, backgrounds, experience, and personalities play out their lives. They share hard work, determination, and perseverance to reach the top of their professions, but they must weigh their achievements against the challenges in their personal lives.

The issues surrounding women like these aren't delineated in a Marine Corps manual, Army regulations, or Defense Department statistics and congressional policies. The women each, individually, have to grapple with the consequences of their career choices. The rewards can be extraordinary, but there is also a cost. Some women service members, in the end, decide the price is too great, and feel they have no choice but to leave. Others—many—stay. Is it worth it? What was gained? What was sacrificed? What's next? These are questions only they can answer. But it's time to ask.

PART I
A FEW GOOD WOMEN

"I believe that it is as much a right and duty for women to do something with their lives as for men and we are not going to be satisfied with such frivolous parts as you give us."

—Louisa May Alcott

2006

The number of American service members killed in Iraq reaches 3,000. Thousands of Iraqis die each month in sectarian violence, culminating in more than 34,000 Iraqi deaths by year's end.

In the fall, a day after a Democratic victory in the House of Representatives, President Bush nominates Robert Gates to replace Donald Rumsfeld as Secretary of Defense, telling reporters a "fresh perspective" is needed on Iraq.

Five days after Christmas, the Iraqi national government hangs Saddam Hussein for crimes against humanity.

Meanwhile, America's focus on Iraq enables al-Qaeda and the Taliban to strengthen support and bases of operation in Afghanistan.

CHAPTER 1
OOORAH on the High Seas

Amy: July 18, 2006. The Mediterranean Sea off Beirut, Lebanon

As the hovercraft's twin engines died, Marine Lance Corporal Amy Stokley knew the day was about to turn miserable.

The air-conditioning withered with the engines, and Amy turned to Hospital Corpsman 2nd Class Miller, a petite blonde wedged next to her, and stated the obvious.

"This sucks, Doc."

As if in response, a wave jerked the boat at an unnatural angle.

"Hope it's not down long," said the Navy corpsman, who was more along the lines of a licensed practical nurse, but when you're the only one on board who can stick an IV, the title "Doc" is fitting.

The twenty passengers in their charge, weary American civilians leaving Lebanon with their suitcases and baby strollers, sat knee-to-knee on benches and eyed the two twenty-three-year-olds dressed in cammies as if pleading, *What now?*

What now? Amy didn't know. She was a Marine Corps truck driver with a knack for surviving IED attacks. Being stuck in the eastern Mediterranean Sea, in the belly of a malfunctioning boat that was getting tossed like a piece of trash was a new experience.

But she knew all eyes were on her and Doc. Never mind that the businessmen, engineers, bankers, nannies, and soccer moms on board wouldn't have given the pair a second thought had they passed the young women in their civvies window-shopping along Maarad Street in downtown Beirut. In situations like this, the uniform lent a sense of authority.

For the last few weeks, Amy had been in Jordan on a training exercise. While there she lived in a pup tent in a tent city surrounded by sand so fine the Marines called it moon dust. Her job was to transport the grunts, the infantrymen, who were training with the Jordanians, and to take them food and supplies. The Marines had left Jordan a week early, after the U.S. embassy in Beirut requested military assistance evacuating Americans who were snared in a Middle East crisis: A deadly border attack by Hezbollah militants followed by a botched Israeli attempt to rescue hostage soldiers had escalated to Israeli airstrikes and a ground invasion in Lebanon that destroyed main highways and the Beirut International Airport. The chaos was front and center in newspapers across the globe, and cable news ran the story nonstop, but Amy, who had no time to watch TV, knew little about that.

What she did know was her mission: Escort Americans on and off the LCAC (which stood for Landing Craft Air Cushion, pronounced "ell-cack") and deposit them aboard the USS *Nashville*, which would take them to safety in Cyprus. But her task was becoming more uncomfortable by the minute.

The stench of sweat mixed with anxiety consumed the already stuffy compartment, which was lit by a set of dim lights. Although no one came to explain what was going on, Amy didn't need to be a sailor to figure out the engines were kaput. The demise of the fanlike 4,000-horsepower engines affixed to the back of the LCAC sounded like a commercial jetliner shutting off at the end of a trip.

"We'll be up and running soon," Amy announced, although she really had no idea.

The LCAC is an armored ship-to-shore assault vessel that can crawl up a beach, open its steel jaws, and regurgitate Marines, weapons, equipment, and cargo during battle. It looks like something Mad Max would love to commandeer. But with no power and no windows, it was like being inside an aluminum can wrenched along the ocean's surface. As the vessel swayed and swooshed with the ocean's swells, children started to whimper; then a woman of Indian origin, her dark skin now gray, began vomiting ceaselessly, to the point of dry-heaving into the white plastic bags that are left on LCACs for this very purpose. Her sickness set off a domino effect among the other passengers, who soon buried their own heads in the bags.

Please, please, I don't want to throw up, Amy thought. Sweat soaked through her green T-shirt, a cotton buffer between her and her desert cammies. The sun had streaked her long, thick hair, which, like many young female Marines, she tamed into a tight bun.

She checked her watch. An hour had passed. It reminded her of an earlier mission, when she'd gotten sick herself while waiting on a small bobbing boat to transport Americans onto the USS *Nashville* under much different circumstances.

That time just last summer had been much closer to home but was still worlds away from the America she knew. It was a place where entire rooftops sat in front yards next to flipped-over couches and uprooted trees. Inside abandoned homes, dirty water-level marks scarred walls near ceilings, and soot and stench covered everything. It looked like a battlefield. Most painful of all, framed family photos lay on the ground, soaking wet. Within days of Hurricane Katrina's landfall, Amy and her Marine unit had been in New Orleans for a month and a half, removing downed trees from roofs and throwing the debris in the back of her seven-ton truck.

While Amy didn't follow the politics and complexities surrounding her current humanitarian assignment, she did know about the Beirut barracks bombing in 1983, when an Islamic terrorist attack introduced the word "terrorism" into America's lexicon. That year, on an early Sunday morning in October, while many Marines slept in their bunks, two trucks laden with explosives and driven by suicide bombers smashed into the barracks, killing 220 U.S. Marines who were serving as peacekeepers in the region.

Amy wouldn't be born until five months later, but the tragedy was seared into Marine memory, as well as into America's, as a dire harbinger of future Islamic extremism.

Until her corps buddies started talking about the irony of it all, Amy hadn't realized that those fallen Marines were from her own unit, the 24th Marine Amphibious Unit (MAU), which had become the 24th Marine Expeditionary Force (MEU) in the late 1980s.

Now, as the LCAC continued to turn and tip, Amy clasped her tanned arms and looked down at her suede boots. She tried to focus on happy thoughts, like her two little nieces, Kayley and Krisenda, her sister Shay's kids, back home in Taylorsville, Kentucky. But the unmistakable hiss of mortar fire kept interrupting. The artillery was too far away to be a threat, Amy knew, but the sound reminded her of Iraq, where mortars and rockets repeatedly hit her forward operating base. Though the chow line should have offered some respite, she avoided it. Amy knew insurgents marked the mess tent with a big bull's-eye. Eating there was a chance she just didn't want to take. So she relied on MREs or the cans of ravioli and Little Debbie snacks her mother sent from Kentucky.

Like a lot of deployed Marines, Amy had kept a "just-in-case letter" in her chest pocket while in Iraq. She had decided to write it after experiencing her first death of a Marine. Though she was just twenty at the time, she tried to address anything she thought might worry her mother. In an attempt to lift her mother's spirits, she kept things light:

> *Dear Mom,*
>
> *Don't be sad. I lived happy and did everything in life that I wanted to do. You better throw a party for me not a funeral.*
>
> *You should be happy for me because now I get to sleep all the time.*
>
> *I know I'm going to heaven so don't worry about that. I'll be watching you and if I see you looking like you're too down, I'll haunt you in your sleep!*
>
> *I was prepared to die and I don't feel like there was any*

unfinished business. I'm happy I died serving our country.
I'm so thankful to have you as a mother. You raised me well
and I couldn't ask for anything more.

Love,

Amy

P.S. Blow every dollar of my life insurance. Don't spend it
on anything sensible!

Despite the joking tone in her letter, Amy had recurring nightmares in Iraq. They were always the same: In one, her family visited her in Iraq and her sister was wounded despite Amy's efforts to protect her. In a second nightmare, Amy was shot repeatedly in her stomach and chest with small-arms fire while manning a vehicle checkpoint, and no one came to her aid. She'd had the nightmare so often, the hot rounds hitting her torso seemed real. It was as if she knew exactly how it felt to get shot.

★

"Lance Corporal Stokley, Lance Corporal Stokley, hey, do you hear that?" Doc said.

The sound was more welcoming than the jangle of a Vegas jackpot. The boat's diesel engines groaned to life, and relief filtered through the cabin. Later that night, finally back on her own ship, the USS *Iwo Jima*, Amy headed to her berthing area on the main deck, two decks below the top deck, where the choppers landed, with plans to shower. A naval ship is designed for efficiency, not comfort, especially amphibious assault ships like the *Iwo Jima*, which are typically darker and danker than the rest of the fleet, since they carry diesel-chugging Marine equipment. The exhaust from those vehicles, aircraft, and hovercraft seeps into every nook and cranny.

On board, the ship's sailors toiled like serfs belowdecks on eighteen-hour shifts, some never seeing sunlight for weeks. As a rapid-response expeditionary force, the *Iwo Jima* was their floating fire hall. The ship carried everything from Humvees, bulldozers, and forklifts to helicopters, mortars, howitzers, and tanks that could be employed when a 911 call came for the Marines to respond with firepower or, as was the case in Lebanon, water, food, and an escort to safety.

In the meantime, though, the 2,200 Marines on the ship passed the monotony of their sea days cleaning their weapons, lifting weights, going to chow, and playing Xbox, dominoes, and spades.

Before reaching her berthing area, Amy checked the head, as the Navy and Marines labeled the bathroom. There were three toilets and shower stalls for the twenty women she shared her quarters with. Water streamed from behind the shower curtains, so Amy went to her room instead. Since everyone worked different shifts, a number of the Navy corpsmen were sleeping.

Amy was glad she hadn't joined the Navy, whose junior enlisted seemed like civilians to her. They were mostly on a first-name basis, and everyone seemed to be friends regardless of rank. There were also more females in the Navy than in the Marine Corps, and being around that many females made Amy feel awkward. The differences between the sexes are pronounced within military culture, a world populated with "males and females," not "men and women."

Amy's sixty-member motor transport detachment had just one other female, whom Amy wasn't that fond of, since she was a slow truck driver and mothered the other Marines.

The sterile, windowless berthing area was the Navy's version of Army barracks. The metal-and-steel room had all the charm of a morgue. An ironing board hanging vertically on a wall looked like artwork, given the room's barren canvas. Personal space was limited to slim wall lockers for uniforms, and bunk beds stacked like shelves three high. Known as "racks," the beds were little more than metal boxes topped with thin mattresses. Sailors often called them "coffin racks," because they opened like a casket for additional, albeit shallow storage, just five inches deep, beneath the metal mattress platform. One tier of bunks sat directly across from another, separated by only three feet of space.

Nevertheless, the first time Amy saw her living accommodations, a sense of excitement and wonderment enveloped her, the way a college dorm room would excite an incoming freshman. She was embarking on a seven-month adventure at sea to destinations unknown. Marine friends who had been on sea deployments told her of "train-ups" in Middle Eastern countries like Jordan, Kuwait, and Afghanistan, and port calls in Italy, France, and Dubai. They also warned her of long stretches of boredom and cramped living conditions.

Fortunately for Amy, she was not the type to crave moments to herself, even when she was feeling down. She always wanted to be surrounded by her family of Marines. Of course, that didn't mean people didn't annoy her.

No sooner had she closed the door than there was a knock. It was a tall, skinny black sailor.

"Is Tanisha here?"

Amy plunked her hands on her hips. She knew where this was leading, and she didn't try to hide her annoyance. It seemed like every five minutes, day and night, Navy and Marine males knocked on the door looking for one of the females.

Amy turned her head back into the room.

"I don't see her."

"I wanna leave a message for her. Can you tell her Briggs came by, and tell her to come to my workstation, and if I am not there, to check the smoke pit?"

"Ah, right," Amy said before quickly shutting the door.

Like that's really something I want to do, keep getting up to answer the door to find out it's for pleasure, not business, Amy said to herself.

Knock, knock . . .

Amy was ready to knock the kid's block off. She swung the door open, and her smirk turned into a smile.

"What's that mean-girl look for?" asked Amy's good friend Tisha Reed, a half-black and half-Filipino Marine from Texas. "You just get back?"

"Yeah, the LCAC I was on broke down for, like, an hour."

"I bet that sucked."

"It was pretty bad. A bunch of the civilians got sick." From the military perspective, civilians are a different species from the military.

"You wanna head over to chow?" Tisha said.

"I don't know. I saw the line coming back. It's all the way up into the hangar deck," Amy said. "You know, it's gonna be hot and nasty in there."

Unlike the other service branches, the Navy segregates its dining facilities by rank, with enlisted and officers eating in separate messes. While the food quality is equal, the waiting time to be served is not. Sometimes enlisted personnel have to stand in line an hour before entering the mess decks, which resemble a large cafeteria, while officers, who have the choice of dining in a traditional mess with white linen or cafeteria-style, usually have no wait time.

The separate dining arrangements often trouble Army officers visiting aboard ship, since Army mess halls both in garrison and in the field are integrated, and, when appropriate, custom calls for soldiers to eat before their officers. It's a tradition rooted in Army culture, where a soldier's needs come before a commander's, since officers ask people under their command to potentially die by their orders.

But Navy culture is different. Aboard ship for months at a time with little privacy, a separate dining mess allows naval officers, who are greatly outnumbered on ships—just seventy-three on the *Iwo Jima* compared to more than two thousand sailors—the only opportunity during the day to be in a setting where they can speak freely, be with peers, or discuss matters like evaluations, management, interpersonal issues, or careers.

"The smoking lamp is lighted on the starboard midships sponson," boomed a familiar voice over the ship's intercom system. Like the PA announcer on the TV show *M*A*S*H*, the boatswain's mate of the watch, who stands on the ship's bridge and "passes the word" as directed by the officer of the deck, was a faceless yet familiar voice everyone on board heard daily. And this was one announcement that made Amy's and Tisha's faces light up.

"Wanna go?" Amy said. She already knew Tisha's answer. Amy smoked a pack a day on ship, mostly out of boredom. Tisha was always by her side, a willing partner on the smoke-filled balcony known as the enlisted smoking sponson. It was such a popular spot they sometimes had to wait in line.

When President Clinton banned smoking in federal buildings in 1997, the Navy followed suit and banned the practice inside the skin of the ship. All smoking now has to be done in a designated open-air topside space. (In late 2010 the Navy also banned smoking on submarines.) Most of the time, the "smoking lamp"—a centuries-old throwback to the days when sailors used a designated oil lamp far away from gunpowder to light their tobacco—is lit from sunrise to sunset.

When the "darken ship" order is passed, though, there is no more topside smoking. A lit cigarette can be seen at three miles on a dark night without night-vision devices, which is a bad way to call attention to your vessel.

Amy and Tisha made their way up for a smoke. The two were inseparable. They ate their meals together, played cards together, and visited the same nightclubs during liberty ports.

Amy liked Tisha because she was real. Her friend was honest and told people like it was, and she liked the way Tisha carried herself. The two had met before deployment at the motor pool back at Camp Lejeune. Tisha was married and had a daughter, and since Amy was dating someone then, the two stuck together. Amy didn't want to spend time hanging out with a bunch of guys, and as a married woman, Tisha didn't either, something Amy respected.

Of course, this meant people assumed the two were lesbians. In the military, perception is reality, Amy knew.

Not hanging with the guys meant a woman had to be a lesbian, whereas hanging out with the men labeled a woman as a slut. Often, the best a young woman new to the military could hope for was to be thought of as a little sister. But once a woman gained rank, responsibility, and military experience, she was no longer anyone's little sibling, and other labels came into play.

Amy always heard rumors about Navy females sleeping around, and with every deployment, some returned pregnant. While little privacy can be found on a ship, countless small, semihidden spaces exist where two young, eager, and flexible people can hook up and not be seen. In a much-ballyhooed story from the Gulf War in 1991, 10 percent of the women on board the *Acadia* (thirty-six servicewomen) were pregnant and had to be transferred off. According to news accounts at the time, more than half gotten pregnant during the deployment. Since then other tales of military Love Boats have surfaced.

Ultimately, having men and women serve together on a ship or at a desert outpost means sex happens, despite orders prohibiting or strongly discouraging such behavior.

In November 2009, one Army general implemented a controversial policy that punished soldiers under his command who got pregnant while deployed to a combat zone, along with the men who impregnated them. While the media jumped all over the sensational aspects of the story—an Army general trying to control a woman's reproductive rights through punishment—what went largely unreported and unexamined was the actual intent of the policy, which was about "readiness."

The expectation that service members in a war zone should act professionally and responsibly at all times, and that their personal behavior shouldn't jeopardize mission readiness, got lost in the uproar over what became dubbed as the "pregnancy ban" and over women possibly being court-martialed for getting pregnant, which was never the intent of the policy. The irresponsible actions of two people can impact an entire unit, since soldiers who get pregnant during a deployment immediately return stateside, leaving a hole that others must fill.

In the end, the policy was rescinded that December, following intense media coverage and criticism, including from four female senators. Meanwhile, the pregnant soldiers provided ammunition for naysayers who believe women shouldn't be in combat in the first place.

On ships or off, official policy dictates that there be no fraternization within a service member's chain of command or unit, and no senior-to-junior relationships. Amy knew she and her boyfriend, Staff Sergeant Saleem Byrd, were bending the rules. When they were stationed together, the couple worked in the same section, and Saleem outranked her by three pay grades. While their relationship wasn't a secret, no one in the section talked much about it, and the two kept it professional at work.

It wasn't uncommon for males and females within the same unit to get involved with one another. But Amy knew problems often occurred when a male Marine was fraternizing with a female of lesser rank. Many times she'd seen how a female Marine would get a guy "by the balls," which allowed her to get away with what she wanted and even to talk to him however she wanted in front of other subordinates.

If someone in the male's chain of command found out, he would get into trouble.

Amy and Saleem had been dating for a couple years. He too was deployed, but aboard the USS *Whidbey Island*. Amy e-mailed him when she was able, and the couple met up at liberty ports. In Jordan she'd been able to see him every day.

But she knew the relationship was coming to an end. Amy wanted to get married and have kids. Saleem, who was six years older, already had three kids and was in no rush to settle down.

"You wanna play spades at the chow hall when it clears out?" Tisha asked as the women reached the smoking balcony.

"Yeah, might as well," Amy said as she lit her Newport.

She had become a proficient spades player since she enlisted in the Marines. The card game was competitive, and it was the only one she and her friends played every day, sometimes in pairs but often with four people. Popular with American service members since World War II, spades has also long been the card game of choice for prison inmates. Which seemed fitting, since being on board a ship was a bit like being in jail.

Amy looked down at the sea through the latticelike netting. The waves looked like swirls of frosting on a cake. She had never seen a body of water this color before. Navy ships like the *Iwo Jima* were painted the color of wet cement to better blend in with a bleak sea and sky. But against the shimmering blues and emerald greens of the Mediterranean, the assault vessel stuck out like a boxer in a boutique.

The weather was perfect, though, on the balcony—in the low eighties with no humidity.

Amy put the sea green package of Newports back in her leg pocket and inhaled deeply. Newports were the only kind of cigarette she smoked. She had her reasons.

★

Sand as fine as cremation ash coated the card table that served as Amy's desk inside the dispatch tent at Forward Operating Base Kalsu, twenty miles south of Baghdad. The desolate outpost was named after the Buffalo Bills' Bob Kalsu, the only active professional athlete killed in Vietnam. The 24th MEU had set up camp there in July 2004. August, though, was the hottest and driest month in Iraq, and the temperature was quickly approaching 120 degrees.

It was just after nine a.m. on Thursday, August 26, and Amy, who was one of two dispatchers for the detachment, studied a spreadsheet of vehicles and drivers that would make a supply run from FOB Kalsu to Muhammadiyah. The destination was one of the cities in Iraq's Triangle of Death, the densely populated and dangerous area south of the capital. Amy thought she had the best of both worlds. It was her job to set up the vehicle matrix showing the order of the trucks and the names of the drivers and A-drivers (assistant drivers). Best of all, she got to drive a vehicle in the convoy. There was no way she was going to be left behind. It was boring back at the FOB, which didn't even have a shower trailer yet. The detachment averaged two supply convoys each day, and everyone knew Amy would put up a fight if she weren't driving in one of them.

The convoy was getting ready to roll when a thin Marine with soft eyes entered the tent. Corporal Bart Hummlhanz was a twenty-three-year-old Pennsylvanian from the MP detachment.

"Hi, Corporal Hanz," Amy said, using his nickname. "What's going on?"

"Can I go on the convoy?" he asked. "Is there any way I can get my name on the manifest?"

Most times, after Marines were assigned to vehicles, Amy didn't like to go back and make any changes, because she'd have to contact the communications center and submit a new matrix. It wasn't that much of a hassle, but she knew the busy communications folks wouldn't appreciate it if the dispatchers made a habit out of bothering them.

Corporal Hummlhanz was a quiet, good guy, however, a by-the-book Marine, so Amy granted his request.

"Okay," she said. "I'll put'cha on here, but you're gonna have to ride in the back of the lead truck with the rest of the Marines who are going. There's no more room in the cab."

"Great! No problem!" he said. "Thanks."

Amy could tell he was excited. He wanted to get outside the wire with his buddy MPs. The convoy wasn't going just to Muhammadiyah but also to BIAP (Baghdad International Airport), a place Corporal Hanz had only heard about. All the Marines wanted to go to BIAP, which was the war zone equivalent to Disney World. The base had the biggest chow hall you could imagine, and the Marines called the PX there Walmart; it was that good. The Marines always returned with shopping bags full of stuff from BIAP.

This was the convoy that everyone wanted to go on.

Now it was time to move. Amy mounted her truck, called a Medium Tactical Vehicle Replacement (MTVR), though in fact there was nothing "medium" about this monster, whose six tires each stood as tall as a person.

"You ready?" asked Corporal Moore, Amy's A-driver, whose job was to help keep Amy awake if she got tired, or to provide any other assistance.

"I've been ready," said Amy, as she placed her radio, a one-eared headset, on her head and adjusted the mic near her mouth. The radio allowed her to communicate with other drivers in the convoy.

"We are Oscar Mike," came a voice through the headset, which meant "on the move."

Amy drove the second truck in the twelve-vehicle convoy. In front of her was the truck with Corporal Hummlhanz and other Marines in its bed. Someone had given them spare radios, so they could hear all that was going on.

Slowly the convoy made its way out the gate.

Most of the drivers were Amy's age, in their early twenties, and had gone from cruising the roads of their hometowns to convoying in Iraq. And, like Amy, it was their first time outside the United States. Before the Marines, the biggest thing Amy had driven was her father's Dodge Ram pickup. Now she drove massive vehicles at night with no headlights by focusing on the red lights of the vehicle in front of her.

When Amy joined the Marines, she came in "open contract"—a recruiter's dream, since it meant the corps could put her anywhere to meet its needs. At the time, Amy didn't care. She just wanted to join up. She later learned Marines can get higher bonuses for reenlistment in other job specialties and that, since one doesn't have to have high military test scores to drive a truck, it was on the same level as a mechanic or cook. Fortunately, Amy loved her job.

Military trucks were lumbering, slow-moving, easy targets in Iraq. But Amy didn't worry about that. She had confidence and admiration in her seven-ton because it was strong, powerful, and seemingly indestructible.

Amy followed the lead truck down the paved main supply route at about forty-five miles per hour. Muhammadiyah was forty-five minutes away, and from there it was another half hour to the airport. She knew the route well, as she'd been traveling it every two days. The highway was one lane coming and one going, with little traffic except for the occasional dusty Toyota pickup. Beyond the asphalt, the countryside was sand-covered flatlands and fields with an occasional house.

Finally, the convoy was just five minutes outside of Muhammadiyah, a disfigured city of crumbling box-shaped buildings, abandoned cars, and loose tires, all covered in sand and grime. Any splash of color was as washed-out as a faded photograph.

Like much of Iraq, Muhammadiyah looked exactly as it smelled—like burning trash.

The road narrowed and the convoy decreased speed, with Amy maintaining a three-vehicle space behind the lead truck, as she was taught. If there were ever any daisy-chained IEDs, the chances of their hitting more than one vehicle were smaller that way.

"It's hotter than—" Corporal Moore never finished his words.

"Oh, no! No! Oh, my God!" Amy screamed.

As the lead truck traveled over a huge bump in the road, the first thing Amy saw was an enormous explosion of smoke, debris, and chunks of concrete. The smoke climbed higher and higher in the sky. Then came the loud boom.

The vehicle was hit mostly on the passenger side, and it skidded to the right as the tires withered. The mighty seven-ton looked helpless.

As the second in line, Amy knew it was her job to push through, so that the rest of the convoy could get out of the kill zone in case there were more IEDs.

But Amy didn't do that.

"Where are you goin'?" Corporal Moore screamed. Amy had jumped out of the truck, and debris from the explosion pelted her helmet. She felt naked. Sure that every Marine in that truck would soon be dead, she ran as fast as she could toward the screams, some hysterical, others yelling for a corpsman.

Then a calm, familiar voice filled her ears: "Push through . . . push through." It was Lance Corporal Kenny Gerhart on the radio, which was still wrapped around Amy's head.

Gerhart was a good friend, a Jersey boy, and the first person she'd met in the fleet. He was someone she looked to for advice when she needed it. And if ever there was a time she needed it, it was now.

"Push through" meant the convoy needed to keep rolling and not stop. At that moment Amy's training clicked in, and she realized the whole convoy had halted behind her. Before she reached the downed truck, she ran back to her own. She edged past the kill zone and pulled her truck in front of the disabled vehicle so that a tow bar could be attached to pull it back to the FOB.

After setting up a perimeter around the convoy, the Marines spread out about twenty-five meters away from the trucks. Most were providing security, while others tended to the wounded. The vehicle was not just a flatbed; it had sides with plates of attached armor, but the armor was short enough that the Marines could comfortably hang their arms over the side, which turned out to be a dreadful idea.

One of those who tried it was Corporal Hummlhanz, and he had gotten the most severe wounds, with shrapnel both on top of and underneath his arm. He was bleeding badly but still awake and alert.

"Medevac! Medevac! Medevac!" Staff Sergeant Rivera, the convoy commander, called into the radio.

After the chopper arrived and whisked Corporal Hanz away, the Marines finished their mission to Muhammadiyah. This time, though, there would be no trip to the BIAP for CDs and burgers.

As night fell, the Marines returned to the FOB in silence. Before turning in trip tickets that recorded mileage and expended fuel, and doing maintenance, Staff Sergeant Rivera gathered his Marines in a circle for a debriefing.

"Corporal Hanz didn't make it," he said. "He died on the bird."

No one uttered a word. Tomorrow they would give written statements, he said. As others walked silently to their tents, Amy realized she was the one who had put Corporal Hanz on the convoy.

"Come on; let's go have a smoke," said Lance Corporal Gerhart. A band of friends—Amy, Corporal Grey, and Lance Corporal Chilton—followed him to an area near the motor pool, just outside the dispatch tent, where smokers had created a lounge covered with camouflage netting that consisted of camp chairs and a white deep freezer that added to the seating.

"What's gonna happen next?" Amy asked from her perch on top of the freezer. It was getting late, but no one wanted to be alone.

The normally gregarious group remained silent. Even Gerhart, the comedian among them, was at a loss for what to say.

"Let's go find them!" he finally said, breaking the silence. A few minutes of tough talk on what they would do to the bad guys seemed to help.

"Here, this'll make you feel better," Gerhart said, as he handed Amy a Newport.

"No, I'm not smoking that," she said. She thought smoking was disgusting. Then she changed her mind.

Maybe it will help me relax, she told herself. "You know what? Gimme one a them," she said.

"Okay, but just one," Gerhart said.

Amy held the cigarette like a pro. She'd been inhaling secondhand smoke and watching young veteran smokers since she joined the corps.

She expected to cough but didn't. Halfway through, however, she felt light-headed and euphoric.

"Here, gimme another one a them," Amy said.

"Nope," Gerhart said, like a father who'd offered his child her first chocolate-chip cookie but limited her to one bite. "You don't smoke, and you're not about to get another one."

Everyone looked at her blankly.

"What? I won't start," she said. "I promise. I just want one more."

"Awright," Gerhart said. "But only 'cause you're havin' a bad day."

──────────── ★ ────────────

"Amy? Amy?"

"What?"

"Look," Tisha said. Amy's cigarette was close to burning her knuckles.

"Ohhhh," Amy said.

"You zoning out or what?" Tisha said.

"It's just been a bad day," Amy said.

Sunset was fast approaching, and the Mediterranean's vibrant colors took on darker hues.

"You wanna check on the chow line?" Tisha said.

"I think I'm gonna turn in early," Amy said.

"You still glad you re-upped?" Tisha asked, as the two women made their way off the smoking sponson.

"Yeah, it's out of my hands now."

While in Jordan, Amy had submitted her reenlistment packet, as her two-year commitment was almost up. She was interested in becoming a police officer back home in Kentucky, but she loved the Marines. Ever since her high school days in JROTC, Amy's dream had been to be a Marine Corps drill instructor. She'd put in the papers, but still had to get a medical record screening, physical fitness test scores, and a commander's approval that showed she was fit and mature enough to attend DI School.

Back in the berthing area, after her shower, Amy climbed into her rack, which was about 70 percent the size of a twin bed. With just eighteen inches of space above the mattress, sitting up was impossible, and side sleepers were out of luck, since you couldn't roll over without hitting some body part on the bunk above. Amy simply slept at the position of attention. She pulled the bed's curtains closed. She wanted to get a good night's rest before morning formation, which on ship was meant to make sure everyone was alive and no one had fallen overboard.

She thought about her decision to sign up again. Only the very best enlisted Marines were chosen for DI School, the top 10 percent. What if she didn't get selected? Even more intimidating, what if she did? While some people lived their lives afraid of taking chances, Amy fell into the other camp.

She was terrified of not doing exactly what she wanted to do.

As the ship made its way through the gentle Mediterranean waters, Amy tried to picture herself wearing the campaign hat, the distinct Smokey Bear headgear of a DI that symbolized Marine Corps perfection.

Amy was over not getting hitched to Saleem. Becoming a drill instructor meant she'd be married to the corps. And DI School would be one fire-and-brimstone betrothal.

CHAPTER 2
The General

Angie: Spring 2006. Marine Corps Recruit Depot, San Diego

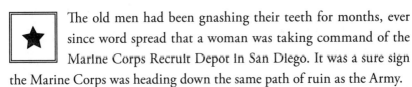 The old men had been gnashing their teeth for months, ever since word spread that a woman was taking command of the Marine Corps Recruit Depot in San Diego. It was a sure sign the Marine Corps was heading down the same path of ruin as the Army.

Sergeant Major Bobby Woods had fielded any number of calls and e-mails on the matter. What the hell was going on? Who was behind this? Donald Rumsfeld? Was it a joke? A rumor? Why weren't they sending her to Parris Island, where the women trained?

"I don't know . . ." was all Sergeant Major Woods could say. He had seen a lot in his twenty-eight years of service to corps and country, but never anything like this. Nor had he ever worked for a woman Marine. Absolutely not.

"Sergeant Major, what in the world is going on in this Marine Corps?" demanded retired Sergeant Major "Iron Mike" Mervosh, who, like all the local retired sergeants major, kept a direct line to the depot's leadership.

With the face and growl of a bulldog, Iron Mike was a legend in San Diego. He had defied death in Iwo Jima, Korea, and Vietnam, earned three Purple Hearts, and after thirty-five years of service, had the distinction of being the longest-serving enlisted member in the Marine Corps. When the first Gulf War had broken out, he was in his seventies, but according to news accounts at the time, he still tried to reenlist. He was sure he had one more good war left in him.

"What are they sending her here for?" Iron Mike barked over the phone into Woods's ear. That was the question everyone wanted answered, especially the sergeant major himself, since he would be affected most. In a few months he would be her top enlisted adviser. They would be together at events, ceremonies, training exercises, and PT . . . always together.

The woman behind the uproar was Angela Salinas, a soon-to-be brigadier general, one of only three women Marine generals on active duty, the sixth woman in the history of the Marine Corps to make it to the general officer ranks, and the first Hispanic woman to be selected to general in the corps.

And word on the street was that she could chew butt better than any male.

"Sergeant Major, your life is going to be miserable," said an officer from the 12th Marine Corps District, who had worked with Salinas when she commanded that district a few years earlier. Woods got an earful about her relentless recruiting efforts and how she was tougher on her officers than on her enlisted personnel.

"Well, that's a challenge; I'm ready to take it on," Woods told the officer.

Woods also knew his future boss disliked Marines with mustaches. Though now clean shaven because he was on drill field duty status, Sergeant Major Woods had had a mustache ever since he was able to sprout one in high school. After boot camp he grew it back the first chance he was allowed.

"That's her problem," Woods remembered telling an officer who three years earlier had informed him about Colonel Salinas's aversion to facial hair. Back then Woods had gotten wind that he was being slated for recruiting duty and might serve under the colonel. He ended up receiving orders elsewhere, though, so the mustachio wars had been averted.

San Diego's Marine Corps Recruit Depot, a sprawling 388-acre complex of yellow stucco known as "MCRD," is the place "Where Marines Are Made." Male Marines, that is. The corps is the only service branch that still segregates recruits by gender for training, and male recruits who live west of the Mississippi attend boot camp at MCRD San Diego. With the exception of Corporal Molly Marine, the depot's four-year-old English bulldog mascot (who can salute with her paw), MCRD is an all-male recruit training base. Now the powers that be were putting a woman in charge of 18,000 male recruits and their 500 male drill instructors. Salinas would also lead Marine recruiting west of the Mississippi to Okinawa, Japan.

Meanwhile, back east in Quantico, Virginia, Angela Salinas's phone and e-mail remained silent. She received no congratulations from anyone at the depot. Sergeant Major Woods was the first to send her a note.

"Ma'am, congratulations," he wrote. "We haven't met, but I look forward to working with you."

A professional gesture, though privately the sergeant major still couldn't wrap his brain around why the corps was sending a woman to San Diego. When he did his homework and looked up her history—where she'd been and what she'd done—it turned out his new commander had greater experience and more years of recruiting and recruit training than any general in the Marine Corps. That could not be denied, the sergeant major noted.

But he also knew that sometimes men were from Mars and women from Venus, and that troubled him. How on earth this relationship was going to work out remained to be seen.

August 4, 2006. MCRD, San Diego

Brigadier General Angela Salinas woke up at three a.m., still on East Coast time. In twelve and a half hours, in a ceremony filled with pomp and pageantry before a thousand people, she would become the commanding general of Marine Corps Recruit Depot, San Diego. Just two days ago she had been a colonel, a successful rank that is the last promotion for most military officers. Now "aboard" the depot, unable to sleep, she pulled on her PT clothes and slipped out of guest housing and into the darkness. Even in the dead of night, San Diego had pristine seventy-degree weather. Lanky king and queen palm trees looked down on the 1920s buildings that dotted the depot and neighboring San Diego Bay. Alone with her thoughts, Angie ran along the perimeter, using a chain-link fence topped with concertina wire as her guide.

Less than 1 percent of Marine officers are selected to be generals, and six months before, Angie, who was hitting mandatory retirement, needed to submit her paperwork. She had already been looked at twice and not selected for promotion. While on her lunch break in Virginia that February, she heard her cell phone ring and went outside to take the call.

General Michael Hagee, the commandant of the Marine Corps, was on the line. Such a call wasn't unusual; Angie was the chief of staff for the Marine Corps Recruiting Command at Quantico, and she assumed the commandant was calling about monthly recruiting numbers.

"Angie, our numbers are looking really good," he said. "We're up."

"Yes, sir."

"Well," Hagee continued. "I hate to put another rock in your pack."

Uh-oh . . . thought Angie.

"I just wanted to tell you congratulations. You've been selected for promotion to brigadier general."

Angie almost dropped the phone.

"Thank you, sir. I'm incredibly honored."

"The list won't be released for a few days," he said. "But you can share the news with your family."

"Thank you so much, sir."

"I'm looking at you going to San Diego," Hagee said.

When Angie got off the phone, she thought, *I swear he said San Diego.*

A woman Marine general had never commanded either of the two boot camps, but unlike MCRD San Diego, Parris Island trained both male and female recruits. Angie had served in a number of positions there over the years. She had commanded 4th Battalion, the only female recruit training battalion in the Department of Defense, and had served there as a young company-grade officer when it was Woman Recruit Training Command.

He must have meant Parris Island.

Clearly, the commandant had not.

What's going to happen in the next twenty-four hours? Angie asked herself as she ran the depot fence line, listening to the sounds of the morning routine of the making of Marines. *This is the beginning of who knows what. . . .* she thought, as she hummed the chant "Mama, mama, can't you see, what the Marine Corps has done to me."

★

Shepherd Field, the parade deck at MCRD, known as the Grinder, stretches for half a mile and is lined with an equally long arcade of historic barracks buildings with yellow stucco facades and red-tiled roofs. From the air, the parade deck resembles a massive parking lot, and it would take ten minutes to walk across, although no one would dare do such a thing, let alone park a car on it. This is hallowed ground, reserved for Marine Corps graduation, drills, and official occasions. Unlike the Army, which marches on grassy expanses known as parade fields, the Marines march on a hard surface called a parade deck, a nod to the corps' nautical roots.

Pendleton Hall, also known as Building 31, was the commanding general's headquarters and sat on the east end of the parade deck like a family patriarch holding court at the head of the dining room table. Perched like a crown on the roof, a white turret served as the pedestal for the commanding general's flag, a field of red cloth with a white star in the center.

Adjacent to the building, on Pendleton Field, generals and admirals sat on folding chairs along with their wives, San Diego's mayor and business leaders, and hundreds of other invited guests, including more than forty of Angie's relatives, many of whom had flown in from Texas. In front of them, on a green knoll, Marines stood by regiment in formation behind their colonels and guidon bearers, with their regimental flags rippling in the breeze.

Angie was dressed in service Charlies—the Marine Corps' equivalent of business attire—with two-day-old silver stars on her collar. She stood next to the outgoing commander, Major General John "Jay" Paxton, who would take over the 1st Marine Division at nearby Camp Pendleton. The physical difference between the two was jarring and reminded Angie of the *Mutt and Jeff* comic strip. At five feet tall, Angie stood fourteen inches shorter than Paxton, though her olive service cap, nicknamed the "bucket cover" by women Marines because of its shape, gave her a few extra inches. She had big brown eyes, highlighted hair, and a dimpled smile.

In contrast, Major General Paxton, an admired and loved figure at the depot, was the kind of general Marines are used to seeing—square-jawed, grizzled, and graying. Despite his commanding presence, the infantryman was known to be kind, gracious, and funny. He never lost his cool. People hated to see him go.

As the two, along with Sergeant Major Woods, passed the organizational colors in a symbolic transfer of authority from the outgoing commander to the incoming one, Angie became the forty-eighth general to lead this fabled depot, following in the footsteps of commanding generals who dated back to 1921, men with Medals of Honor, Silver Stars, and Purple Hearts, a line of men who had fought in every battle from the Spanish-American War through the conflicts in Iraq and Afghanistan.

After Paxton welcomed his successor and made his farewell remarks, which were casual, off-the-cuff, and without a podium, he handed the microphone to Angie. All eyes turned to her. Most in the seats and on the field knew little about her other than what they read in the papers, where she was front-page news: Headlines read, "Highest-Ranking Latino Woman Assumes Command of Marine Corp Recruit Depot"; "Female General Takes over Marine Corps Recruit Depot San Diego"; and "Marines Name First Woman to Post."

When Angie had pinned on her general's stars, it was like flipping a light switch to reveal a new world. She liked to joke that she instantly became funnier, better-looking, taller, and started winning at golf. Flag officer rank brought power, real and perceived. But she couldn't help wonder, were people being sincere? Who was really a friend? Were people hanging out with her because they had to? It wasn't always easy to interpret people's motives. Plus it was like living in a glass house. People analyzed what she said and how she said it. They noted her mood, facial expression, weight, gait, what she ate, and how she dressed off duty.

It was a little like being in the center of a minefield. She knew more than a few people present would not have minded if she failed. Some of her former male peers perceived that Angie's opportunities and successes came at a cost to their own career advancement. Such a perception of successful military women is more prevalent than one might expect, given all the advancements women have made in the armed forces.

But it would not have been politically correct for Angie's detractors to publicly criticize her strictly for her gender. It was more acceptable to note that she was not a combat veteran and to question her ability to oversee the training of male recruits who would almost certainly deploy to Iraq and Afghanistan within a year.

The underlying message, though, was: *She's never really been tested.*

That argument was a potshot. During the general's thirty-two years in uniform, women had been barred from ground combat. Only after the Iraq War broke out, and events on the ground superseded policy, did a new generation of women Marines and soldiers, many of them young truck drivers, medics, and MPs, find themselves in combat despite what Congress ordained. By then Angie was a full colonel who had made her name in recruiting and was commanding a recruiting district, the first woman assigned to a critical component of the corps' mission.

And, as a Marine, she was always up for a challenge.

Angie had never planned on joining the corps. In 1974 she was a twenty-year-old college student approaching the end of her sophomore year at Dominican College, a small Catholic school outside San Francisco founded by the Dominican Sisters of San Rafael. She was the first in her family to attend college and was there with the help of a scholarship, student loans, and work programs. Angie had chosen the school with the thought of possibly becoming a nun. In her all-girls Catholic high school, the teaching sisters had been funny, bright, outspoken, strong-willed women of character. Angie was looking for role models; she found them in the Dominican nuns.

But once she was at school, she realized the religious life wasn't for her. She was president of her sophomore class, an office she had also held her freshman year, and captain of the basketball team she had founded, despite her size. She was also having a lot of fun partying. Too much fun. Her grades were suffering, she owed several thousand dollars for some knee surgery, and she was on the verge of dropping out. She felt alone and afraid.

On the last day of April she went to the post office to mail a bill payment, and out stepped a tall, handsome Marine recruiter. He looked confident and sharp in his uniform.

"Why aren't you a United States Marine?" he asked, looking her in the eye.

"I'm trying to mail a letter," said Angie, glaring back at him.

Seven days later, to the dismay of her parents, she was across the country at Parris Island, getting screamed at by a drill instructor and thinking, *What the hell have I done?*

But the good-looking recruiter in his flawless uniform represented something to Angie that she wanted for herself. She had joined the Marine Reserves, which afforded her the opportunity to go back to college. Angie graduated from Dominican in 1976 as the "most outstanding student" in her class. The following year she attended the first gender-integrated class of Officer Candidate School and became a Marine officer. Years later she would joke that she looked better in her dress blues than in the black-and-white capes the Dominican sisters wear.

"Ladies and gentlemen, I'm very honored and I'm very humbled to have this responsibility entrusted to me," Angie said as she addressed the crowd at Pendleton Field. "But I will tell you, it's not me. It's truly the Marines that are before you who will accomplish the very task asked from the commandant of the Marine Corps and asked of this very nation to fill the ranks of the United States Marine Corps."

Angie's whirlwind week had started back east, with packing and moving out of her quarters in Virginia. Two days ago in a wood-paneled standing-room-only auditorium in the Gray Research building at Quantico Marine base, Angie's mentor, Major General Walter Gaskin, commander of the 2nd Marine Division, had presided over her promotion ceremony, replacing her colonel's eagles with the stars of a brigadier general. The next day she, her ninety-two-year-old mother, Florita; and sisters, Janie and Irene; brother, Amado; and sister-in-law, Gloria, had flown to San Diego.

Despite the hurried time line, one of Angie's first stops was at Pendleton Hall for a quick hello to her staff. She especially was eager to meet her sergeant major face-to-face before the change-of-command ceremony.

"I've heard a lot of great things about you," she said to Sergeant Major Woods.

Sergeant major is the highest enlisted rank in the Marines, and Woods wore the mantle well. Even in civvies people knew he was a sergeant major. He was broad-shouldered and fit, with wide-set brown eyes and hair shorn close to his head. Like many of the corps' top sergeants major, he was black.

Wow, what a little tiny woman to hold such a high position, he thought. "It's nice to meet you, too, ma'am," he said aloud, with only a hint of a Southern accent from growing up in western Tennessee.

The two shook hands. And although her hand was about half the size of his, her handshake was firm, the sergeant major noted. A good sign. He found her to be polite and inviting.

Angie thought the same about the sergeant major. He had a great handshake, not a weak one, like she sometimes got from men. Very professional. Angie was a hand shaker and a look-them-in-the-eye kind of person. The direct engagement came from her old recruiter training. Recruiters are constantly shaking hands—before, during, and after a conversation. A good handshake said a lot.

"My early mentors were my sergeants major, and I have that same expectation," she told Woods. "I rely a lot on the sergeant major to tell me the truth about what is going on. If I screw up, I expect you to say something."

"Aye, aye, ma'am," he said. Then they parted ways.

He'd never had a commander tell him that before.

Angie left satisfied. *This wasn't a hard introduction*, she thought.

Just as she'd done in every position, her way of doing business included treating her Marines with firmness and fairness, dignity and compassion. She wouldn't demand of them anything she wouldn't demand of herself. Whether that would be enough here remained to be seen.

———————————————— ★ ————————————————

One month later

Brigadier General Angela Salinas walked through the entrance of Wesley Palms, a retirement and assisted-living community in the Pacific Beach neighborhood of San Diego, and took off her camouflage cover, the military term for her hat. Before she could say a word, a woman approached.

"You must be here to see the general," the receptionist said. "I'll call for a golf cart to take you to his house."

In San Diego circles, a community filled with retired Marine Corps generals, *the* general was a title reserved for just one: Lieutenant General Victor "Brute" Krulak. Though he had served in three wars, the general was more than a battlefield hero; he is considered by historians as a visionary and architect of today's Marine Corps. Krulak designed amphibious assault landing craft that helped win World War II, and his employment of helicopters on the battlefield in Korea affected how wars are fought today. Most notably, he is credited with saving the Marine Corps when the government wanted to do away with it after World War II and Korea.

Never mind that the general had retired from the Marines when Lyndon Johnson was in the White House, or that Angie was six years old when he took command of the very depot that she now led. What mattered was that this man's support—or lack of it—could mean success or failure for the commanding general of MCRD San Diego.

Brute Krulak was the key to good relations in both the corps and the community. After retiring, he became a newspaper executive and columnist in San Diego and still penned opinion pieces. Across the country, at the Pentagon, he held the Marine Corps commandant's ear. Despite his ninety-three years, Krulak retained his brilliant mind. He was a philanthropist and a player in San Diego leadership.

That was important, because in addition to running the depot, recruiting, and training the recruits, the MCRD commander was very much the "Marine mayor" for San Diego. The depot sat on valuable downtown real estate, adjacent to both the harbor and the airport, surrounded by a bustling metropolis that had grown up around it since the 1920s. More than a few San Diego business developers and community leaders eyed the property and its possibilities. The only Marine base in the country within city limits, MCRD had come up on the Base Closure and Realignment Commission's chopping block in the past, only to be saved by the corps' and the San Diego community's urgent pleas against such an action.

"Whatever you do, go see my dad," Chuck Krulak, himself a four-star general who retired in 1999 as the commandant of the Marine Corps, had advised Angie. The senior Krulak was old-school and known to judge people based on their customs and courtesies. In bygone military days a newly arrived officer went to his commander's house with a calling card in hand for a formal introduction. Tales abounded of a depot commander who blew off the retired general and as a result never gained community support or earned a second star. And so every few years, when a new general came to town, he would make the pilgrimage to Brute Krulak's house to pay his respects—and hopefully gain his blessing. It was the corps' version of kissing the godfather's ring.

Angie climbed into the golf cart, and the driver followed the winding sidewalk path of the retirement community, whose 1960s-era cottages with low-slung roofs were perched high in the hills overlooking the Pacific Ocean's coastline. The morning was one of those crystal blue, sunny days San Diego is known for.

She had debated which uniform to wear. Not only do the Marines have the nicest-looking duds of all the service branches, but they also have as many uniforms as Macy's does dresses. Angie decided on cammies, since those were her "uniform of the day," the apparel she wore to work. The Marines don't wear their cammies in the "public domain," but this uniform certainly fit the occasion for her first official meeting with the Marine icon.

"Be sure to go to the front door," advised another retired general, who had found out the hard way that General Krulak's side entrance was not acceptable. Angie had heard many other things about Krulak. He could be polite. He could be a gentleman. And then there were all the horror stories.

Brute Krulak didn't get his nickname from being Mr. Rogers. A 1965 *Life* magazine profile summed up his personality this way: "In the course of minutes, he can be alternately avuncular, terrifying, expansive, withdrawn, and, always, inquisitive . . . he is about as tolerant of mistakes as a well-oiled rat trap."

As the golf cart approached Krulak's bungalow, Angie wondered which version of the general would show up. What if he grilled her with questions she didn't have answers to?

She had been in command for only one month. The leap from colonel to general was vast. What if Krulak was so unimpressed with her that the moment she left he dialed up General Hagee and berated him for sending a woman to command MCRD?

She already knew that after she arrived everyone had run to Krulak asking, "What do you think?"

In a story that ran the day after her assumption-of-command ceremony, the local *Union Tribune* had asked Krulak to comment on Angie's lack of combat experience. Krulak responded that her lack of combat credentials wouldn't hamper her ability to effectively inspire the boot camp's staff and recruits.

"Training recruits is not the same as training for combat," he was quoted as saying. "[This phase involves] learning the discipline and philosophy of the Marine Corps."

Angie was grateful for that public show of support. But what if now, behind closed doors, the general let her have it? She had no intel on how the general really felt about her presence on his hallowed San Diego Marine turf.

She steeled herself for the worst-case scenario. *Despite what I said in a public forum, I don't think you should be here*, she envisioned him saying.

She had reason to worry. Sixteen years earlier, when the military was facing a drawdown after the Cold War, the retired general had written an opinion piece in the *Evening Tribune*, offering a solution for making the Marines a leaner force: Cut out the women Marines.

Under the headline "Can Women Fulfill Role in Military?" Krulak said the corps had to focus on "competence and readiness . . . There will be little room for those who are not conditioned for and fully capable of fighting," he wrote. "This raises the troublesome, albeit delicate, question of women in uniform." Assessing women's contributions to the military, Krulak argued that women have a higher rate of attrition than men and, because of the turnover, are a more costly investment. He said they are four times more likely to report ill, and their percentage of being medically nonavailable is twice that of men. He added that somewhere between 10 and 17 percent become pregnant, which limits their abilities. "They can drive a large truck, but need a man's help if they have to change its tire. They can be assigned to an artillery unit, but they can't handle the ammunition."

He went on, "The first reality is that the manifest physical and physi-ological limitations of servicewomen are only the beginning. They are mag-nified by instinctual and emotional limitations, as well," he said. "Put plainly, as a group, and in a lesser degree than men, women do not want to fight, to kill, to risk being killed or captured."

At the time, Angie had been the first woman Marine to command a maintenance battalion headquarters company, but what bothered her the most was that her base commander had reprinted the article in the base newspaper.

Marines have always been proud of their warrior ethos and unapolo-getic for it. Brute Krulak's son Chuck, upon assuming the top Marine position in 1995, had told reporters that while women were important to the success of the corps, they had no place in ground combat, a sentiment shared by most military leaders, politicians, and the public at the time.

"Why? Because I don't think they can do it," the general was quoted as saying, noting later in the interview that he was "more on the side of women than most Marine generals."

Though such frank public remarks from an active-duty general would be unlikely today, mostly because times have changed and women have been tested on the battlefield, young female Marines still come across male Marines who believe that women not only shouldn't be in combat but shouldn't even be in *their* corps.

Angie's attitude on being a woman in places she was not wanted was always: "Get over it." And if anyone thought she'd gotten to be a commanding general because she was a woman, they didn't realize she had earned it *in spite of* that.

At ten thirty on the nose, Angie took a breath and rang the doorbell. The sound was quickly followed by the yelps of a small dog. A moment later the door opened, and a cinnamon-haired dachshund greeted her. Krulak and his wife, Amy, who died in 2004, had always owned dachshunds, and they were big supporters of the Humane Society. Brute had also served as president of the city's zoological society. Behind the dog she saw a stooped-over man dressed in slacks pulled up above his waistline and a cardigan sweater over a collared shirt.

"Hello, sir, how are you? I'm Angie Salinas."

"Hello," Krulak said. "Please come in."

The retired general was officially five feet, four inches tall. But official military heights can be vertically generous, depending on the mood of the measurer and who is getting measured. Angie was "officially" five-foot-one. And perhaps in her youth, before five knee surgeries, a back surgery, and thirty-two years of Marine life, she had been. But even at five feet, Angie could see clear over the general's balding head. He stood no taller than four feet, ten inches, and she outweighed him.

As the dog pranced around Angie's feet, she followed Krulak, who in his prime had been known to sprint rather than walk. Now he shuffled into the living room.

"Please have a seat," he said, motioning to a 1960s-era couch. The only other seating in the room was a recliner, which was clearly where the general always sat.

Though the Krulaks had once lived in Point Loma, an affluent area of San Diego, overlooking the harbor, this house seemed more like an efficiency apartment. It was nothing remarkable, but perfect for an elderly man who could no longer see or hear well. In addition to the recliner and couch, an impressive number of books filled bookshelves, and there was a table where a longtime personal assistant could handle correspondence.

Except for the dog, which jumped in and out of Angie's lap, the general was alone, which only added to her discomfort.

"Sir, I'm sorry you weren't able to be at the change of command. I'm honored to be here at MCRD. . . ."

And so began the pleasantries and pregnant pauses of an official visit. Less than fifteen minutes later, the general and his dachshund escorted Angie to the door.

Near the front entry he stopped. "I want to show you something," he said, pointing out some personal memorabilia, including a framed photograph of his three sons in uniform at Chuck's graduation from the Naval Academy.

"If you ever need anything, let me know," he said. "I can help you."

"Sir, thank you," she said. "I look forward to seeing you again."

"Until next time," he said.

Angie raised her hand and saluted.

Outside, the San Diego sun embraced her. The courtesy call had gone better than she'd hoped.

Two weeks later

When the members of San Diego's Rest & Aspiration Society heard that a woman would command MCRD, the men went into a panic. They faced an awkward dilemma: Should their all-male organization extend membership to Brigadier General Salinas?

The R & A Society was an old-boys' club of San Diego's successful and powerful—executives, physicians, bankers, attorneys, and judges. Founded after World War II, the society had a devil-may-care vibe. "We don't aim at nothing, so we can't hardly miss," was the club's motto, and monthly gatherings were part drinking club, part networking group. Membership was by invitation only, and the society always presented an honorary membership to the depot's new commanding general, which was less an invitation to join than an expectation. And every September on the third Thursday, the members, in turn, expected the commanding general to host the group, about a hundred men, at his residence, Quarters One. The party was the highlight of the year, even more popular than Ladies' Night Out, held at the famous Hotel del Coronado and the one event wives could attend.

After lots of discussion, society members made the decision not to break with tradition—the tradition of the party at Quarters One, that is. Gender aside, Brigadier General Salinas was grandfathered into the bylaws.

It was left to R & A Society member Major General Don Fulham, seventy-eight, who had commanded the depot from 1986 to 1988 and had resided in Quarters One, to call on Salinas.

Angie sensed the retired general was uncomfortable about something.

"We're real excited you're here," Fulham began. "Congratulations. And, ah, we have this group. . . ."

Four weeks after that, Angie stood in her backyard welcoming members of San Diego's establishment with her five-star handshake. The party had been moved to the last week of September because of Angie's travel schedule, though someone from the R & A had suggested Angie needn't be present, if the original date didn't work for her. After all, the society catered the party, and it would be held behind the house, like most events at Quarters One.

"Uhh . . . no," Angie said. "I wouldn't think of not being there. I couldn't miss the opportunity to meet some of San Diego's best men."

Quarters One sat upon a lawn of green velvet where Pendleton Avenue and Wharton Road came to a vee in front of a traffic circle. Two palm trees stood sentry in front of the residence, which was one of only five officers' quarters on the depot. The 4,000-square-foot Spanish Colonial home was dressed in beige stucco with a red-tiled roof. Built in 1925, it is one of twenty-five depot buildings on the National Register of Historic Places. It was easy to see why people wanted to come back again and again.

The men filed into the backyard, which was named Butler Gardens, after the estate's first occupant, Major General Smedley Butler. Calling the area behind Quarters One a yard was like calling Buckingham Palace a house. The area covered five acres of gardens. Hundreds of plants, trees, and flowers, including eucalyptus, azaleas, ferns, camellias, star jasmine, and bamboo from Okinawa, flourished in the Japanese-themed garden. In the center sat a large, rectangular pond for koi, which turned the water into a liquid rainbow.

The story goes that Major General Butler had ordained that any Marine who donated a plant, tree, or bush to his garden would receive a three-day pass. The offer was so popular that before long the grounds blossomed with colorful vegetation. That is, until the general received a letter from San Diego's mayor welcoming the Marines to San Diego and closing by asking him to please stop his Marines from stealing plants from nearby Balboa Park.

President John F. Kennedy gave a speech from Butler Gardens in front of a C-shaped hedge that came to be known as the "Kennedy Hedge." Another hedge of roses commemorated the ladies of the manor. A bush was presented to each wife at her husband's change-of-command ceremony and planted in her honor.

Now Quarters One was home to three ladies and no men. Angie's widowed mother, who had been against her daughter's joining the Marines, had come to see her in 1980 when Angie was a lieutenant stationed at Parris Island. Petite like Angie—just four feet, six inches tall—Florita, too, fell in love with the Marine Corps way of life and never left. When Janie visited in 1996, she stayed on as well.

"Everyone else who comes to visit has to have a round-trip plane ticket," Angie joked.

From the moment her daughter joined the Marines at age twenty, Florita had worried about her finding a husband.

"Mom, there are two thousand female Marines and two hundred thousand male Marines!" Angie had told her. And while she never married, her mother still held out hope.

"I'm not dying until you get married!" she proclaimed.

Meanwhile, Angie often relied on Janie to fill in where a wife was expected. Janie ran the household, and their mother was its commandant.

"You might tell people what to do everywhere else, but not here," Florita once told her.

Marines and their spouses usually knew Angie's marital status before she arrived at a new posting.

"She's single. What about the families?" was the usual response.

Traditionally a commander's wife offers leadership, mentorship, and, when appropriate, friendship to the legions of wives on base. The military entrusts her with a high level of responsibility—albeit without the authority of a person in uniform—and there's an unspoken expectation that she will provide selfless service and focus her attention on the welfare of families in the unit. In fact, through networking, she often brings to her husband's attention issues that have fallen through the cracks.

At the general officer level, a wife is the honorary president or adviser of the spouses' club, leads and advises family readiness group leaders, attends every ceremony and event on base, and hosts large events at her home.

But Janie was in her seventies and wasn't part of the circle of spouses, so Angie worked hard to connect with them herself and to stay on top of their concerns. She had "eyes on target."

Janie *was* a key volunteer and the queen of entertaining, whether it meant hosting a dinner party or decorating the house for the spouse club's tour of homes at Christmas. It was proof that things could still get accomplished outside the traditional norm.

As far as protocol, though, no one knew what to do.

Invitations were usually addressed by name to married couples or single Marines, but the Salinas clan didn't fit that model.

Playing host, however, was never a problem. The R & A guests filled Quarters One and admired the splendor of a bygone era. The military relics of former occupants—including Major General Butler's Mameluke sword, which hung on the center wall in the sunroom—made for excellent conversation pieces and were permanent fixtures in the historical landmark. Now Angie's personal furniture was mixed in with the government issue in the historic rooms, and there were family photos on the wall next to Major

General Butler's medals, which included two Medals of Honor. Angie thought it was important for others to see who they were as a family.

All the grandeur was quite a change from Angie's humble beginnings in public housing in Kingsville, Texas. Her parents had been born into proud families in south Texas and worked the *ranchitos*. Her father had a sixth-grade education and made a living as a mechanic, and her mother, who finished the fourth grade, cleaned houses and sewed shirts to help support their five children. When Angie was eight, her parents moved the family to northern California to escape the discrimination they found in 1950s-era Texas. Their American dream was to have all five children graduate from high school. Angie was the youngest. When she graduated, her mother told her what she had told her other children: "The rest is up to you. Make a difference with what you have that maybe someone else does not."

Now Angie was shepherding guests into the solarium and the "Kennedy Room," where JFK relaxed during his visit to the depot.

This was actually the second party she'd hosted at the house. The day after her assumption-of-command ceremony, Angie had invited her family and personal staff, including her chief of staff, secretary, and sergeant major, to a catered Mexican fiesta. It was probably the only time in its history that Butler Gardens featured tacos, fajitas, and a mariachi band. The general loved margaritas; they were her drink. And her brother was making pitchers of them that night.

I'm not going to drink that sissy drink, Sergeant Major Woods told himself as he held the margarita in his hand. The former drill instructor had never tried one and wasn't about to now. However, his Hawaii-born wife of twenty-four years, RhodaAnn, who normally didn't drink, gave the tequila concoction a try and loved it.

Among the guests at this inner-circle gathering, Sergeant Major Woods was surprised to see Colonel Jim Guerin, a tall, gray-haired widower who had retired in 1999. Woods had last seen him a decade ago.

I wonder why he's here? thought Woods. Colonel Guerin had been the sergeant major's commanding officer in the 1990s, and the two caught up about their days together on the drill field. But Woods never asked questions about the colonel's presence.

Beyond the hospitality, the evening was a way for Angie to bring her team together in her home and explain her command philosophy.

"You're stuck with me . . . like family," she told them. "We're all one big family."

Her first week, Angie had told the sergeant major about her thirty-day rule. "There are no hurt feelings if you feel you can't serve with me," she told him, adding that he was free to request a new assignment within a month. "But we've got to sing the same song for the sake of the troops. We have to have that relationship, because the Marines are not naive. We can fight like cats and dogs behind closed doors, but when the door opens . . ."

"Aye, aye, ma'am," Sergeant Major Woods responded. "I'm here. I'm good to go."

He just wasn't going to drink any margaritas.

The R & A crowd, though, was happy with any libation on offer, and the event was humming along, when, out back, Angie heard someone say, "Look! Is that General Krulak?" She looked up to see the elderly man stepping out onto the back porch.

The party came to a standstill.

Due to declining health, Krulak hadn't attended an R & A Society event in years. But here he was, shuffling along in plaid trousers, a khaki-colored cardigan, and a cap.

"Welcome to Quarters One. . . . Thank you so much for coming, sir," Angie said. "May I give you a tour?"

The general had lived in the home forty-five years earlier, but he might not have recognized the place. The home had gone through a major renovation the previous year to accommodate the demands of entertaining and now had air-conditioning as well as double-pane windows to block some of the airport noise.

The home also had someone who brought out the best in the house. Janie had a designer's eye and decorated Quarters One, as she did all of their homes, as if it had come straight out of *Better Homes and Gardens.* She could pull off plaids, stripes, polka dots, and cheetah print all in one room. She never relied on a traditional layout of a couch bookended by two end tables. Instead, furniture was placed at interesting and unexpected angles.

At the end of the evening Lieutenant General Krulak came to say good night.

"I just want to thank you both so much for allowing me to tour your beautiful home," he told the sisters. "I must say, this has got to be the most unmilitary home I've ever been in."

Janie and Angie burst into laughter. The comment gave them a lot of joy.

The party had been a success, but Angie had nothing to prove. Her objective was for the R & A men to see nothing had changed by her membership.

Nevertheless, she was keenly aware that the old general's presence spoke volumes to the crowd. Whatever anyone was thinking about her stayed merely a thought.

CHAPTER 3
The Cadet

 Bergan Arsenault was more nervous than nauseous, which was a good thing, considering the Black Hats were clear: "Throw up inside your shirt, or you won't pass jump school."

I've made it this far, Bergan told herself, as the C-130 lumbered along through the sky above Fort Benning, causing her stomach to lurch into her throat. "All I have to do now is jump five times, and I get my jump wings."

It was anticipating this moment—parachuting from an airplane at more than 1,200 feet—that had kept her up the previous night. Before airborne school, Bergan had never even been on a plane, which put her in the company of many World War II paratroopers, whose first plane ride didn't include an airstrip landing. Bergan, at least, had experienced that.

"Call me when you get there," her mother, Amy, had told her a few weeks ago during a teary good-bye following a two-and-a-half-hour drive from their hometown in the Adirondacks to Albany International Airport, where Bergan boarded a plane to Columbus, Georgia. She was to attend the Army's three-week Basic Airborne Course, better known as "airborne school" or "jump school." Such schools provide the preparation and confidence building needed to handle the rigors of leading soldiers in combat.

The flight to Georgia wasn't as bad as Bergan imagined. But she was about to do something travelers with thousands of frequent-flier miles would never attempt.

What mattered now was jumping out of a plane four times in daylight and once in darkness so she could earn her jump wings. Being airborne-qualified was a big deal at Norwich, a military college in Vermont where Bergan was a rising junior. Slots at jump school were limited, and cadets competed against one another just to get selected to go. They had to have excellent PT scores, top grades, and be an ROTC scholarship recipient. All the "high-speed" cadets wanted to go, and when they returned to campus, they not only wore their accomplishment on their chest, but also showed it in their gait. Bergan wasn't about to fail and do the duffel-bag drag back to Norwich.

Being here meant she was one step closer on her journey to becoming a military officer, a dream set into motion two years ago when she entered Norwich University, the nation's oldest private military college.

Bergan had been a few weeks shy of her sixteenth birthday when planes struck the World Trade Center and the Pentagon. She had wanted to serve in the military since she was a kid playing Army in the woods, and 9/11 only solidified her decision. But being a soldier wasn't enough. Bergan wanted to *lead* soldiers. To do that, she needed to go to college and receive a military commission.

Her worried parents hoped their goal-oriented daughter was merely going through a phase, but they knew that when she made up her mind, there was no changing it. Bergan's goal was to become an MP. Since women weren't allowed to serve in the combat arms, the military police corps was the closest she could get to that.

But first, she had to get through Norwich and jump school.

• • •

"Ten min-uuutes!" bellowed a jumpmaster over the roar of the plane's engines. Jumpmasters are the lead paratroopers who ensure soldiers' safety before jumps. The steady baritone was the only voice they'd hear on the flight, since the students weren't permitted to talk. Bergan and the others on board—a mix of young officers, enlisted soldiers, and cadets from across the country—sat limb-to-limb like packaged hot dogs in the stifling belly of the cargo plane on one of Georgia's triple-digit July days. A distinct smell—a tang of sweat, anxiety, and Bengay—permeated the plane.

The Air Force's C-130 is like a flying school bus, and today's students were on a one-way trip. Bergan had eaten a wedge of pizza washed down with Gatorade from the gut truck early that morning, though she hadn't been hungry. She knew enough about the Army to know it was best to eat when food, even bad food, presented itself.

The weight of her four-pound helmet made her head sway like a bobblehead whenever the plane hit turbulence. Taped across the front in black block print was, "C-21," her roster number. The "C" stood for cadet. College kids from the service academies and ROTC programs attended airborne school in the summer months. Since they weren't yet in the military, they ranked below privates in the eyes of the Black Hats, as the drill sergeant–like airborne instructors were known.

"Oh, these are our future officers?" the Black Hats would respond if a cadet did something stupid. Bergan just tried to blend in, a good idea at any school where push-ups are part of the punishment.

But she stood out nevertheless. During Tower Week, in the middle of the course, students needed three qualifying jumps off a thirty-four-foot tower. Hooked to a harness, each student steps off a platform that resembles a mock airplane door and descends to the ground suspended from a cable. It is equivalent to falling out of a fifth-floor window. Many find the towers more terrifying than an actual airplane jump. Up in the tower, waiting for one's turn, there's too much time to think. About the tops of the trees. About the pavement. About all the things that could go wrong.

Bergan was one of the few in her platoon who did three good consecutive tower jumps. That caught the eye of Staff Sergeant Dillard, an instructor whose ego matched his large size. Like all the Black Hats in the 1st Battalion, 507th Infantry Regiment, he wore a black ball cap expertly placed on his head and adorned with his rank insignia and a parachutist's badge.

"Come here, my little paratrooper," said Staff Sergeant Dillard.

"Yes, Sergeant Airborne!" Bergan answered with as much gusto as she could muster, and trotted over to her Black Hat. At jump school, students never walked anywhere; they double-timed. After a week in Georgia, Bergan's cheeks and pixie nose had turned the color of rosé wine. She hadn't bothered to pack the tube of SPF 50 sunscreen on the school's required-items list.

Dillard liked to brag about Bergan's tower skills to his fellow airborne instructors, who sometimes had to push their students off the tower. Bergan's roommate, another cadet, had washed out when she injured her knee after continually hitting it against a wall while descending from the tower.

When Bergan arrived at airborne school, a clerk had told her to pick a room. Ineligible to stay in the Bachelor Officer Quarters (BOQs), she and the other female cadets were to share a barracks floor with enlisted women going through the course. Dorm duties included trash detail and latrine cleaning.

I don't want this room; there's no door, Bergan thought, as she passed the first quarters she came to. The second room had no door either. She quickly realized none of the rooms had doors. She chose a mattress and placed her duffel bag on it. Except for the sunscreen, she had diligently packed everything on the school's list, including five pairs of underwear, three towels, three washcloths, five pairs of black- or green-soled socks, and five pairs of white "civilian" athletic socks (with no stripes or logos) that covered the ankles.

As the school instructed, she brought no more than $50 in cash. The other big rule? Clothing worn during off time that presented a "provocative appearance" was prohibited. That meant no tube tops, tank tops, or muscle shirts.

"Make sure you eat right, because the heat can take you as quick as not being able to do the physical stuff," Bergan's boyfriend, Tom, advised. "During runs, make sure you don't fall out. Just keep up with the person in front of you."

Tom Flannigan was a year ahead of Bergan at Norwich, and since he had attended airborne school the summer before, she had peppered him with questions. Bergan also knew she'd have to attempt ten pull-ups every time she entered and exited the company area. Thanks to her practicing on a pull-up bar that she had her parents hang in the doorway to her bedroom that summer, she'd gone from zero pull-ups to three or four. It wasn't ten, but most of the guys couldn't do that many either.

Males and females had to meet the same standards at airborne school. That didn't necessarily satisfy crusty airborne veterans who wondered why women were even allowed to attend, since the job of a paratrooper was forced entry by parachute into hostile territory. But women had been attending airborne school at Fort Benning since 1973, the same year the draft ended and the military converted to an all-volunteer force. Five years later women were allowed to join the 82nd Airborne Division at Fort Bragg, despite the grumbling of its leaders, who thought their presence would constrain the leaders' ability to conduct airborne missions.

"Get rea-daaay!"

After getting the go-ahead from the pilots, the jumpmasters unlatched the aircraft doors as if opening a vault. Wind whipped around the plane. The engines were even louder now.

Bergan scanned the plane's interior through the lenses of bulky brown eyeglasses ugly enough to repel any enemy. The large Army-issued frames gave her round twenty-year-old face a cartoonlike appearance. To keep her glasses from falling off, a strap held them firmly in place. She wore no makeup, jewelry, bobby pins, or barrettes, per the school's instructions.

Anything that could fall off—eighty pounds of helmet, boots, parachute, reserve chute, rucksack, and weapon case—Staff Sergeant Dillard had rigged, strapped, cinched, tightened, knotted, and bound so tightly to Bergan's body that sitting and standing up were athletic feats.

Airborne school was all about learning safety procedures, jump commands, how to exit the aircraft, how to land, and, yes, how to rig equipment.

So, earlier that day during Jumpmaster Personnel Inspection (JMPI), Staff Sergeant Dillard had gone over every inch of nylon, canvas, and metal, looking and feeling for twisted cotton webbing and waistbands, incorrectly routed straps and ties, improperly tied safety wires, and frayed static lines.

"Squat!" he said, and then cinched the parachute harness straps that were routed around the groin even tighter. The painful procedure was necessary to ensure that the chute wouldn't come loose. It also made bathroom breaks impossible unless one removed every piece of battle rattle and then went through inspection all over again.

"Outboard personnel stand up!"

Bergan struggled to her feet, lifted her folding seat, and secured it. Then she faced the ramp at the back of the plane. She was so physically uncomfortable she couldn't wait to be set free. She had feared boarding the plane that morning, but now she was more afraid to stay on it. Anyplace was better than this prejump purgatory that had started at four a.m. with a one-mile jog to the parachute hangar, followed by four or five hours of waiting, before heading to the plane. Finally things were happening quickly.

"Inboard personnel, stand up!"

Bergan was one of the only women on the plane, but under helmets and with parachute humps on their backs, you couldn't tell. Everyone looked like turtles. Terrified turtles. For two days straight, the Black Hats had drilled into their heads what to do if they hit water, telephone wires, trees, or another jumper. And if they lived through it, what to do if they became a "towed jumper" dragged behind the plane like an aerial banner. "Collisions," "entanglements," and "parachute malfunctions" are grave words in the paratrooper business. Bergan didn't think about what could go wrong. She had to trust her equipment and her training. That was the Army way.

"Hook up!"

As turbulence rocked the plane, Bergan steadied herself, reached up, and latched the snap hook from her universal static line onto the plane's anchor line cable. At five-foot-three, Bergan was just tall enough to reach the cable, which resembles a clothesline and runs the length of the plane. Once again she was in good company with the World War II paratroopers, who tended to be short so they could easily fit through the small doors of the military planes of the era. Tall airborne volunteers of that time were often sent to glider regiments.

"Check static lines!"

Bergan traced her static line and the one attached to the soldier in front of her. The fifteen-foot static line is a school bus yellow nylon cord with a tensile strength of 3,600 pounds. It is a paratrooper's lifeline. With one end now attached securely to the plane, the other end was at the top of Bergan's chute inside her deployment bag. If everything functioned properly, the static line would pull the main canopy from the bag on her back once she jumped. When the canopy inflated, her weight would cause the static line to break away from the chute and she would descend to the ground.

"Check equipment!"

Bergan checked the straps on her helmet and her parachute harness for the umpteenth time. *Just get out the door and count to four,* she told herself. *One one thousand, two one thousand, three one thousand, four one thousand . . .*

No one wants to get to five. Pass that fateful number, and it's time to pull the rip-cord grip, a metal handle on the Modified Improved Reserve Parachute System (MIRPS), the reserve parachute that lies against the stomach. In a way, the MIRPS was like the godfather: Know your place, treat it properly and with respect, and it could spare your life when death was seconds away. But make a bad judgment call or an innocent human error, such as accidentally deploying the spring-loaded MIRPS inside the plane and getting sucked out the open door, and the MIRPS will snuff out your life in such a brutal way that your funeral would have to include a closed casket. The MIRPS was the ultimate "frenemy."

"Sound off for equipment check!"

The jumpmaster placed both hands behind his ears, forming triangles with his arms and elbows.

"Okay! . . . Okay! . . . Okay!" Each soldier sounded off after patting the bottom of the trooper in front of him, until the one closest to the jumpmaster yelled, "All okay, Jumpmaster!"

"One minute!"

Heartbeats quickened as the plane slowed to 131 miles per hour. Jumpmasters on each side of the aircraft stood in the open doors, gripped the skin of the plane, leaned out as far as they could, and performed a "clear to the rear," which was a safety and ground reference point check. Then they pulled themselves back inside.

"Thirty seconds!"

Once again the jumpmasters leaned out the doors.

This is it, thought Bergan. *"Aggressive exit off of the platform. Maintain a tight body position. Count to four. . . ."*

"Stand by!"

Bergan was sixth in line from the door and shuffled toward it with the others. The plane's light flashed from red to green.

"Go!"

There could be no hesitation now, or someone could be seriously hurt, and as quick as a lemming running off a cliff, the first jumper disappeared out the door, then the second, third, fourth, and fifth. Bergan glanced quickly to make sure her arm wasn't tangled in her static line, looked the jumpmaster in the eye as she had been taught, handed him her static line, then took a step with her lead foot and disappeared from the plane. Like the others she fell sideways into the prop blast like make-a-wish seedlings from a dandelion.

In the excitement and terror of the moment, Bergan forgot to count to four.

Suddenly she felt a tug and a jolt on her body.

"Oh, my God, it opened," she thought. Above her head, a nylon canopy thirty-five feet in diameter and bowed like a mushroom slowed her descent; it might as well have been an angel's wings. Now she started falling vertically at twenty-two feet per second. She used her risers to steer herself away from other jumpers, so as not to collide with them or take their wind. On the drop zone white smoke billowed from smoke pots.

An air pocket caused her to pop back up in the air. After the rattle of the plane engines, the sky's stillness and silence enveloped her. But she wouldn't enjoy it for too long.

"Holy crap," Bergan said, as Mother Earth grew larger. All those Parachute Landing Falls (PLFs) she'd practiced over and over, suffering bruise after bruise under the scrutiny of the Black Hats—this was why.

Feet and knees together . . . Bergan told herself. *Balls of feet, calf, thigh, butt, back.* Falling at such a fast speed, paratroopers tend to land like a pile of bricks. The purpose of a proper PLF, where only the balls of the feet touch the ground before the other body points—calf, thigh, buttocks, and side—make contact with the ground is to help absorb the shock of landing and reduce injuries.

Bergan kept her knees slightly bent and her eyes on the horizon as she had been taught. As her feet touched the ground, like a winning gymnast she struck a perfect landing. Bergan remained in place for a few seconds, unable to move, unable to think.

"C-twenty-one . . . PLF! C-twenty-one . . . PLF!" It was the voice of God, Staff Sergeant Dillard on a megaphone.

Bergan quickly fell on her side, then onto her back. She activated the canopy-release assemblies so the chute wouldn't drag her across the drop zone. Because of her weight, she was the last to land despite being one of the first out. The Black Hats shouted through megaphones for everyone to hurry and pack their gear and get on the buses.

One down, four more to go, Bergan thought.

One month later. Norwich University, Northfield, Vermont

It was obvious to Bergan that her rooks needed a lot of work. Especially the girls. They looked clueless. As for the guys, some thought they wouldn't have to work as hard with a female cadet drill sergeant as their platoon leader.

Wait until our first PT session, thought Bergan, her large hazel eyes almost hidden under the black visor of her white service hat. *They're gonna learn I'm not to be fooled with.*

Bergan went into everything she did knowing she was going to have to prove herself just to earn respect, and she worked at it constantly. She never once wanted to be told she couldn't do something because she was female.

THE CADET ★ 61

Sometimes, though, she was mistaken for a different female on campus, her identical twin sister, Bethany, who got a kick out of being saluted by mistake on the small campus where everyone knew one another. Despite their similar looks, they were very different in personality. When the girls were eight, their mother, Amy, had looked out the window at the field next to their house and seen Bethany on the side in her cheerleading outfit, shaking pom-poms, while Bergan was wearing her bike helmet and a life preserver as she played football with the boys. Bergan remained rougher and tougher than Bethany and had no fear of anything.

As close as they were, the twins had originally wanted to be apart during college. But after three weeks away at school, Bethany, who had always leaned on Bergan, was lonely and missed her sister. The next year she enrolled in Norwich's small civilian undergraduate program with the goal of becoming a teacher. The sisters shared a psych major and many classes, but when it came to the military, that Bergan did alone.

Norwich's Corps of Cadets was about 85 percent male. But such stats meant little to Bergan, as the newest class in the college was about to discover.

Forty rooks—thirty-six boys and four girls—were standing in front of Bergan on the Upper Parade Ground of Norwich's postcard-perfect campus in the Green Mountains of central Vermont. All of them looked so young, Bergan thought, as she tried to seem as stern as she possibly could. Although they were only two years her junior, they may as well have been a generation apart.

"Eyes!" Bergan yelled.

"Snap!" the rooks responded, as all eyes focused on her.

"Get it back!" Bergan yelled.

"Pop!" the rooks said, voicing the required reply. After twenty tries, they had pretty much mastered where their eyeballs needed to be on command. Their facing movements—about-face, for example—were another story.

The process was an introduction to the profession of arms and would provide the basic building blocks in developing confidence and competence, attributes they would need as the military's junior leaders in the years ahead. While central Vermont was a place of covered bridges, ski slopes, cider mills, and festivals that celebrated everything from chamber music to cheese makers, the world beyond Norwich looked increasingly like a doomsday clock. The summer had brought reports of intense fighting in southern Afghanistan, an average of a hundred civilians dying each day in Iraq, Israel and Hezbollah reaching the breaking point, and North Korea launching a nuclear device in its own mountains.

But "UP," as the cadets called the parade field, was a nugget of emerald-colored grass lined with ancient maples and redbrick dormitories, many of them named after the generals and admirals who had graduated from the military college more than a century ago. UP was the heartbeat of the campus, where the 1,200-member Corps of Cadets gathered each morning in the dark for reveille, each evening for retreat, and on Friday afternoon for parades. Except during drill and ceremonies, cadets were prohibited from walking on the grass.

On this cloudy Monday in late August, a week before classes began, UP was mayhem, with sustained levels of ranting and shouting at four hundred slices of fresh meat dressed in khaki trousers, collared white short-sleeved dress shirts, black neckties, and ball caps. Today was Rook Arrival Day, the first day of Norwich's version of basic training. It marked the transition and transformation of the recruits from teenage sloths to Norwich cadets, a process that required pouncing on their every word, movement, and facial expression. Aside from its being a lot of fun for the upperclassmen, the purpose was to prepare the rooks to think quickly on their feet and make sound decisions under duress.

Wearing maroon ball caps with "ROOK" stitched in gold across the front was like having bull's-eyes on their heads (though being called rooks wasn't really so bad, considering the Citadel labeled its freshmen "knobs" and Virginia Military Institute named its first-years "rats"). Unlike the rest of the outfit, which would be replaced by a uniform in a few days, the hat stayed until the end of their "rookdom," months into the future, when, as a class, they would officially be welcomed into the Corps of Cadets.

A gold-colored chain with a gold whistle hung from Bergan's uniform as she walked through the formation, correcting lopsided salutes and body postures. Unlike some of the pudgy rooks who showed up in trousers a size too small, Bergan fit her uniform smartly. Because of her petite stature she had to have her trousers hemmed her freshman year. She'd been growing her hair out since then, and it was just long enough to tuck into a bun. She'd changed from the camouflaged BDUs (Battle Dress Uniform) she'd worn that morning, when she greeted the rooks and their parents, into her "Super Summer" Class Bs—gray slacks and a white collared shirt adorned with ribbons and the sign of her newest accomplishment, silver jump wings.

Staff Sergeant Dillard had pinned them on at graduation with a customary shove for good measure, a nod to the bygone tradition of "blood wings," when the newly initiated actually had the exposed metal spikes of their jump wing insignia pounded into their chests. The Pentagon cracked down on that tradition in 1997 after a macabre video of Marine paratroopers getting their blood wings appeared on CNN. When the Pentagon ordered the service branches to investigate the hazing ritual, an Army spokesman with a nose as long as Pinocchio's was quoted as saying, "The Army has yet to discover any blood pinnings," but would be on the lookout for such ceremonies. In the end, the Army let the Marines take the fall. But blood wings at Fort Benning had quietly gone the way of beer machines in the dayrooms.

Bergan zeroed in on a rook looking up at the overcast sky.

"Keep your eyes forward!" Bergan snapped.

"Oh, sorry . . ." said the girl, whose necktie was off center. For most of the girls it was the first time they'd ever worn the accessory, but Bergan's father had taught her how to tie one before her freshman year.

"The correct response is, 'Yes, Platoon Sergeant'!" Bergan was just inches from the girl's face. "Straighten your tie!"

"Yes, Platoon Sergeant . . ."

"Speak up!"

"Yes, Platoon Sergeant!"

The next two rooks seemed a little too relaxed.

"You think this is a joke?"

"No, ma'am . . ."

"The correct response is, 'No, Platoon Sergeant'!"

"No, Pla—"

"Wipe that look off your nasty faces! Drop and give me twenty! Noooow!"

The startled boys got down on their hands and knees, as did Bergan, who led them in push-ups. It was important that cadre members show they could do everything they told the rooks to do, and she had prepared for her new role by being in the best shape possible. She had had to compete for the position, too, going in front of a board of upperclassmen and answering questions related to standard operating procedures and school rules. Out of the thirteen cadet drill sergeants chosen, she was one of only two females.

Bergan's own drill sergeant her first year had been a female, which influenced her decision to try out for the role. Platoon Sergeant Lauren Fernando was always hard on the rooks, especially the girls. Bergan never wanted to disappoint her. Proving oneself is a recurring theme in the military, since service members change jobs regularly, which means a consistent flow of new bosses, peers, subordinates, and job responsibilities in a competitively charged environment. But women had the additional challenge of proving they could hold their own and excel *despite* their gender.

"You have two minutes to get changed," Fernando used to say. "Let's be the first outside in the hallway." She always wanted the females to be first.

It hit Bergan harder when Fernando yelled at her than when a male cadre member did. Fernando stood shorter than Bergan, but despite being small, she was physically strong. Bergan could tell she didn't let anything stop her, and that was an attribute Bergan wanted to emulate.

"Those were a sorry excuse for push-ups!" Bergan barked. "Get back in formation! Today! Move it!"

By now most of the rooks looked scared; some looked lost; others looked like they had no idea what they were getting themselves into.

When Bergan had shown up on her first day at Norwich, at least she had an idea of what to expect, thanks to an upperclassman who gave her a heads-up. She knew that as soon as her parents left, all hell would break loose.

Bergan had come a long way from her own Rook Week, when she and her new roommate, Meghan Richard, a dark-haired, blue-eyed Irish girl from Liverpool, New York, found themselves in a quandary late one night in their fifth-floor room in Hawkins Hall. They had spent part of the day learning how to properly roll their underwear, socks, and shirts. Their cadre had instructed them to go to bed, but the girls knew that the next day there would be an inspection of their bureau drawers. It was well past the mandatory ten p.m. lights-out when Bergan and Meghan dug out their flashlights and started rolling their clothes on Meghan's bottom bunk, making sure they didn't flash any light under the door.

"Want some?" Bergan said. She had pulled out her stash of Laffy Taffy, contraband that she had brought from home.

"Sure," Meghan said. She had never tried the candy, but it was late and she was hungry. It was the first night the roommates had had a chance to talk for more than a few minutes at a time, and it marked the start of their friendship.

Everyone remembers the first day at Norwich. It is always the same. Freshmen show up nervous, expecting people to be yelling at them and running around, but it is actually the opposite, a mind game of sorts. The upperclassmen help rooks carry their luggage to their rooms, they talk to parents, answer questions, help inventory gear, and make sure rooks have everything they need. Then comes lunch in the Campus Center with parents. Little do the rooks know it will be the last time they can talk during a meal.

With stomachs full, the newcomers stride across campus to Shapiro Field House to hear the college president's welcome address and to say good-bye to their parents. Soon they will walk only in the gutters, silent and forced to look down. Walking and talking are privileges at Norwich and have to be earned back as a class.

The school's "What Not to Pack" list—which included cell phones, bicycles, gum and candy, framed pictures, music CDs, rugs, plants, stuffed animals, and civilian clothes—should have tipped off even the most clueless as to what was in store. Where did the rooks think they were, anyway? Party State U? Norwich was a military college, a place where leadership, honor, discipline, morality, and citizenship were front and center.

Instilling such disciplines apparently required lots of yelling.

★

Three weeks later, September 14

Freshly showered and in jeans and a sweatshirt, Bergan bounded down the stairwell from her fourth-floor room in Alumni Hall and out into the damp autumn air. Wearing civvies after the duty day was an upperclassman's privilege.

It had been overcast and rainy all month, as evidenced by the soggy grass and sidewalk puddles. The gloom would linger until April. Fortunately, Champlain Valley's birch, beech, and sugar maples, dressed in yellows, oranges, and reds for fall, provided spectacular relief.

Now after dark, the lit-up lampposts offered up a bit of bling to an otherwise dank evening. Bergan nuzzled deeper into her coat as she walked along the Upper Parade Ground one dormitory over to Ransom Hall, an upperclassmen barracks, where Tom lived. The couple was going to Pizza Hut in Barre, an old quarry-and-rail town near Northfield. Barre also had an Applebee's, and that was about it as far as chain restaurants in the area, which was fine with Bergan and Tom. Neither was a gourmand. They'd choose fast food any day, which would serve them well in the Army, since most post towns specialized in takeout.

Bergan had last seen Tom an hour ago on the obstacle course at Rangers. Both of them were in the Ranger platoon, a high-speed extracurricular ROTC club on campus. The Ranger Challenge, a two-day competition held each November, was the club's big event of the year. Norwich's team would compete against the Ranger teams of other colleges in military skills that included marksmanship, patrolling, grenade assault, weapons assembly, and physical fitness, topped off with a timed ten-kilometer road march.

Tom was Norwich's Ranger Challenge commander. Strict about the training plan, he kept platoon members busy with two hours of PT in the morning and three hours of drill practice and training on the obstacle course and rifle range each afternoon. Unlike the U.S. Army Ranger School, which is open only to men, ROTC Ranger clubs and Ranger Challenge are open to both male and female cadets. (By the spring of 2012 the Army's leadership would begin to examine the possibility of opening Ranger School to women.) As with everything else, Bergan had to compete for a spot in the platoon and then compete again to be on the nine-member A-team. She had worked extra hard for the privilege, since it was Tom's last year and she wanted to compete with him.

She and her roommate, Ambre Hayes, were the two females on the A-team, but Tom didn't cut Bergan any slack—nor did she want any—just because she was a girl *and* they were dating. To ensure everyone received equal treatment, Tom had an NCO, Sergeant First Class Estrada, grade all events. To him, Bergan was just another cadet on the team. An exhausted cadet. She had Rangers and drill sergeant duty and also had to find time to study and sleep.

At least Bergan's rooks had finally bonded. They referred to one another as "rook brothers" and "rook sisters" and were deep into their "rook books," a handbook of knowledge on all things Norwich, including the 183-word honor code they had to memorize and recite upon the demand of upperclassmen.

But Bergan's female rooks continued to frustrate her. They still had no military bearing nor any idea what Norwich or the military was about. The little things bothered Bergan the most: They consistently kept their long hair in sloppy buns, aligned their toothbrush and shampoo improperly in the drawer, and often forgot to square the hallways and "sandwich their sentences," leaving off the "sir" or "ma'am" at the beginning and end of every utterance. One female rook had dropped out of school earlier that week.

Norwich had begun voluntarily admitting women cadets in 1974, two years before the service academies were ordered to do so by Congress, and now about one in seven cadets at Norwich was female. Ironically, while the females had higher attrition rates than the males early on, they also consistently held a high percentage of leadership positions in the corps. The regimental commander, the highest-ranking cadet at Norwich for the 2006–07 school year, was a woman, the second to hold that position.

Being in the minority didn't really bother Bergan, since most of her friends—except for her sister, Bethany—were guys anyway, and she figured it would prepare her for life in the Army.

But she did push her own females a little harder than the men, because that was the way she had been trained. She wanted her young women to do the best they could without the excuse of being a female.

Bergan put all that out of her mind as she entered Ransom Hall, which was as cold inside as it was outdoors. Antiquated heating systems meant cadets living in unrenovated barracks often studied bundled up with gloves on in their rooms during the coldest months. Tom lived on the first floor, and his door was ajar. Cadets weren't allowed to decorate their quarters. Except for the TV, a senior privilege, the room looked like all the others, with a bed, a weapons rack affixed to a wardrobe, a bookcase, and a desk with a computer and an issued desk blotter.

"Hi, you ready to go?" Bergan said. "I'm starving."

"Hey," said Tom, who was seated at his desk. "I'll be ready in a sec. I gotta finish up something." The twenty-two-year-old kept his blond hair clipped in a high-and-tight, which topped his handsome, square-jawed face. Like many male cadets, he was skinny, with the body of a boy-man. Filling out could take until he reached the rank of major, when many officers also had to start watching their weight.

Bergan sat at the edge of his bed, which was a bit like sitting on a gift-wrapped box. Tom's bed was covered with a maroon wool blanket with "Norwich" stamped in large gold letters and expertly centered on the bed with the blanket's edges tucked under the mattress at forty-five-degree angles. The second of two gold bars near the bottom of the blanket was lined up exactly along the foot of the mattress. A gold dustcover—a blanket folded in half lengthwise—covered the pillow and was also tucked in at forty-five-degree angles. The tradition dated back to the Army's cavalry days, when the covering was needed to keep dust and debris at bay. Tom's pillow rested under the dustcover with the white pillowcase opening facing the wall.

Such laser focus to detail is important both at military schools and in basic training, because it clearly translates to success and failure during deployment, where minutiae could range from a complicated operations order to conduct counterinsurgency in Iraq to recognizing subtle changes in the behavior of a tribal leader in Afghanistan.

"What are you working on?" Bergan asked.

At that moment Toby Keith's hit song "Huckleberry" filled the room.

It was their song. Bergan didn't really like country music, but she liked that one. The previous year Tom had given her a framed photo of the two of them at the Regimental Ball with the song's lyrics imposed on the print. Tom was in his cadet blues, and Bergan wore a green cocktail dress. Female cadets were allowed to wear dresses to the ball—if they had dates.

As the song played from the computer, Tom turned in his chair to face Bergan and knelt on one knee.

"Berg, will you marry me?"

Bergan could tell he was trying not to cry as he held up a diamond ring.

Bergan's eyes widened. She said just one word, the most essential one: "Yes."

And with that Bergan and Tom were on their way to becoming "dual military," a term describing a married couple who both wear the uniform. The planning, compromising, calculating, forecasting, and "working the system" on how to have a life together while in service to their country had begun.

Tom placed the ring on her finger. The center diamond, a half-carat, had two smaller friends on each side, and tiny diamonds surrounded the band. Like most cadets, he purchased it on a payment plan that would go into effect when he started accruing a paycheck on active duty.

Tom and Bergan had met during her freshman year, when Tom had been Bergan's corporal cadre. Back then she hadn't liked him because he was constantly yelling, while Tom's initial impression of Bergan was simply that she was a freshman he needed to train. Bergan was a rook, and he viewed her as such. But he did consider her one of the high-speeds in the company, good with uniforms and room inspections.

During Rook Week he persuaded her to switch from Navy ROTC—Bergan had planned on joining the Marines—to Army ROTC, by convincing her there were more opportunities for women in the Army. Of course, most of Bergan's cadet cadre were in Army ROTC and naturally wanted her to join their service branch.

That summer, after her rook year, Bergan texted Tom on a whim, while he was at airborne school. He didn't know how to text, so he called her back instead. From that moment on, they talked to each other every day until they went back to school in August. They have been together ever since.

As soon as they started dating, Bergan knew Tom was the one. They had the same goals, the same stubborn and independent personalities, and the same values, backgrounds, and conservative views. Both were from small towns in the North; both their dads were building contractors; both came from close-knit families with parents in long marriages. If there were differences, it was that Tom was more of a people person, while Bergan was an introvert.

While it might seem surprising for a young woman like Bergan, with big plans, to marry while still in college, as with many military couples, practicality played a role in the timing of their engagement. Tom and Bergan hoped the Army would assign them to the same post if they were already married before Bergan went on active duty. And unlike the service academies, Norwich allowed cadets to marry—although living together was forbidden. It was a bit like being authorized to purchase a bottle of water but prevented from drinking it. It didn't matter that much; Tom, who also wanted to be an MP, would be in the Army and stationed elsewhere by that time anyway.

In Norwich's orderly world, with its taut bedding and drawers of rolled underwear, where preparation and planning equaled success, the couple's personal lives now appeared aligned with their future in the Army.

Meanwhile, on the other side of the world, bombs rocked Baghdad. One of the dead was Sergeant Jennifer Hartman, an Army cook Bergan's age with the 4th Infantry Division. Two other soldiers were killed in the blast that wounded thirty.

Between schoolwork and her cadre duties, Bergan rarely caught the headlines, and she missed this one. Little would she realize, headlines like this were the norm in the profession she was about to enter.

"Okay, let's go eat," Tom said.

It would be an early night. Ranger PT started at five the next morning.

2007

Four days into the New Year, President Bush nominates Lieutenant General David Petraeus to replace General George Casey as the senior commander in Iraq. Less than a week later, Bush announces that efforts to secure Baghdad have failed. His change in strategy includes committing an additional 20,000 American troops to improve the security environment in Baghdad.

At the end of February, Vice President Dick Cheney, while visiting Bagram Air Base in Afghanistan, escapes an assassination attempt by the Taliban.

The insurgency in Afghanistan grows, and the employment of IEDs and suicide bombs increases and many provinces of the country are increasingly violent. Reconstruction efforts stall because of a poor security environment.

In September, General Petraeus travels to Washington and tells Congress the military needs more time to meet its objectives in Iraq. September also brings a standoff with Iran's nuclear program.

The Washington Post's February exposé on wounded warriors at Walter Reed Army Medical Center and their poor living conditions, inadequate care, and management results in the dismissal of Major General George Weightman, who oversaw the hospital. Army Secretary Francis Harvey also steps down. The scandal results in a review of the VA health care system and improvements in treatment for soldiers with traumatic brain injury and post-traumatic stress syndrome.

CHAPTER 4
Doyenne of the Depot

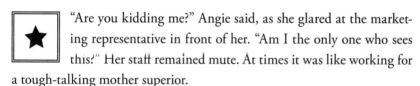

Angie: Spring 2007. Pendleton Hall, MCRD, San Diego

"Are you kidding me?" Angie said, as she glared at the marketing representative in front of her. "Am I the only one who sees this?" Her staff remained mute. At times it was like working for a tough-talking mother superior.

Angie held the Ultimate Fighting Championship program brochure up as if she were holding dog crap. Each page had a scantily clad woman in a provocative pose. Except for the last page. On that page was a large prototype advertisement, a close-up photo of a sharp-looking African-American Marine.

Finding markets to reach a target audience—in this case young males—to recruit into the military was a challenge four years into an unpopular war. But clearly, the Ultimate Fighting market was not a venue to be pursued under this general's watch. And Angie was far from finished taking a wire brush to the marketing rep's ass.

"The idea is to show Marines as elite, tough, proud, and honorable," she said. "Somebody's mother is going to see our ad in this brochure, and you think she's going to want her son to join the Marines? She's spent eighteen years trying to inculcate in him values that include respect—one quick look at this program and she'll be slamming the door in the recruiter's face."

The adman opened his mouth to speak, then quickly closed it.

"There are some who believe Marines are individuals who had few choices in life and became Marines. They also think the Marine Corps enlists high school dropouts and criminals. *You* think this endorsement of UFC will enhance our elite image, while I think it will only cement their impression of how Marines view women," Angie said. "I can't see spending scarce advertising resources on this. I think you can do better."

If there had been any doubt as to how Angie viewed the mixed-martial-arts discipline, which was part sport, part spectacle, she had made herself clear. Angie would not support any UFC Marine recruitment advertisements.

After the meeting, the adman fled from Pendleton Hall like a scalded cat.

Meanwhile, down the hall in Sergeant Major Woods's office, a district commander needed the sergeant major's opinion.

"Do you think the general is going to pass this?" he asked. It was a frequent question since Angie took command. She had a reputation for being tough on tattoos, even those already on recruiters. On those, she'd been influenced by a parent's comment.

"You won't let my kid join," a mother told her at an event, "but you've got your recruiters with tattoos selling the Marine Corps."

Angie realized the woman was right. After the exchange, she met with Sergeant Major Woods to discuss the best course of action. Recruiters with inked arms were to wear dress blue Charlies (long sleeves and a tie) all year long, no matter how hot it was outside.

"Look, ma'am, it's a bulldog!" a Marine told her, proudly showing off his forearm when she visited one of the recruiting stations.

"When you're eighty-five, it's going to be a Chihuahua," she warned. "And it's going to be on your wrist. How much did you pay to get that done?"

"This one was cheap. Less than a thousand dollars, ma'am."

"Aren't you married with two children?"

"Yes, ma'am."

"Bet your wife would like that thousand dollars back."

Now Woods looked at the photo of a recruit prospect and his tattoo.

"You can try . . ." he said, sounding doubtful.

Racist, sexist, gang-related, and other offensive tattoos had long been banned by the corps, but in March 2007 the policy was amended to prohibit excessive tattoos on arms and legs. Those on the head or neck were also unacceptable. General James Conway, who had become the Marine Corps commandant the previous November, had authorized the overhaul, noting, "Tattoos of an excessive nature do not represent our traditional values." The corps was all about image, and that had to be protected. Since the service branch was small, it could afford to be selective, though fighting two wars had made it more difficult.

But the new policy was vague, and what was considered "too big" or "too many" was left open to interpretation by commanders.

Regulations directed any applicant with four or more tattoos to be reviewed and approved by the first general officer in the chain of command. Any single tattoo bigger than a hand had to be approved by Angie herself. Everybody with a questionable tattoo got the opportunity to plead his or her case in her court.

First up, a photo of a skull tattoo. Wearing a fedora hat. With snakes coming out of its eyeballs.

"What does that tell you?" Angie said. It was important to her to connect the dots. She felt that tattoos reflected a person's thoughts and said something about the individual's character.

"Nothing, ma'am," the commander said.

"No, it's something," she said. "Is this the type of person we want in the corps? Would you trust your son or daughter to this person or would you want them to be their friend?"

She flipped the page to the next photo. This one had a naked woman on a forearm.

The commander read Angie's look. "Ma'am, he said he can put a bikini on her."

"No," Angie said.

"Ma'am, would it be better if he put a dress on her?"

"No," Angie said.

"It's just a tattoo, ma'am."

"No, it's not," Angie said. "It's not just the tattoo; it's everything that it represents."

"He didn't know what it meant."

"Yes, he did," she said.

"He's a good guy. . . ."

"He might be a good guy, but we're looking for a good guy who has common sense, who realizes a naked woman on his forearm is a bad idea," Angie said.

Case closed.

Her chief of staff stuck his head in the office.

"Hey, Chief, there's trash blown up against the fence between us and the airport," she told him, which was his cue to get it taken care of. The day before, Angie had gone for a bike ride across the depot, a chance for exercise and more specifically an opportunity to notice every detail of what was—and was not—happening on MCRD.

Like many generals, she hated seeing litter on her depot. The second time she told her chief of staff about the trash, his reaction was, "Certainly we have bigger things to do than that." But he came to realize that insistence on litter removal was not so different from the Marines' cherished close-order drill, which taught discipline and organization. He also knew that each year more than 100,000 visitors entered the gates at MCRD San Diego expecting everything from manicured pristine lawns to barking drill instructors. Trash was a disappointment and would ignite a flurry of calls to the general's office.

Angie rubbed her temples. It was only nine a.m., but like most Marines she had been up for almost five hours. It came in handy that Quarters One was a quick two-hundred-yard walk from Pendleton Hall. She started off her day the way she always did, in her basement with one precious hour—four thirty to five thirty a.m.—carved out on the schedule for herself, to run on her treadmill. After that, things that needed to be done that day often occurred to her while she was blow-drying her hair. Her staff started calling them "the hair-dryer taskers." Impressively, two-thirds of the hair-dryer notes usually turned into positive accomplishments by the end of the day.

Later, on her way to a Wounded Warrior golf tournament, Angie was still steaming about the adman. As she walked to the car with Sergeant Major Woods, her driver, and an aide, Angie reached down and picked up a candy wrapper.

"Can't say I'm not setting the example; even the general picks up trash—a Kodak moment," she joked.

Sergeant Major Woods removed the offending paper from her hand.

Before getting into the car, Angie zeroed in on a meaty Marine walking along the sidewalk. She walked over to her unsuspecting target, a chunky enlisted recruiter.

"How much do you weigh?" she said.

"Ma'am?"

"Do you know you look overweight?" Angie said. "Do you understand you have to look good? You represent the corps on the streets of America and may be the only Marine they ever meet! It's important not only that you look good but that you are proud to be a Marine. How you look tells me a lot about you."

Then she left the job of fixing that problem to Sergeant Major Woods. It was teamwork at its best.

Angie was the first woman general whom most of the staff had worked for. There weren't any real differences when it got down to doing the job. But she had her own style. To be sure her intent was understood, for example, she often said to her staff, "I know what I said; now tell me what you heard."

The command was a complex one. The corps needed to be 202,000 strong, which required enlisting 40,000 recruits each year during an un-popular war. The general and the sergeant major oversaw the recruiting and training of about half of those, and Angie was responsible for more than 1,600 recruiters in twenty-four recruiting stations. The 8th, 9th, and 12th Marine Corps Districts of the Western United States and more than

3,000 service members, including close to 500 drill instructors on the depot, fell under her authority. She was also in charge of MCRD's day-to-day operations—everything from paying the light bill to reviewing VIPs staying in the Bachelor Officer Quarters.

Since she'd taken command, she and Sergeant Major Woods had fallen into a comfortable, albeit hectic work rhythm. Every week she traveled with Woods and other staff members, often on a six thirty a.m. flight on Monday morning, to visit recruiting stations. The goal was to return by Wednesday evening so they could be on the depot for the weekly Family Day on Thursday, and Friday's graduation ceremony.

Along the way, the two forged a connection. One day as they walked the grounds of the depot she said, "Sergeant Major, pinch me. I just never thought I'd be at this level."

Woods knew his boss never doubted her talent or perseverance, but it was a humbling moment for him to see a side of her that not many generals would have shared.

And for Angie, even a golf tournament was a chance to get her message across. At the buffet lunch before playing, Angie and Sergeant Major Woods, now in civilian clothes, carried their trays over to where two young Marines were eating.

"Do you mind if we sit with you?" Angie said. She parked her tray next to one of the men, a lance corporal who was covered in tats.

"How many tattoos do you have?" Angie asked.

"Five," he said.

"So how much does it cost to get one of those?" she said.

"Anywhere from two to three hundred dollars."

Sergeant Major Woods listened as he ate his chicken. He knew where this was leading.

"Did you know that with those tattoos you wouldn't be able to go on recruiting duty?" Angie said. "And here's another thing . . ."

With more questions, Angie found out the Marine was an instructor at the School of Infantry at Camp Pendleton.

"But you're from North Carolina," Angie said. "Why didn't you ask to be assigned to the School of Infantry at Camp Lejeune?"

"Because I don't want to be at a school that trains women," he said.

Sergeant Major Woods saw his boss's antennae go up and her eyes flash.

Be careful what you are saying, thought Woods, staring at the young man, who was on the path to verbal suicide.

"Tell me more about why you feel this way," Angie said.

"Real Marines aren't women," he said. "I'm combat arms."

"Don't you think after twelve weeks of boot camp everyone has earned the title of Marine?" Angie said. "Everyone went through the same training. Don't we teach that everyone, male or female, is a Marine?"

By this point the Marine's buddy had figured out something was amiss, but the lance corporal had an audience. He continued to pontificate.

"Yeah, but I don't have to put up with it," he said. "I'm a grunt. I don't have to work with 'em."

The sergeant major had heard enough.

"Did you know we're Marines?" Sergeant Major Woods said. "This is Brigadier General Salinas. She's the commanding general of MCRD San Diego, and I'm Sergeant Major Woods."

"Really?" the lance corporal said, still unaware of the deep pit into which he'd fallen.

After the meal, Sergeant Major Woods pulled the Marine aside and lit into him like a vulture ripping into roadkill.

"Are you out of your mind? To say that to a general? And to a *fe*-male general? That you're not too fond of women in the corps?"

"Sergeant Major, she asked me my opinion. . . ."

"Who's your sergeant major?"

Later that day Woods contacted the Marine's sergeant major to have him counseled.

At the end of the day Sergeant Major Woods crossed the hall to his boss's office to discuss the rest of their week. She was just getting off the phone on what appeared to be a personal call.

"Did you know Jim Guerin was my significant other?" she said.

"I do now," Woods responded.

She and Jim Guerin had met in 1999, when he left the corps. Six years older than Angie, he was a widower whose wife had died of breast cancer a few years earlier, and the father of three grown daughters. After retirement, Jim had stayed in San Diego, working for the United Way and raising money for the Combined Federal Campaign.

In 2001, when Angie was based in San Diego as the 12th Marine Corps District commander, she had needed a date to the Marine Corps Ball and invited Jim. Angie's aunt, uncle, cousin, sister, and mother all shared the table.

After that, she and Jim would go golfing as part of a group, and gradually their friendship deepened into a different relationship. By 2004, they were "an item," showing up at events together.

"You're my eye candy tonight," Angie would joke.

And now that she was the general at MCRD, there was a natural fit that worked perfectly for them. She didn't have to explain to Jim about the corps or her role as commander, though at parties people sometimes assumed he was the general and went to shake his hand, and Jim would promptly point to Angie and say, "*She's* the general."

★

On an early spring morning, Sergeant Major Woods was perched atop a town house roof with some other Marines hammering sheeting into rafters. It was the last place he expected—or wanted—to be during the duty day. Everyone knew the general was into giving back to the community in terms of volunteer service. But what about the making of Marines? All he could think was, *General, we have recruits to train, and I'm going to be spending today pounding a nail for Habitat for Humanity?*

The lot below was a muddy mess, the result of three days of rain. One roof over, Angie, dressed in jeans, a turtleneck, a Marine Corps sweatshirt, and a white ball cap, was pounding nails like a pro. It was evident this wasn't the first time she'd used a saw and claw hammer.

The twenty or so Marines they were with had been at the work site one day the previous week as well, framing a row of town houses in a low-income neighborhood of small bungalows on West Sixth Avenue in Escondido, a town with a large Hispanic population just north of San Diego.

Later on, Woods moved inside, nailing brackets into walls, hammering nails into studs, and contemplating the recruit training he was missing. From time to time he noticed the general talking with reporters.

The next day, back at MCRD, Woods held up the *Union-Tribune* and read the headline: "Sharing Their Skills: 20 Marine Volunteers Get Habitat Project Back on Schedule."

"Marines coach Little League, contribute to the United Service Organizations and feed the homeless," Angie was quoted as saying. "But something like this is especially important to Marines because we spend so much time away from our families. Ten years from now, we can drive past this site and know that we helped people who would not necessarily have been able to own a home. Marines appreciate how important a stable home is."

The sentiment would later be echoed in another publication, which said: "Among the modest volunteers were the depot's top leadership Brigadier General Angie Salinas, Commanding General, and her right-hand man, Sergeant Major Bobby Woods."

Sergeant Major Woods put the paper down. "What a great thing we did!"

The Habitat for Humanity foray was hardly Angie's only outreach into the community. She was equally comfortable with a gaggle of Girl Scouts sending cookies to deployed Marines through Operation Thin Mint and speaking to chapter members of the Daughters of the American Revolution at their tea.

Word had quickly spread about the general's charismatic style and self-deprecating humor, and invitations flooded in. She turned down none of them, and soon she was doing three speaking engagements a week, often standing on her toes or on a box at the podium so she could be seen. It was too much, Angie knew, but she felt that she had a rare opening to engage the public, particularly those who knew little about, or had little interest in, the Marine Corps. What group wouldn't want a commanding general as the speaker at its monthly meeting? She used the opportunity to get an articulate and consistent message out, which was critical in shaping public opinion, improving community relations, and helping recruitment for the corps.

Before long, women's and Hispanic groups were showering her with awards. In March, just seven months after taking command, she was recognized on the floor of the State Assembly as the 76th Assembly District's Woman of the Year. *Latina Style* magazine gave Angie its Leadership Award, and she was named by *San Diego Magazine* as one of six women who moved the city.

Sometimes when addressing a Hispanic group, she'd confide that her parents made her and her siblings speak English at home. They didn't want the kids to speak English with an accent, for fear they would be discriminated against. Lamenting her Spanish-language skills, she noted ruefully that she could order "two burritos, two tacos, and a beer, please" in Spanish and be understood perfectly.

As a Marine, Angie hadn't always embraced her heritage. Until she was a lieutenant colonel, she hadn't wanted to be singled out as either a good female Marine or a good Hispanic Marine. She just wanted to be a good Marine. But her mind had changed in the late nineties, after she flew to Texas to attend a cousin's wedding. When the ceremony's emcee started recognizing out-of-town guests, Angie clapped along with the others.

But Janie told her, "I think they're talking about you!" As Angie made her way to the front to say a few words, everyone in the room stood up. The applause was thunderous, and she realized that the guests were looking not only at her but also *to* her. At that moment she represented the dreams they had for their own children, and from that point forward, Angie understood the legacy of her heritage and her responsibility.

The sergeant major had caught on to his boss's pop star status in the Hispanic community when he accompanied her to a school in Chicago following a recruiting visit. The principal, who knew little about the military, introduced Woods as Angie's "bodyguard." She meant well, though that wasn't appropriate for a sergeant major. When Angie got up to speak, she corrected her: "To be quite honest, the sergeant major is not my body-guard; I'm his."

But that day, Woods felt like Angie might actually need a protector. After her speech, the general was mobbed as she signed copies of a magazine she was featured in. The students were getting way too close, Woods thought. He'd never witnessed such a reaction to a Marine, and it scared him. *We have ten minutes to get out. I'll throw her over my shoulder and take off.*

He had come to realize Angie was a voice for people who didn't always have one.

Later that year the *San Diego Business Journal* awarded her its 2007 "Women Who Mean Business Award." During the celebratory evening dinner, the emcees from the local TV station, who were modeling the sponsors' clothes and jewelry, talked about what they were wearing and the prices of the items. When it came time to give out awards, Angie walked up to the podium in her dress blue-white uniform.

"Come on, say something," the emcee urged. Angie had been told she wouldn't have to speak, and she hadn't prepared any remarks. But she stood there and looked out at the one thousand attendees, mostly women, gathered around countless tables.

"Shoes? Forty-five dollars," she said. "Haircut? Thirty dollars. Cubic zirconia earrings? I think were fifty dollars. But to wear the uniform of a United States Marine is priceless."

It was classic Angie Salinas.

August 23, 2007. Washington, D.C.

Angie and had just returned to her hotel room for the evening. She took off her boots, turned on the TV, and cracked open a beer. She was out of town, sitting on a promotion board, a closely guarded proceeding to ensure the integrity of the promotion process. No one was supposed to know who sat on such boards until the promotion lists were released months later. Some people at MCRD thought Angie had simply taken leave.

As she unbuttoned her cammie uniform blouse and sat in her T-shirt, she glanced at CNN. The volume was turned low.

"That looks like San Diego," she said. "That's MCRD. . . ."

Then she caught part of the crawl on the bottom of the screen: ". . . worst case of Marine drill instructor abuse since Ribbon Creek . . ."

"What the . . ."

Angie knew the drill instructor in question. Sergeant Jerrod Glass was being charged with, among other things, physically abusing a platoon of recruits. In February, Angie had relieved a team of drill instructors who served with Glass—the most junior drill instructor on the team and a recent DI School honor graduate—for failing to supervise him properly. She had gone on to approve Glass's case for court-martial months ago, but no one had informed her of the arraignment date, which, according to Wolf Blitzer, was today.

She immediately called her chief of staff.

"Do you think you could have told me?" she said.

"We didn't think it was going to be a big deal, ma'am."

"The commandant is going to think this is a big deal," she said.

As the commanding general, Angie had the authority to dole out punishments and send Marines accused of offenses to court-martial. The San Diego paper had noted that disciplinary actions "jumped markedly" when she took command. The year before she arrived, six drill instructors had been disciplined for misconduct, a number that rose to twenty-one after she came to the depot in 2006, and another seventeen in 2007.

Angie had two unbreakable rules: A drill instructor never touches a recruit with malicious intent, and a recruiter must never be involved in an unprofessional or personal relationship with any applicant, even if the applicant is of legal age.

"There are things you don't do," she told her people. "No parent expects their kid to be abused by an institution that you trust." If DIs or recruiters crossed the line, she expected them to be held accountable for their actions.

Angie always looked for intent. If a DI closed the blinds, it indicated he was going to commit an act intentionally. Angie wouldn't tolerate that.

"I'm holding each of you as peers to be accountable to each other," she told her drill instructors, not because of fear, but because they wanted to do the right thing. "Parents have accepted that their son or daughter may go in harm's way, but they shouldn't have to worry that something is going to happen during the twelve weeks at boot camp."

She also zeroed in on recruiters who had flings with high school girls. In her mind, the most heinous offense a recruiter could commit was to violate a parent's trust.

Recruiting is considered a special-duty assignment for which Marines are handpicked, since they are in the community with little supervision, interact daily with civilians, and influence public perception of the corps. Recruiters often meet teenagers on high school campuses or at job fairs, and being involved with a female applicant is known as "dipping in the pool." Angie had no tolerance for the practice; nor did local law enforcement, which prosecuted and jailed recruiters who had sex with underage girls.

Sergeant Major Woods could see the situation from what he called a man's viewpoint. Sure, the recruiters may have crossed a line, but many of these girls aggressively preyed upon the Marines' weaknesses by flirting and inviting advances. He thought Marines accused of lesser offenses and who had excellent records deserved a second chance.

Angie didn't buy it. "Every recruiter should have a high standard, and we're holding them accountable," she insisted. And she did.

"I don't care if you're single or married," the general told her recruiters. "When you say, 'Hi, my name is Sergeant John Smith, and I'm a recruiter,' you have established a professional relationship. When you drop your daughter off at school, do you expect the gym teacher to be inappropriate with her? Is it worth losing your marriage or a stripe over?" she continued. "I don't care if you have a ten who's in front of you stark naked. You have to walk away. You think she's a notch in your belt? You're wrong. You're a notch for her. I'm not trying to be a prude here. This is the one place we need to be absolutely honorable."

Such talk, especially coming from a woman general, was probably a first for the recruiters. But Angie knew that one twenty-four-year-old sergeant having a romance with a high school junior poisoned the community against the corps. While other officers may not have appreciated that this might have far-reaching consequences, she did.

She never came to a decision lightly. If she faced a complex issue, she would take her time, wait, and think. Sure, that was different from how combat arms officers usually operated. Ask them a question—boom, you got an answer on the spot. But what some might see as indecision on Angie's part was actually a deliberate process.

"You make no decision before its time" was a recruiter saying. She knew that sometimes an answer wasn't really needed for twenty-four or forty-eight hours, and before then relevant new information might come in. She wanted to make a decision once and once only. Very rarely did she have to second-guess herself.

Now the media was touting the Glass case as the biggest at the depot in decades, and she knew right away what she had to do. She had to get to San Diego. If she could have, she would have flown with her arms. Immediately wouldn't have been fast enough for her.

CHAPTER 5
Toy Soldiers

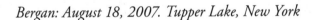

Bergan: August 18, 2007. Tupper Lake, New York

Just weeks before, Bergan had been rappelling off a hundred-foot wall and navigating through a forest after dark at the Leadership Development & Assessment Course at Fort Lewis, Washington. Better known as Advanced Camp, the five-week mandatory summer course for Army ROTC seniors-to-be evaluates cadets on various military skills in garrison and tactical settings. Bergan's favorite part was the field training exercise, even though she didn't get to shower and it rained nine out of the ten days she spent in the woods.

Now she stood in a light satin wedding gown with its floor-length hem hiding her feet. They still resembled hamburger, a raw, red mess covered in blisters, thanks to days of being wet in the field. Bergan didn't mind, since she was wearing ballerina slippers with her gown. She hated heels. If she could have found a pair of sparkly white Converse high-tops, she'd be wearing those today.

"Kneel down," said Bethany, the maid of honor, as she bent over her sister and secured the gown's halter-top straps around Bergan's neck.

Choosing her wedding gown had turned out to be easier than selecting bananas at the supermarket. Bergan saw the dress on a mannequin in the window of a New Hampshire bridal shop, tried it on, and that was it. The big day out to find a gown with her mother and Tom's mother ended almost before it began.

"Do you want to try on some more?" her mother had asked, in an accent similar to that of Canadian neighbors a few hours to the north.

"Nope," Bergan said.

Despite the urging of the salesclerk, Bergan wouldn't entertain the idea of extra padding in the bust to fill out the gown. Bergan was a sports-bra kind of girl, and her mother knew the clerk was wasting her breath.

While Bergan had been tossing grenades that summer, her mother and sisters were finishing the details of her wedding—from addressing and mailing invitations to rolling and cutting out hundreds of star-shaped sugar cookies and wrapping them in cellophane bags for party favors.

Aside from her dress, she did contribute to a few decisions. She chose green and yellow—military police colors—for her wedding colors and helped pick the venue, music, and cake. But most of the choices that came with planning a traditional wedding didn't spark Bergan's interest.

"Everything is great. Whatever you want to do," was Bergan's answer when her mother and sisters asked her opinion.

Bergan had prepared more for Advanced Camp than for her wedding. Doing well there would set her future in the Army, making it more likely that she'd get her first choice of branch. Chances were high that would happen; Bergan had graduated first in her platoon of men and women at camp.

"There," Bethany said, fastening the clasps. She stood up and pulled at the midsection of her own lemon meringue–hued dress.

"I swear I'm going to split out of this thing," said Bethany, who was a jumble of nerves over her twin's upcoming nuptials. "What am I gonna do? It's way too tight." Bethany had been lamenting her dress's fit all morning. Whereas Bergan preferred comfort when it came to clothes, Bethany wasn't afraid to show off her shapely figure.

"Well, that's what can happen when you want it fitted," Amy said, giving her daughter a knowing glance. Amy was the mother of four and the matriarch of the Arsenault family.

"It'll be okay; you look beautiful," assured Brooke, who, at twenty-six, was the oldest of the Arsenault daughters. She had her mother's blond hair, pale skin, and nurturing personality. Brooke was Bergan's matron of honor.

Now, with her hair swept up in a bouquet of curls, and a veil trailing down her back, Bergan looked more like a child bride than a cadet company commander, her new title at Norwich.

Sunlight streamed through the white cotton curtains of Amy's bedroom, ground zero for the day's wedding prep. It was where the twins, who shared a room growing up, often dragged their blankets to camp out on the floor. Sometimes, when she was home from college, Bergan still crept down the hall to sleep near her parents.

Next, Amy helped Bergan put on a silver necklace with two dangling lilac-colored pearls, a gift from Tom that spring.

"What am I going to wear for earrings?" Bergan said. She hadn't given it much thought until now. She assumed she'd wear a pair of her mother's.

"Don't worry about it," Amy said. "I'm sure we'll find something."

All Bergan cared about was marrying Tom in two hours. They would exchange vows in front of 150 guests "uptown" at St. Alphonsus Church, where she and Bethany had been baptized as babies. Growing up, the twins had been altar servers at the "downtown" church, Holy Name, back in the days when little towns like theirs had two priests and two Catholic churches.

The couple had decided not to have a military wedding, since some of Tom's groomsmen weren't in the military. But they did plan to cut their wedding cake with Tom's saber, a graduation gift from his parents.

Bergan's rook sister and old roommate, Meghan, and some other classmates were driving in for the wedding. They had to be back at Norwich that night, in time to train the newest class of rooks on Sunday for Rook Arrival Day, an event Bergan would miss.

Amy took a wooden container, about the size of a shoe box, from her dresser drawer. She knew what was in the box, but she would never dare open it. That morning her soon-to-be son-in-law had repeated explicit instructions: "Please give this to Bergan when she's in her wedding gown."

She was aware it would be a long year for her daughter, who would start off married life separated, as was the case in so many military marriages. Bergan, who would turn twenty-two the next month, still had a year of college, while Tom had already graduated and had been commissioned into the Army a few months ago. Tom was a good guy, with a good head on his shoulders, and this was the next step for the couple. They had the same goals. They wanted to be together. They *loved* each other. Just like Amy and her husband, Billy, when they married at Bergan's age on this very same day twenty-eight years ago.

"Bergan, Tom wanted me to give this to you," Amy said as she handed her daughter the gift.

"What's this?"

She clasped the box in both hands like a treasure chest.

"You'll have to open it to find out," Amy said.

It wouldn't be Bergan's only surprise. A white stretch Hummer, thanks to Tom, was on its way to the Arsenault house.

"Don't spend your money on it," Bergan had told him. But he splurged, knowing she'd love it.

"Open it, Bergan!" urged Bethany, who had momentarily stopped looking at herself in the mirror. Brooke had a camera ready.

It was a jewelry box that Tom had fashioned from a fallen ash tree he and his dad had milled off his parents' property.

Bergan lifted the lid. She put her hand to her mouth as her eyes focused on a pair of pearl drop earrings that matched her necklace. Tucked next to the jewelry were their wedding invitation and a sheet of typing paper folded into a square. Bergan put the box aside and unfolded the paper.

To give her daughter some privacy, Amy puttered near the ironing board she had used to smooth wrinkles out of the bridesmaids' dresses. Bethany stood near Bergan and fiddled with the strap on one of her yellow high heels.

As she read, Bergan teared up, something she rarely did. Tom had typed an entire page. He had majored in science, and English wasn't his strongest subject. He hoped Bergan wouldn't think he was lazy for typing a love letter on the computer. He just wanted all the spelling and grammar to be correct.

Dear Bergan, my little duffer, today is our wedding day. By now you are in your gown, and soon we will be married. I want you to know that my life started when I met you. I will always love you, and I will always be there for you in good times and bad. I will do everything I can to give you everything you've ever wanted. I can't wait to start our life together. . . .

"Girls!" came her father's voice from downstairs. "The photographer's here!"

★

September 3, 2007. Norwich University

"Sirs! Good morning, sirs! This is the outstanding Norwich University Charlie Company! This is the third day of the ninth month of the year of our Lord 2007! This is the first call for reveille formation! Uniform for this formation will be PT gear! You have twenty minutes to fall in!

"Seniors! Attention, seniors! You have fifty-five days until Regimental Ball! You have two hundred and sixty-two days until commissioning! You have two hundred and sixty-three days until graduation!

"Juniors! Attention, juniors! You have two hundred and thirty days until Junior Ring Ball. . . ."

It was five forty in the morning. No one needed an alarm clock at Norwich. Bergan rolled over in bed and reached for her glasses. Every day at this time, rooks assigned as the "morning callers" stood at one end of each hallway and barked in a new day.

As Hawkins Hall came to life, Bergan got out of bed and put on her PT clothes. She was probably the only newlywed sleeping in a twin bed with two stuffed animals—Minnie Mouse, a souvenir from her honeymoon at Disney World, and Bum-Bum, a well-worn gray mouse she'd had since she was two.

She and Tom had spent a week at Shades of Green, a discounted Walt

Disney World resort for service members and their families. She had missed Rook Week, but it was worth it, since she wouldn't be seeing Tom much over the next year. He would leave October 1 for military schools, first at Fort Benning, Georgia, and then at Fort Leonard Wood, Missouri. Till then, Tom filled in the time working construction with his father. Since his hometown was close by, the newlyweds tried to see each other as much as possible, but Norwich's rules dictated that they couldn't live together.

Was I really on my honeymoon a week ago? Bergan wondered as she tied her running shoes. The memory seemed so surreal since returning to her old cadet life at Norwich. But this morning wasn't just the start to any day. It was Labor Day, and for the cadets that meant one thing.

Three hours later

"Right shoulder arms!" Bergan called out with clipped enunciation as she marched her company, forty rooks and forty upperclassmen, dressed in their Super Summer uniform—white service hat, creased gray trousers, and white short-sleeved collared shirt—from the Upper Parade Ground over to Sabine Field, the school's athletic stadium and home to "Sabine Sally," a World War II Sherman tank. In an hour the entire 1,200-member Corps of Cadets would march from campus through town in the 33rd Annual Northfield Labor Day Parade, the largest of its kind in the state and the culmination of three days of festivities.

Norwich cadets had marched in the parade annually since its inception in 1976 as part of the Bicentennial celebration. Each year they were the highlight of the parade, resembling a rippled ribbon of white stretching along hilly Vermont Route 12 as far as the eye could see.

With clear blue skies and temperatures in the low seventies, today was the perfect day for a parade, but the cadets were dreading it. The pace was slow. The rifles got heavy. The march was boring. But the 8,000 people who lined the parade route with lawn chairs and coolers loved it.

On the other side of the world, President Bush had slipped out of the White House for a surprise Labor Day visit to Iraq's Anbar Province, a former Sunni stronghold in the western part of the country that had seen a drop in violence since the surge was announced earlier. Under pressure in the polls and in Congress to cut troop levels, Bush told service members at Al-Asad Air Base that any troop drawdown would be based on progress and would "be from a position of strength and success, not from a position of fear and failure."

Back along the parade route, Bergan's parents were delighted by the fact that this year they would actually be able to easily spot their daughter. As a cadet company commander, Bergan marched in front of her company during formation and parades. Because of her height, she had always been relegated to the back row. Military formations go from tallest to shortest. Those over six feet tall are in the front rows, while average-height cadets spend their lives hidden in the middle. Short cadets invariably bring up the rear.

In her new post, Bergan was responsible for running formations, accountability, training, and discipline. No longer a drill sergeant, she didn't really yell anymore. Except when she had to. Since she didn't spend as much time with the rooks as last year, Bergan made her way over to the young cadets and used the fifteen or twenty minutes of waiting in formation to see how things were going and, of course, to drill them on their rook knowledge, which included knowing the cadet creed, the three general orders, the school's Medal of Honor recipients, the members of the honor committee, the chain of command within the corps, and school history in chronological order, from 1819 to the present.

Her uniform was identical to those of the rooks, except she wore a purple sash around her waist and carried a saber instead of a rifle, which signified she was an officer. Encircling her left shoulder, red and gold cords showed she was on an ROTC scholarship. Three rows of ribbons adorned her shirt, and their weight made it sag slightly. Pinned to the left side of her chest was her new black nameplate with "Flannigan" etched in white letters.

"Williams, what are the first two of the three general orders?" Bergan asked a skinny rook.

"Ma'am, the first general is 'I will guard everything within the limits of my post and quit my post only when properly relieved,' ma'am.

"Ma'am, the second general is 'I will obey my special orders and . . . and . . .'"

"'And perform all of my duties in a military manner,'" Bergan said.

She moved on to the next rook. "Barton, what is the history of Ransom Hall?"

"Ma'am, Ransom Hall was built in . . ."

"In 1957," Bergan said.

"Ma'am, Ransom Hall is named after Lieutenant Colonel Truman B. Ransom, the second president of Norwich University. Colonel Ransom was killed in . . ."

"In 1847, Barton. What was he doing when he was killed?"

"Ma'am, this recruit does not know the answer, ma'am."

"He was leading the charge on Chapultepec during the Mexican-American War."

Bergan moved on.

"Berkhardt, how did the cow die?"

"Ma'am, the cow choked on an apple, ma'am."

Finally a correct and complete answer.

Bovine trivia was an academy tradition. West Point had its own question: "How's the cow?" To which the proper answer was: "She walks, she talks, she's full of chalk, the lacteal fluid extracted from the female of the bovine species is highly prolific to the nth degree."

Bergan moved on to the next rook.

"Cardinale, who was Norwich's last living Medal of Honor recipient . . . ?"

Eight weeks later

The day's rain had stopped by nightfall on Saturday, October 27, and a full moon hung above Plumley Armory, the site of Norwich's Regimental Ball. Inside, cadets had draped parachute canopies across the ceiling, and balloon

columns edged the dance floor and stood between white linen–covered tables. The only hint that the ballroom was used for other purposes was the
maple floor with the markings of a basketball court.

Just before midnight, the lights dimmed, and as the haunting sound of
rotor blades and unmistakable piano notes from Billy Joel's "Goodnight
Saigon" filled the cavernous armory, a thousand cadets ditched their dates
and scrambled to huddle in circles with their companies. Bergan and Tom,
wearing dress blues with the crossed pistols insignia of the military police
pinned on his uniform, took off together in search of Bravo Company.
Both had been rooks in Bravo, and that meant so much to them that the
previous year the couple got identical bull skull tattoos, with the company
motto: "Bravo Rules the Hill." Bergan wore hers on her lower back with her
graduation year, '08. Tom's was on his shoulder, with '07.

The song was the unofficial anthem for Norwich cadets and, as a
contemplation of war and lost innocence, it articulated their journey and
the camaraderie they shared. After graduation, for many, the song would
come to take on a darker and deeper meaning. It was always the last song
of the evening at "Regi," as the cadets called the ball.

Regi was one of the most anticipated social events of the year, and one
that Bergan had planned to miss. Though the ball recognized seniors, without Tom there Bergan didn't feel like attending. She volunteered for guard
duty instead.

But Tom had called a week ago. "Guess what," he said. "I've got a long
weekend and can fly up for Regi!"

Bergan could barely contain her excitement. She hadn't seen Tom since
he left for Fort Benning.

"Michele, can you do guard duty for me?" she asked a rook sister who
wasn't going to the ball. Next she called her mother. "Mom, can you get me
a dress?"

Amy knew her daughter's taste: nothing pink and nothing too frou-
frou. She found a gray baby-doll dress with sequins and spaghetti straps
that, like those of her wedding dress, wrapped around her neck. Amy over-
nighted it to her.

Bergan's asking for a dress made Amy chuckle, since her daughter had refused to wear dresses since she left kindergarten. For First Holy Communion, Amy made Bergan white culottes with a matching vest and a wreath plopped on her head. Meanwhile, Bethany was a princess for the day in a white dress and veil.

Bethany, who was dating a cadet, was a princess at Regi, too, and she made sure her sister was equally pretty. Bethany knew her way around a mascara wand and expertly applied Bergan's eye makeup and pinned her hair in an updo similar to her own.

On this night the girls looked identical. For the female cadets, the opportunity to dress like the other dates was like being Cinderella for the evening. The issue is a gray one for the Army, where individual commanders decide whether dresses are allowed. Supporters believe it is a morale boost and a special night. Detractors argue that it sets a separate standard for male and female soldiers, that if men must be in uniform, women soldiers should be as well. And while many college ROTC programs allow female cadets to wear gowns to their unit balls, West Point forbids it.

The rooks seemed shocked to see their company commander all dolled up, but they didn't dare say anything. Though they were allowed to have a good time at Regi, with no yelling, at midnight they would turn back into pumpkins.

In the darkness, with only strobe lights to light the room, Bergan and Tom joined the chants of "Bravo, Bulls! Bravo, Bulls!" and tried to outshout the other companies. By this time of the evening the male cadets had shed the formal brass-buttoned jackets that made them look like toy soldiers. In their suspenders and company T-shirts, many sat on top of buddies' shoulders and pumped their fists. Bergan's camera dangled from her wrist as she swayed to the music arm in arm with Tom and the rest of the Bravo Company cadets, who had formed a large circle. The couple had last heard the song at their wedding reception, a must on the playlist for any Norwich wedding.

Meghan and Bergan also locked arms and stayed along the outer perimeter of the company during the playing of "Goodnight Saigon." Meghan was an inch shorter than Bergan, and they had learned the hard way during their rook year that being short and in the center of all the craziness meant getting stepped on and pushed over.

This night, still far away from posts that awaited them in Iraq and Afghanistan, the cadets continued to sing.

When the music stopped, Bergan and Tom said their good-byes to friends and, with the other cadets and their dates, poured out of Plumley's giant doors. They hurried down the steps and past the two cannons that flanked the armory. As a senior, Bergan didn't have a roommate, and Tom was staying with her this weekend. Technically it wasn't allowed, but Bergan was in charge of her barracks, and, after all, they were married.

Bergan's ears tingled from the night of blaring music, and the cool air felt good against her face. The season's first snowfall was a week away and would overstay its welcome with daily snowfall through April, turning Norwich into a snow globe, happily secluded from the rest of the world.

CHAPTER 6
The Burn

Angie: Autumn 2007. MCRD, San Diego

"My knees are killing me," Angie said under her breath to Sergeant Major Woods. It wasn't something she'd admit to just anyone. She had turned fifty-four almost a year earlier, but as a commanding general, she wasn't about to broadcast any signs of wear and tear.

"Ma'am, pain is weakness leaving the body," Woods reminded her. The expression was the Marine Corps' version of encouragement. But the sergeant major knew the general's body was broken. Scars like road maps crisscrossed her knees, and a metal rod with five bolts kept her lower back in place. She sometimes walked gingerly, and when Woods ran beside her, he could hear her moans mixed in with the cadence calls, something he kept to himself.

They had just finished leading 450 skinny, buzz-cut eighteen- and nineteen-year-old recruits dressed in green PT shirts and shorts on a quick-paced, four-mile moto (short for "motivational") run in front of cheering parents, grandparents, and siblings who hadn't seen their kids since they left for boot camp thirteen weeks earlier. The run took place every Thursday morning at ten thirty as part of Family Day, twenty-four hours before the recruits graduated from boot camp to become the corps' newest Marines. Angie and Sergeant Major Woods led the weekly run, which was like being in front of a herd of colts.

"Ma'am, you're the one at the front of the pack. You control the pace," Sergeant Major Woods often told her. But moto runs were fast, and Angie wasn't going to change that, even if the guys at the back of the formation would have welcomed a more moderate speed.

"She's taking it easy because she's a woman," was something Angie never wanted anyone to say. So every morning at four thirty she went into her basement and ran for four or five miles, punishing her knees on the treadmill, and every Thursday she led teenage boys on a spirited sprint. She often joked that her motivation was looking over her shoulder and seeing five hundred young men chasing her.

Following the run, the action switched to the depot's movie theater, where Angie addressed the parents.

"Welcome, families and friends, to MCRD San Diego!" It was showtime. And it was evident to this crowd, many of whom were wearing T-shirts with "Marine Mom" or "My Grandson's a U.S. Marine"—which the depot's exchange restocked with the alacrity of a grocery store putting milk on shelves—that she was the one in charge.

"It's great to see all of you here this morning. I can tell our newest Marines come from good stock. Very soon you'll be embarking on a journey with your new Marine . . . " The sound of an airplane taking off drowned out her words, a common occurrence at the depot, which shared a fence with the San Diego International Airport.

"We call that the 'San Diego pause,'" Angie told the crowd. "To us, it's the sound of freedom, and every day with that sound your loved one is reminded why they raised their hand and said, 'I do solemnly swear to support and defend the Constitution of the United States.'"

Then she continued, "You, the parents and family, are now part of our beloved Marine Corps. Your new Marine has been entrusted with the legacy of those who have gone before, and they now stand on the shoulders of all who earned the title Marine. We tell them it's a two-way street. They've got to give as much as they've been given . . . "

While Angie was not physically commanding, she had a palpable presence, and people knew it. Perhaps it was the intonation in her voice, or her attitude. Whatever it was, she had it.

"You'll see many positive changes in your young men," she went on. "While here, they learned to use words like 'deck' and 'head' and 'ladder well,' and along the way they began to learn the meaning of words like 'honor,' 'courage,' and 'commitment.' They now get out of bed with little complaint; they get dressed, brush their teeth, and make the bed. They even learned what their waist is for—to wear their pants straight!"

The line always drew laughs. So much so that the sergeant major tried borrowing it a few times, only to get a deadpan response. But Angie was great with a crowd. She was probably the only general in the history of the armed forces who could pull off using words and phrases like "heinie," "rat's patootie," and "woo-hoo" to great effect. No one knew that as she stood with a mic her knees were as stiff as two-by-fours.

The trouble had started on her college basketball court. She blew out her ACL and had to have an operation, which was followed by four more surgeries over the years on her other knee. But it was Angie's back that almost ended her military career. Years of running and rucking with heavy loads in specially ordered size-two-and-a-half men's boots had taken their toll by the time Angie was a lieutenant colonel. (This was before the corps realized, in the mid-nineties, that a man's boot in a smaller size was actually harmful for a woman's foot. Before that, the attitude was: "If it's good enough for us, it's good enough for them.") Decades of carrying the same weight for the same distance and at the same pace as men—but carried differently on a woman's hips—had ravaged her lower back. One day in 1990 while she was on a run, a piercing pain shot down Angie's leg. She tried everything to get relief—exercises, therapies, acupuncture, and a chiropractor. It reached the point where she had to take eight hundred milligrams of Motrin to get out of bed in the morning and couldn't walk from her car to her office without severe pain.

Five years later, while she was serving on the joint staff at the Pentagon as the deputy special assistant for general and flag officer matters, with the sciatic nerve pain still making her life miserable, she received new orders: She was slated to go to Parris Island to command the 4th Recruit Training Battalion, the boot camp unit responsible for training all female Marine recruits in the U.S.

My back is killing me. I can't do this, she thought.

She declined the command in writing and sent in her retirement papers. Marines who knew Angie were shocked that someone who had been "deep-selected," that is, promoted early before her peers, to the ranks of major and lieutenant colonel would turn down command and abruptly leave the corps.

"What are you doing?" demanded her boss, Major General Carlton Fulford, with her paperwork in his hand. "I'm going to hold on to this."

The general's reaction was a typical response, since it made little sense why a rising star like Angie would abruptly retire. Like other servicewomen of her caliber, Angie kept her medical problems to herself. To do otherwise put women in a position of vulnerability, a card no servicewoman wanted in her hand. In a culture of "no pain, no gain," health issues, even the severe kind, invited others to question a woman's physical and intestinal fortitude. Top-shelf military women never wanted to be labeled as weak or as using a medical problem as an excuse for their performance.

"Sir, I'm just going to retire," she insisted. "It's time to try new things." How could she admit to anyone that she was almost overcome with pain? Angie wasn't about to sully her own reputation or those of other women Marines. Her mind was made up. She was going to leave the corps from a position of strength, on her own terms.

"Pack your bag; you're going to Andrews," Major General Fulford told her two days later.

"Where am I going, sir?"

"Don't worry about it."

The next afternoon Angie, dressed in her service Bravos uniform, sat with her overnight bag in the waiting area at Andrews Air Force Base, just outside of the nation's capital. She looked out at the flight line and wondered where the hell she was going and why. All she knew was that she was waiting for a flight and she'd be told what to do.

As if on cue, a gunnery sergeant approached.

"Are you Lieutenant Colonel Salinas?"

"Yes, I am."

"Come with me, ma'am."

She grabbed her bag and followed the gunny onto the tarmac and into a Learjet. On board she passed the front VIP section, which had four spacious seats facing one another. She had never been on a plane like this.

"We're going to the back, ma'am. Here's your seat," the gunny said. Then he disappeared. No one else was on the plane, and Angie peered out the window.

What is going on? she wondered. Then a large, dark sedan with "1775" plates—the birth date of the Marine Corps—pulled up to the plane. Out bounced a short man in uniform with four stars on his shoulders.

Oh, my God. It's the commandant of the Marine Corps! Angie said to herself. *Where's he going?*

Her eyes grew wide as General Charles "Chuck" Krulak, one of Brute's sons, followed by an aide, bounded up the steps of the Learjet.

Oh, my God . . .

The Marine Corps commandant is like a deity to Marines, one of only two officers in the corps to wear four stars, and Angie was on his plane. As the engines revved up and the plane's doors locked, General Krulak appeared in the aisle.

"You!" he said, pointing at Angie. "Get up here!"

Me? thought Angie. As she made her way up to the front, she had little time to figure out how the commandant of the Marine Corps would even know she existed.

"Sit," Krulak said, motioning to the seat directly facing him.

Angie did as she was told and peered into the commandant's blue eyes, which seemed to be perpetually squinting. Years in the sun had freckled his skin. Like all Marine generals who weren't bald, he wore his hair shorn on the sides and just long enough on top to hold a part.

"Are you stupid or what?" General Krulak said.

"Sir?" By now the plane was airborne and had hit some turbulence.

Angie wasn't fond of flying to begin with and tried to disguise her discomfort.

"Do you know what kind of record you have?"

"Yes, sir," she said. "I do. Do you?"

"That's why you're here. Why are you declining command? You're one of the few women in the Marine Corps who can do that job, and I need someone good."

"Thank you, sir," she said. "If I'm so good, why am I leading a women's command?" It was a bold response, but Angie and other fast-track female Marines were eager to break into the sought-after operational commands.

"Gunny! Bring us something to eat!" Krulak ordered, adding in his next breath, "This is where I need you now, and here's why . . . "

Over cookies, as the plane bounced and jerked, the general laid out his vision for changing recruit training and the entire transformation process from civilian patriot to Marine. Krulak wanted more emphasis on values, moral courage, and character.

All Angie could think was, *I'm going to hurl on the commandant.*

The general noticed her grip on the armrests.

"This is a piece of cake," he said totally relaxed. "This is one of the safest planes ever. Gunny, bring out more cookies!"

"Sir, may I ask where we are going?"

"Biloxi."

The general was giving a speech in Mississippi, and the only available time in his schedule to talk some sense into Lieutenant Colonel Salinas was during this flight. General Krulak then explained how he wanted to make boot camp harder and longer and to have it culminate in an exercise so physically, mentally, and emotionally challenging that each recruit would have to *choose* the Marine Corps way of life. He wanted that kind of dedication in his Marines, both male and female.

"I need someone to take the lead," he said. "And based on your record and reputation you are the right person for that."

"Thank you, sir, but . . ."

"The best commander, the best female commander, needs to be in that position," Krulak said. "The time is right now."

"Thank you, sir," she said, "but I'm still going."

The following day, when the plane landed back at Andrews, General Krulak looked at Angie. "This isn't over."

A few weeks later, Colonel Russ Appleton, military secretary to the commandant, stopped by Angie's office.

"Have you got your ticket for the ball?" he asked.

"The ball" was the Commandant's Marine Corps Birthday Ball, a huge annual affair steeped in tradition and held all around the world on the anniversary of the corps' November 10 founding. In Washington the gala was attended by senior Marines, elected officials, and other bigwigs. Former Marines such as John Glenn, Senator John Warner of Virginia, and Secretary of the Navy John Dalton would all be there. Angie hadn't planned on going, and it was too late to get a ticket now.

"No, I don't, sir," she said.

"You have one now," Colonel Appleton said, and handed her a ticket. "Bring me a check for sixty bucks."

The night of the ball Angie found herself in a cavernous ballroom at the Hilton with 3,000 other guests. She was seated two tables over from the commandant's spot, along with his parents and the pilots who had flown his plane the previous month. It was a bit like being at the kids' table, near the grown-ups. With all the important people there, Angie never had an opportunity to greet the commandant. But she suspected Krulak was using the camaraderie of the occasion to remind her of why she became a Marine.

And within a few weeks, after years of trying to get a referral to neurology—by coincidence or perhaps intervention—she had an appointment scheduled with the head of neurology at Bethesda National Naval Medical Center. A month later, in December, Colonel Appleton called her at home. He needed an answer about the command.

"I'll make a decision after this interview, sir," she told him, referring to an appointment she had with a private company. She had started looking into civilian jobs and was about to go to her first meeting.

The next day she sat across from a human resources manager at a Fortune 500 firm.

"You're very marketable, and you'll have no problem getting a job," the HR manager told her. "Do you have any questions?"

"What motivates you to come to work every day?" she asked. She assumed he would say money, but his response took her aback.

"What?" he said. The man looked at Angie as if she'd asked him whether he'd ever taken a day trip to the moon. "If you think you're going to find what you have in the Marines here, you're not," he went on matter-of-factly. "We have a high turnover rate. People don't stay more than a year. You're not going to find loyalty or camaraderie here like you're used to."

After the interview Angie called Colonel Appleton. She'd made her decision.

"I'll take the command, sir, but I have to take care of some medical issues first."

In April 1996, five months after the ball, Angie had back surgery. She came out of anesthesia to find that the pain that she'd lived with for more than five years was gone. Her thirty days of rehab were supposed to be followed by nothing physical for six months. But her command date was pushed up, and she was at Parris Island on August 1. Unbeknown to anyone, she wore a body cast under her uniform at her change-of-command ceremony. She had perfect, erect posture. But if anyone had touched her, she'd have clinked like the tin man.

Eleven years later, she was a menopausal general officer conducting weekly runs for boys who had more energy than windmills. Her commitment to PT meant a lot to Sergeant Major Woods. At forty-nine years old, he could outrun 90 percent of his recruits. As with most sergeants major, physical training was important to him, and he wanted a commander who was as fit as he was.

And he got one. Just in a different way than he expected. Before Angie's arrival, Woods had asked around and found out the general had been a "three hundred PT-er" for years, meaning she maxed her twice-a-year physical fitness tests. These days, she still passed all her tests, always scoring first class—the highest bracket—though considerable grit and pain were involved. Angie was one tough Marine.

CHAPTER 7
Typhoon Season

Candice: December 5, 2007. Schofield Barracks, Hawaii

  Major Candice O'Brien's eyes jolted open before dawn to the sound of her cell phone ringing in its charger. Like most Army officers, Candice kept her lifeline on the nightstand for middle-of-the-night calls. Through swollen eyes, she made out her husband's number and mustered a pleasant greeting.

"Hey, honey, what's going on?"

"I cannot believe this shit," said Major Will O'Brien, his words clipped as short as the hair on the sides of his head. "We missed the fucking flight. I've been waiting in line forever, and fucking United Airlines isn't doing anything to help us out. I'm almost outta diapers, and I have no idea what to do in an airport if we run out of diapers."

Candice rolled over her bulging belly. Will's predicament required her to reach for another lifeline, her eyeglasses.

Years earlier, after her eye exam for entrance into West Point, the elderly lady administering the test studied then-seventeen-year-old Candice

Frost, a thin, freckled Iowa girl with pale blue eyes and a shock of copper red hair.

"You wanna be a pilot?" asked the lady, whose pouf of gray hair added a few inches to her height.

"No, ma'am."

"Good, 'cause there's no way you'd qualify, honey. One of your eyes is close to failing for depth perception and the other barely passed."

Candice kept quiet and waited for the other shoe to drop. Since she'd been a kid, she couldn't make out the big E on the eye chart.

"But I'm gonna pass you because the military needs some more good women."

And with that, the fluffy-haired lady winked at Candice and finished her paperwork.

Fifteen years later, it was that kind of encouragement and promotion that continued to feed Candice's drive not only to stay but also to excel in the Army. And she did just that, from graduating from West Point, to parachuting out of perfectly good airplanes at Fort Bragg, to commanding troops in Afghanistan, and achieving early promotion to the rank of major.

But at the moment Candice had to calm a raging husband who was somewhere on the mainland. In the Army, news was always delivered with the bottom line first and finer details later. In that regard Will never disappointed.

But where was Will, and what time was it? Candice glanced at her battery-operated alarm clock.

It was only five a.m. She'd had a fitful night sleep. Throughout the night, high winds and thrashing thundershowers had pounded on the walls and ceiling of her bedroom as if a cave-in were imminent.

Six months pregnant, Candice wasn't sleeping well anyway.

"Where are you?" Candice said from bed.

"I'm in Denver. One of the fucking flight attendants had a diabetic episode and didn't have her medication with her, and we had to do an emergency landing in San Francisco," Will said. "I think she was hungover, too. They always party in Waikiki before these overnight flights. That's what screwed up the time line and caused us to miss the connection in Denver. We were on that plane eleven fucking hours. All my bad experiences in life have been on United. I'm going to fucking—"

"Will, honey, slow down," Candice said. "It's gonna be okay. Remember, you're with your daughter. Get in the right frame of mind. What are you doing now?"

Their conversations always ran in this mode when Will was upset. Candice would never accept such tirades from anyone at work, but with Will most of the time she thought, *How can I defuse this? How can I get him to calm down and think rationally?*

So things weren't going Will's way. What was she supposed to do about it from a rock in the middle of the ocean? She had to get ready for her twelve-hour shift for Yama Sakura, a huge joint exercise the U.S. military conducts annually with the Japanese. Candice was the deputy G2 (intelligence) operations officer for United States Army Pacific. As she was the operations battle captain for the exercise, Candice's job was to brief the operational commanders in Japan and Hawaii on the intelligence situation of the last twenty-four hours and assess what would occur in the next twenty-four hours. She had to make sure her staff was prepared and her briefings were spot-on. It wasn't exactly an opportune time to coach her husband through his meltdown over the airlines.

The night before, Will had taken an overnight flight from Honolulu with Kate, their one-and-a-half-year-old daughter, en route to Kansas City to visit his parents for a pre-Christmas holiday. With deployments and other work commitments he hadn't been home in two years. Will's unit, which had just returned from Iraq, was on leave this month. The plan was for Candice to join him and Kate in a week, after the completion of her role in Yama Sakura, which translates into "mountain cherry blossom," a name better suited for a spa day package than a military exercise.

Like most dual military couples—the category for a husband and wife who are both on active duty—the O'Briens were used to their time lines not matching up. They had spent half of their seven-year marriage apart.

Fully alert now and on her feet, Candice rubbed her head, which at the moment was topped with a tangle of red hair. She always had her hairdresser cut her tresses to the borderline of the Army regulation, which prohibits women's hair from "extending below the bottom edge of the collar" when in uniform. Hair was a woman's crown and should be treated as such, in Candice's mind. She always tried to make it look good.

The copper color was an inheritance from her maternal grandmother, Bunney Kalick, who had joined the Navy WAVES (Women Accepted for Voluntary Emergency Service) during World War II. Despite her military service as a seaman first class, Bunney cried when she heard her granddaughter was going to West Point. The former WAVE didn't want Candice to be treated the way she had been in the military. The other seamen called her "carrot crotch" and other crude names. She had never experienced such coarse and raw behavior in her life, and she didn't want her granddaughter to either.

But both felt a call to duty.

As Will rambled on about poor airline service, Candice shuffled in darkness down the hallway of their Schofield Barracks quarters. Schofield Barracks was in the middle of Oahu, nestled at the edge of tropical rain forests and pineapple plantations near the North Shore and away from the Waikiki hotels to the south. It was Hawaii's version of the country. The O'Briens' home at 112 Millet Street sat on a corner lot in a cramped officer and senior NCO neighborhood nicknamed the Cinders. The cookie-cutter one story duplexes with attached carports were constructed out of cinder blocks, which gave them the feel of grade-school classrooms. It certainly made hanging pictures and curtains a challenge. But living in a cement box had its advantages. It meant you didn't hear your neighbors making love or waging war. In a typical Army neighborhood, where everyone knew everyone else's business, the privacy was a plus.

The carpeting was another matter. Considered an upgrade because it covered the industrial gray flooring typically found in sixties-era quarters, the carpet was a mixed blessing in Hawaii, since the island's rich red dirt stained everything beyond repair.

Many residents complained about living in the Cinders, especially since the Woodies sat across the way, just beyond the gate. The Woodies were the large, old wooden Craftsman-style homes built between 1919 and 1923. It was in the Woodies where the impossibly handsome Burt Lancaster, who played a first sergeant, shared a passionate and forbidden kiss with his commander's wife, played by Deborah Kerr, in the 1953 Academy Award winner, *From Here to Eternity*. Most everyone stationed at Schofield Barracks had seen the black-and-white film classic at least once.

The O'Briens didn't mind living in the Cinders, which were scheduled to be torn down in a few years. To them it was typical old-school Army housing and was to be expected for junior field-grade officers. They had a fenced-in backyard, and they enjoyed their crumbling screened-in back porch, which everyone called a lanai in Hawaii. Both of them liked the sense of community that comes with living on an Army post. Will loved that he could walk across the street and be at work in the Quads, the historic quadrangles attacked by the Japanese, where the 25th Infantry Division, known as the "Tropic Lightning" Division, still houses its battalions of soldiers. As he was a rear detachment commander for the 2nd Battalion, 35th Infantry Regiment—the officer who fills in for a deployed unit commander—Will's close proximity to work came in handy when mayhem went down each night, as it always did, whether because of deadly incidents in Iraq or due to crazy or wayward spouse problems on the island home front.

As Will railed on about the airlines, Candice reached the kitchen. All she wanted was to put on a pot of coffee. Black was the only way she drank it. Ever since she'd received a coffeemaker for her sixteenth birthday, she'd been hooked. She knew she shouldn't drink too much while pregnant (she switched to decaf after her first cup), but coffee was what got her through nights studying discrete dynamical systems at West Point, and missions in the mountains of Bosnia and Afghanistan.

But like a magician with no rabbit in his hat, the flip of the kitchen light switch brought no magic, only darkness. There was no power. And no coffee.

"Shit, this is taking forever, and Kate is freaking out," said Will, his words blasting through the dark. "She's hungry and running all around."

Now seated at the kitchen table, Candice wanted to say that that was because she'd just been cooped up on an airplane for eleven hours. "Will, she's a little girl who needs to get some of her energy out. Let her run in a circle. Take a deep breath and calm down. It'll be okay. Are you with someone who could rebook your ticket?"

"Hey, I'm at the front of the line. I gotta go."

Candice could picture Will approaching the counter armed with tickets, a diaper bag, and an energetic toddler, all while being exceptionally calm with the agent. He rarely got upset or hurtful with people he didn't know.

During his company command, Will's first sergeant gave him the nickname "Angry Will" because he was always pissed off at someone or something. Will thrived on a routine, and when things didn't go according to the plan, he never had a good reaction. While the phone tirade wasn't all that unusual for Will, the sense of desperateness and hopelessness in his voice was, and it alarmed Candice.

The next call came from PACOM (Pacific Army Command), announcing a late duty call. She was to report in at noon to the Sim (Simulation) Center. The generators were up and running, but the computers were down. For a simulated computer-driven war exercise, this was going to be a nightmare.

She walked into the living room. The large Afghan rug that she bought during her deployment felt good beneath her feet, providing a kind of comfort she never had in Afghanistan. For much of the time she lived in a tent with no running water. She discovered you could do a lot with baby wipes, but 122 degrees was 122 degrees. She was convinced the devil vacationed in Tarin Kowt in southern Afghanistan.

Still, commanding troops in Afghanistan was a true honor, and Candice was among the first female military intelligence captains to lead soldiers there. She considered herself fortunate to have good platoon leaders and strong NCOs.

Candice watched as the room slowly changed from dark to dim, and the Hawaiian dawn unveiled nature's crime scene.

"Oh, my God," said Candice, as she looked out a back window that separated her from the soggy world outside. Part of the lanai's rippled plastic roof had been ripped off, and farther back in the yard the storage shed with all of their bags of military equipment had been blown over. Her potted plants lay on their sides.

The brunt of the storm had struck Oahu at three a.m., with wind gusts at Schofield Barracks recorded at seventy miles per hour, the highest on the island. The storm knocked out power, felled trees and utility poles, damaged roofs, and caused some flooding. On Millet Street neighbors' tangles of Christmas lights were now strewn in front yards, along with door wreaths and debris. The O'Briens' neighbors fared worse, with a cracked umbrella tree limb jutting through their family room. Military families called all trees on Schofield Barracks umbrella trees because of their distinctive dome shape. Years ago the Army had planted these monkeypod trees, native to South America, for natural camouflage and shade around Schofield Barracks. Hawaii now lists them as an invasive species.

Another tree that didn't belong in Hawaii was the Christmas kind. Near the double doors leading to the lanai stood the O'Briens' slightly askew artificial one, topped with an angel dressed in shiny white. The tree resembled a plain Jane at a dance in need of fancier attire. But it looked better than the poor sad and dying trees shipped in each year from the mainland. Those trees had about as much chance to thrive in Hawaii as a polar bear.

Just then, Candice's cell phone rang. Will again. She exhaled and picked up.

"Shit, Candice, this is fucking impossible. Kate went running down the moving sidewalk when I was talking to the agent. I have to wait in the airport another four hours with Kate and a limited supply of diapers. I cannot believe I had to do this alone. You need to be here."

I am going to do this alone next year with two children when you're deployed, Candice thought.

"It's okay, honey; what are you going to do next? Have you eaten? Is Kate hungry?" she said. "Why don't you find a place to just get some foo—"

Click. Will hung up.

Candice took off her glasses and rubbed her eyes. For the last year Will had been a jerk, on edge nonstop. Candice did her best to avoid him when he was like that, because she didn't want to start a fight. She just wanted her husband back.

It's never easy. It's never ever easy, she thought. The entire horrible, sad year had taken a toll on her marriage. When Will's unit had been posted to Iraq, he had still been "nondeployable," since he'd been back from Afghanistan less than the regulated twelve-month "dwell time." Rather than let the Army PCS him out of Hawaii—that is, put him on permanent change of station—Will had asked to stay on as the rear-D. It made sense. Will had been with the unit for five years and knew all the soldiers and the ins and outs of the unit. But volunteering for the job was like impaling yourself with your own sword.

And 2007 had been the deadliest for U.S. soldiers in Iraq since the war started in 2003. That translated into Will's making 136 notifications to a spouse or parent that his or her soldier was in one of two official classifications: "seriously" or "very seriously" injured. Twenty-one soldiers in his battalion died in IED attacks and a chopper crash where half of the platoon was lost. Will was the point man for the memorial services and hometown funerals on the mainland. He was there with grieving wives and children during their first moments of shock and the following months of grief. He broke the news to parents that their sons had lost body parts. He saw friends return with TBI (traumatic brain injury), now shells of their former selves. With each loss of a limb and loss of a life, Candice seemed to lose a piece of her husband as well.

This morning's phone calls were a shaping moment for her: *Why are we doing this to ourselves?* Candice was not the first person in a dual military marriage to ask that question. A female mentor at West Point, Kathy Derrick, once told her it was nearly impossible to have a first-rate marriage, two hard-charging "top block" officer careers, and children. Something had to take a backseat, and it was often the marriage.

The day had barely started, and Candice's face looked more drawn than it should for a thirty-two-year-old. Staring at the destruction outside made her feel as helpless and hopeless as Will. Candice couldn't wait to see 2007 end. It was as if the storm were a treacherous grand finale, a careening, out-of-control crescendo crashing down on the awful year.

• • •

"Good morning!" said Captain Laura Gulick, as she bounced into the family room with her sunbeam salutation. Candice's houseguest was a brown-eyed blonde with a big smile, dressed in ill-fitting ACUs (Army Combat Uniform), the Army's digitized camouflaged utility uniform.

"What's wrong?" Laura said. "You look exhausted, and we haven't even started our shift."

"Good morning," Candice said. "We have a late duty call. The power's out. Did you look at the mess outside? I hope all the phone calls didn't wake you."

"No, other than the storm, I didn't hear a thing. What's wrong?"

"It's Will. He's on a roll," Candice said. "Things are not going his way. He's delayed in Denver. His flight was rerouted, and he's freaking out stuck with Kate."

Candice let out a half laugh. It was one of those laugh-or-cry moments. Laura knew Will well, and the two women could both picture the infantryman trying to manage in an airport with dolls, diapers, and a little girl.

Yet Candice couldn't help but feel resentment, against the storm and against Will. This was supposed to be her time with Laura. No kids. No husbands. Just fun girl time—Army style. Laura was a reserve officer who had flown in from Virginia Beach two days ago to participate in the exercise. But after that they planned to watch movies, go out to eat, and catch up. The women had met six years ago, shortly after 9/11, at a swim test, when both were in-processing at Schofield Barracks. Since an average of one 25th Infantry Division soldier drowned each year in Hawaii, all soldiers at Schofield Barracks were required to take a swim assessment test, in full uniform minus boots, upon reporting for duty. The two women, both West Pointers and intel officers, had been friends ever since. They went on to serve together in Bosnia, and Laura had been there to witness Kate's birth. Since high school, Candice had always had many good friends, but never a best friend and very few exceptionally close friends. Laura was a close friend.

"You okay?" Laura said.

"I'm fine. But there's nothing I can do from here to fix this."

Laura took a seat next to her friend. "Sometimes you can't always fix things, Candice. You're going to have two kids now, and sometimes things just happen."

Like Candice, Laura had one child. And like Candice she was pregnant, but with twins.

She tried to make her friend laugh. "Do I look as uncomfortable as I feel in this uniform?" Laura asked. She was thirteen weeks pregnant and thought she could make it through her two-week reserve tour by borrowing some bigger ACUs from Will's closet. After all, the man stood six feet tall and weighed two hundred pounds. But by day two she was so uncomfortable she could barely stand it. With twins in her belly she had abandoned the unspoken Army motto of "pride over pain."

Candice could relate. After breakfast and a shower she appeared back in the family room sporting her own uncomfortable uniform from Will's side of the closet.

"Laura, I know I said I'd make it to the end of the pregnancy in Will's uniform, but this isn't going to cut it." She lifted her blouse, as the camouflage jacket is known in the military, to reveal pants buttoned so tight she could hardly breathe.

The Army is the only service branch that does not have a utility uniform designed for a woman's body. Instead, the women wear men's uniforms and boots. That means stocking men's uniform trousers sized "X-small, X-short" and jackets sized "X-small, XX-short." For women with small feet, it also means the hassle of special-ordering men's boots in size 3.5. (By the summer of 2010, however, the Army announced it would begin developing and testing women's ACU prototypes, with a women's version possibly fielded by 2014.)

Unbeknownst to anyone, for years pregnant servicewomen married to soldiers have quietly worn their husbands' uniforms until they grew out of them. The Velcro strips on the ACUs make it simple to swap out name tapes, ranks, and unit patches, and make borrowing all the easier.

The larger-size uniforms worked well for pregnant women who had either not yet announced their pregnancies or were putting off wearing the maternity uniforms that the Army had finally begun to stock.

The fact that Will was six inches taller than Candice mattered little. She cinched the sleeves at the wrist with Velcro and rolled up the pants and stuffed them into her boots.

But this solution worked for only so long.

"We'll try the PX again tomorrow to see if the maternity pants arrived," Laura said. Finding Army maternity pants in out-of-the-way duty stations such as Korea, Alaska, or Hawaii was like trying to buy a beer in Saudi Arabia. Supply and demand, mixed in with an archaic military clothing & sales and post exchange ordering system, often resulted in no maternity uniforms for pregnant female officers, who were required to pay for their uniforms, and a three-month waiting period for enlisted women, who had a uniform allowance but who ordered uniforms through the Army's slow-moving Central Issue Facility.

In any case, like most Army women, Candice wanted to put off wearing the Army maternity uniform for as long as she could physically stand it. The ACU maternity duds held a stigma that no one talked about openly, but that everyone had an opinion about. The tentlike design flattered no one, and on a subconscious level, since ACUs were designed and worn by those going into the field or into battle, when soldiers spotted a woman wearing the maternity version, it was as if they'd seen a man wearing a tutu.

Candice considered the maternity uniforms obnoxious-looking. And she hated that the jacket had no pockets on the chest or arms, which meant no place to put a cell phone or pens. It wasn't like she was carrying a purse around.

But during her first pregnancy one of the most beautiful things Candice ever saw appeared in the waiting room at Tripler Army Medical Center at Fort Shafter, Hawaii. It was a "superpregnant" female lieutenant colonel. Candice usually saw only young, pregnant privates and specialists, not often a peer and rarely a superior. But there she was: a colonel. She had the glow of motherhood while still personifying the confidence and military bearing of a leader. It was an empowering moment.

I want to look like that, Candice decided on the spot.

But at the moment, Candice's eyes were still swollen (a condition she woke up with every morning), she couldn't breathe in Will's pants, and she had one more dilemma: getting her damn boots on. She'd perfected a technique that had to be done sitting on a sofa or bed. First, the ties had to be loosened; then she leaned to the side, flipped on the boot, grabbed the top, hooked her foot inside, and swung the boot over and onto her foot.

While Candice had outgrown her uniform, she did not want to outgrow her boots. Sneakers worn by pregnant women in uniform were officially authorized with a medical waiver, but again other soldiers, both men and women, considered them an embarrassment and a desecration to the uniform and all that it stood for. Fair or not, sneakers denoted weakness, a label most military women tried to avoid at all costs.

As she laced up her boot, the phone rang. It was Will.

"I'm okay, sweetheart," Will said. "I got the tickets changed. We'll be on a flight at two. I convinced a Mexican restaurant here to make some eggs for Kate, and there's this big play area for the kids. We'll play in there forever. I also bribed Kate and bought her every *Sesame Street* doll I could find."

"Good, I'm glad it worked it out," she said.

Candice could picture Will sitting in the airport, sipping a grande-size Starbucks Irish crème latte, calm and order restored to his world.

It was the old Will. The Will whom Candice had fallen in love with on Sicily Drop Zone at Fort Bragg. It was the Will she rarely saw much of anymore.

She remembered back to a time when she was a lieutenant in the 82nd Airborne Division and was so sure of herself and determined to be part of the action. Once, during the division's All-American Week, an annual homecoming celebration each May filled with socials and sports competitions, Candice had spoken with a former 82nd Airborne Division commander.

"Back when I was division commander, there were no women in the division," said the general in a tone that conveyed that he thought there still shouldn't be.

"With all due respect, sir, it's no longer your division," replied Candice.

That day she had just run a ten-mile race neck and neck with her brigade commander, and she was breaking her back at work. She was in no mood for snide remarks, even from generals.

Eight years later, Candice still had that same determination and tenacity. What *had* changed—she was not only committed to her nation but also to a family. As with other women like her, she would have to be prepared and ready for whatever came next.

PART II
DOUBLE TIME

"Because I am a woman, I must make unusual efforts to succeed. If I fail, no one will say, 'She doesn't have what it takes.' They will say, 'Women don't have what it takes.'"

—Clare Boothe Luce

2008

By March, the number of U.S. service members who have died in Iraq reaches 4,000.

Violence persists across Afghanistan. According to UN reports, Taliban insurgents are responsible for civilian deaths increasing by 60 percent in Afghanistan; American and allied deaths have increased by 40 percent over the prior year.

In August the U.S. agrees to remove combat troops from Iraqi cities by the end of June 2009 and—if Iraq is stable—to pull out all combat troops by the end of 2011.

Wall Street crashes, shaking U.S. and world economies. Oil prices hit a record high, unemployment rises, and foreclosures lead to a housing crisis. Barack Obama wins the presidential election against John McCain.

CHAPTER 8
Return to Parris Island

Amy: January 2008. Marine Corps Recruiting Depot,
Parris Island, South Carolina

 Before dawn Amy stood in darkness in her green cammies on the basketball court across from the three-story Osprey Inn, the Bachelor Enlisted Quarters (BEQ) on Parris Island.

She was finally here, ready to prove to the corps she had what it took to be the best of the best, a drill instructor. And Parris Island was going to test her in ways unlike any she'd experienced before, even in Iraq and Lebanon.

A winter wind from the nearby Atlantic chilled the air, but it wasn't enough to deter the sand fleas that infested this swampy sweep of land that jutted like a witch's finger into Port Royal Sound.

Amy was now a sergeant, which meant more duties and responsibilities. Making amateur mistakes was no longer acceptable. But here, at this place, *no* mistakes were acceptable.

As other Marines, her fellow students, trickled onto the basketball court, wafts of Avon's Skin So Soft and alcohol, which everyone had slathered on in hopes of keeping the biting buggers at bay, mixed with the sea air. The smell instantly transported Amy back to when she was an eighteen-year-old recruit. She was as nervous now as she was then.

Two days ago, she'd driven over the causeway and arrived aboard the depot, where she showed the MP at the gate her military ID. She was a month shy of her twenty-fourth birthday, and even with her five years and two deployments in the corps, knots formed in her stomach.

The same feeling of, *Oh, my God, what did I get myself into?* washed over her as she had driven along Malecon Drive, a serpentine road lined with palmettos that straddled saltwater marshland to the east and west. Much of the 8,000-acre island is uninhabitable marsh, infested with mosquitoes and home to alligators, water moccasins, and beds of scalpel-sharp oyster shells. Malecon Drive was like the scenic road into hell.

As she reached civilization, known as Mainside, she passed the parade deck and reviewing stands where she had marched on graduation day as a new Marine, and then she saw it: the "We Make Marines" banner that stretched across Boulevard de France like a shotgun barrel.

"Making Marines and winning battles" are tenets of the corps, and while every drill instructor was a little different in personality, they all shared the same desire to make the best Marines possible. Now Amy would get her shot.

There was no turning back.

When it came to personality, the "schoolhouse," as many military schools are called, was looking for one thing in particular in a student—the desire to give back to the Marine Corps. Training recruits meant helping to mold the corps' future and secure its legacy, a responsibility the corps didn't take lightly.

Amy had found out when she reenlisted in the fall that her orders had been approved for DI School.

"You're gonna love it, but it's gonna be hard work," cautioned Sergeant Major Paul Archie, who had never lost his raspy voice from his own drill instructor days. Amy worked for him as the motor pool platoon sergeant for a medical battalion at Camp Lejeune, after she returned from ship deployment and attended sergeants' school. "The real payoff is at the end of every cycle," Archie went on, "when you watch those recruits that you made into Marines march across the parade deck."

She wanted the challenge so badly. And this was a big one—Drill

Instructor School was the most rigorous enlisted leadership school in the corps. Not until 1977 were women Marines allowed to attend, with the first class graduating in 1978. Before then, the women who trained female recruits were considered to be troop handlers, and their official titles were platoon sergeants and platoon leaders, although their recruits called them DIs. In those days the male DIs taught the female recruits to drill, and it was only in 1996 that female DIs could become primary marksmanship instructors on the rifle range and were finally allowed to wear the iconic Smokey Bear campaign cover.

Will I be physically strong enough? Amy wondered. *Will I have the endurance?* In the Marine Corps, females who aren't good at running are the ones males tend to think don't belong in the corps. Marines are so focused on PT that those who have a hard time with it are labeled a "shit bag," a common term used by Marines.

To make sure, she started running long distances five days a week, usually eight miles but never less than five. And she began memorizing some of the "knowledge" she'd be tested on.

Amy was filled with excitement, pride, and love for the corps. The last thing she wanted to do was let anyone down—Marines like Sergeant Major Archie, others from her previous chain of command, her family, or herself. She knew becoming a drill instructor was going to stress her mind and body, but she was determined. Failure was not an option.

But that didn't prevent the jitters.

None of the sixty Marines in class 2-08, which included six women, talked on the basketball court. To be in this formation, everyone had to be debt-free, PTSD-free, clear of marital problems, not going through divorce or separation, and had to have no pattern of disciplinary infractions in the corps. Marines had to be at least twenty-three years old and no older than thirty-seven, and be a minimum rank of sergeant and a maximum of gunnery sergeant.

A voice cut through the darkness.

"Moonbeams on the deck!"

Far in the distance three flashlight beams lasered in on the basketball court like hunters marking their prey. The lights grew larger, and Amy could see the distinct shape of the Smokey Bear hats.

Oh, God, here they come. . . .

The drill instructors pounced, immediately making corrections on the Marines' position of attention.

"Get yer head and eyes straight forward!"

"Aye, Gunnery Sergeant!"

"Is yer mouth broke?"

"No, Gunnery Sergeant!"

"Open yer face!"

"Aye, Gunnery Sergeant!"

Amy felt as if she were standing on those yellow footprints with her feet at a forty-five-degree angle all over again.

The ranting was meant to simulate battle stress. And Amy had had her first taste of the real thing on her first day in Iraq. The Marines had rolled in from Kuwait, then staged their vehicles and gotten in formation for accountability. Within moments mortars struck the FOB. The threat was real; their lives were in danger, Amy knew, but that wouldn't sink in until later.

"Thumb along trouser seams!"

"Aye, Gunnery Sergeant!"

And so went the barking and bellowing, with a hearty, "Welcome back to Parris Island." Just because the students were in the top echelons among enlisted Marines, the DIs made it clear that distinction only got the students a spot at the school. They weren't entitled to anything, and just like they had to earn the title Marine, they would have to earn the title of drill instructor.

Following the glow from the flashlights, the students marched behind the DIs into the darkness.

Three weeks later

As the sun rose over the DI playground, a yard of packed sand with patchy grass behind Crawford Hall, a drill instructor with a whistle stood on a squat, square wooden platform, like a gladiator trainer overseeing his charges. In a fast-paced frenzy, students were cranking out pull-ups, push-ups, and crunches, climbing ropes and lifting cattle bells. At the sound of the whistle they moved to a new station.

It was just after six thirty and the beginning of two hours of combat conditioning, a term Marines use to describe physical fitness exercise that will benefit them in a combat environment.

Amy was on her twentieth push-up when a pair of tiny booted feet appeared near her hands.

"Stand up, Sergeant Stokley!"

With this latest exception, most of the yelling had subsided by week two. This wasn't boot camp. The students were already Marines, and the focus was on "training the trainers," with an emphasis on leadership, command presence, instructional ability, and physical conditioning.

Amy scrambled to her feet. It was Gunnery Sergeant Kelly, a petite Hispanic drill instructor and the only woman at the schoolhouse. Amy was at her calisthenics station.

"I guess you think you're gonna have all the time in the world to maintain those nails, Sergeant Stokley."

"Aye, Gunnery Sergeant," Amy said, which was the correct and only acceptable response when acknowledging a DI's statement.

Gunnery Sergeant Kelly moved on and Amy resumed her push-ups, planting her acrylic French-tipped fingers in the dirt. It wasn't something most male Marines would have brought up, but women Marines police their own, since the reputations of all of them are on the line. Some male Marines complain that they don't want to correct a female because they are leery of being accused of sexual harassment, or they don't know what the female regulations are for the proper fit and wear of the uniform. That leaves it up to female Marines to correct other female Marines' "deficiencies." Motivated ones who love the corps are quick to make corrections pertaining to proper hair and nail length.

Amy knew it was hard to maintain a good reputation and gain male respect, so when females stepped outside the box, it was upsetting to other females. Exerting one's civilian side by drawing attention to physical appearance through unusually colored hair highlights, hairstyle, or nails is considered "eccentric" in the Marines.

I'm within regulations, Amy told herself as she pumped out more push-ups. *My nails are not too long.*

She knew Gunny didn't like them because they were fake, but Amy had memorized the regs: "Nail length will be no longer than a quarter inch from the tip of the finger." And hers were exactly a quarter inch. She measured.

Unlike the Army's regulation on nail polish color, which is partly left to interpretation, the Marine policy is clear: French manicures, along with press-on and acrylic nails, are authorized, as long as they are maintained within the length and style regulations. And the only polish color Marine women are authorized to wear in their dress uniform is red. Scarlet red. A color the Army calls "fire engine red" and specifically prohibits.

But "scarlet" is one of the corps' official hues, and red nails are considered to complement the service uniform's red collar and cummerbund, which are worn on special occasions.

Amy thought her nails looked professional, and she found them easier to maintain because her regular nails cracked easily.

But Gunny had certainly made her point.

★

One month later

You will continue to march without stiffness or exaggeration of the movement, taking 112 to 120 thirty-inch steps per minute, swinging the arms six inches to the front and three inches to the rear of your legs, until given another command . . . Amy repeated to herself as she waited outside in a line with other students who were also practicing, before it was their turn to show the drill instructor they had "mastered" the "teach back," a method of instruction DIs use to teach recruits drill movements. A single drill movement can have as many as twenty steps, all of which must be memorized from the drill manual and recited verbatim without using any references. The process ensured that drill was taught consistently to all recruits. But memorizing the instructions was like trying to recite the owner's manual for computer software.

Assume you are marching forward at double time and you receive the command, "Quick time, march." The command of execution may be given as either foot strikes the deck.

Amy used the five- and ten-minute breaks to sit with her nose buried in a manual in Crawford Hall's main classroom, a small auditorium filled with desks and blue chairs. In case anyone forgot why they were there, an enormous red-lettered banner with "Honor, Courage, Commitment" against a gold background hung above the stage at the front of the room.

Hundreds of pairs of eyes looked out from framed class graduation photos on the back and side walls. It was as if their predecessors were peering down upon them saying, "Live up to our legacy."

In the hallway, past a wall of vintage recruiting posters—"We Don't Promise You a Rose Garden," "We Still Make 'Em Like We Used To," "The Marines Are Looking for a Few Good Men," and "We Don't Take Contracts, Only Commitments"—is the Hall of Heroes, a corridor of more photos and unit citations dating back to the Civil War acknowledging Medal of Honor Marines, many of whom received the honor posthumously. More pressure.

"We're always looking down on you" was the effect the school's leadership was after.

Amy's brain was like an overloaded circuit board as she tried to memorize thirty-six drill movements that took up the pages of five books. The class had about two weeks to master each volume.

With a memory like mine, how am I going to do it? she often wondered.

Between their learning the teach backs and the regulations and policies governing recruit training, time management was another skill the students had to master if they were going to make it and be successful on "the streets," a term used for training recruits.

"Don't let 'em in," Gunnery Sergeant Fortune would tell the students, pointing to his head when something was hard or painful. "Don't let the doubts in."

Gunnery Sergeant Fortune was one of the most demanding and motivating of the instructors. He lived, breathed, and slept the corps. As the drillmaster, he taught all the drills at the schoolhouse. And he never let up.

And Amy was trying not to either. She spent hour after hour each night studying.

To help with memorization the students recorded themselves reading a drill movement and then listened to it over and over. Amy would go to sleep playing her recorder. A number of students bought memory pills from the GNC on the base, but Amy never tried that.

She could have used an energy pill, though.

She was tired from the daily physical training, which included two hours of PT and everything from ten-mile forced marches with a thirty-five-pound pack and rifle to sprints and the obstacle course. Then there were the late-night field days, when students cleaned the entire school, inside and out, including cutting the grass. Anything the recruits were expected to do, the DI students did, too. It gave them added credibility and also helped them understand the environment their future recruits would be in.

"I gotta go, Mom; I gotta study," she'd tell her mother at night after talking for a few minutes. Four o'clock came quickly each morning, and Amy was in class formation by five a.m.

Back home in Kentucky school hadn't come easily for Amy. She had to work hard to do well. By age fourteen she had her first job because she wanted to make her own money, and she went on to work in retail at a number of department stores. She learned her work ethic from her mother, Diana, a single mom, who put in overtime on the assembly line of a factory and often held more than one job to make ends meet when Amy was growing up. With her two daughters in tow, Diana cleaned a beauty shop on Mondays as barter for free haircuts for the girls, and she made wedding and birthday cakes and sold Pampered Chef and Tupperware on the side.

When Amy was in first grade, she drew a picture of a car and said,

"Mommy, when I grow up I'm gonna buy you a Lamborghini." Later she tacked on, "And a mansion."

Years later she gave her mother her old fully loaded Chevy Cobalt.

"That's my Marine Corps Lamborghini," Diana would tell people with a laugh.

Her junior year, Amy worked as a receptionist for a local company. When she graduated, the company wanted to promote her to human resources manager and offered to pay for college. Diana was thrilled, but Amy came to her with a different plan.

"Mom, I'm going to join the Marine Corps."

"What?" Diana said.

"I've been thinking about it for a long time," Amy said.

"What?"

"You always told me not to wake up when I was forty and have regrets about not doing what I wanted to do."

★

Now, in a be-careful-what-you-wish-for moment, it was Amy's turn to recite. She approached Gunnery Sergeant Kelly and handed the instructor her book. Kelly readied her red pen in case she had to cross a line through any missed words.

Screw it up and students were told, "Go away," and to the end of the line they go. Failing teach backs can get a student dropped from DI School.

Amy did an about-face and walked twenty paces away from the gunny. Then she did another about-face. Facing Kelly, she placed her left hand behind her back and formed what DIs call a "knife hand" with her right hand—fingers and thumb extended close together. It's a DI tradition used for emphasis when giving instruction. Behind Amy, students still in line knifed through the air as they rehearsed the teach backs.

"The movement I will explain and demonstrate is quick time," Amy screamed, while pumping her hand. (Teach backs were always screamed.) "The purpose of this movement is to march at one hundred and twelve to one hundred and twenty steps per minute taking thirty-inch steps. There are no counts involved with this movement. This movement is executed when halted at attention, marking time, marching forward at double time, and marching at half step. The commands for this movement are, 'Forward, march,' 'Quick time, march.' When executed it will sound and look like this: 'Forward, march,' 'Quick time, march.'"

The gunny's pen hadn't yet touched Amy's book.

Just one more page of recitation to go.

"Assume you are halted at attention. . . ."

★

March 26, 2008

Amy looked in the mirror. It was the first time she'd seen herself wearing the campaign cover.

"Am I really a United States Marine Corps drill instructor?"

Her mother and nine other family members had driven the twelve hours from Kentucky to be there for graduation, which was at nine that morning inside the base theater.

Diana noticed that her daughter always carried herself differently when in uniform, poised and with head held high. They even got her to crack a few smiles for photos.

Like the other four women graduates—one had dropped out because of an injury—Amy wore a skirt, but not by choice. The women thought the skirt looked silly with the green DI belt cinched around their waists and the black low quarters, the same flat dress shoes they wore with their trousers.

But the coveted Smokey Bear hat on their heads was the real prize. As a class, 2-08 raised their right hands and, with the vocal cords of Godzilla, grunted out the Drill Instructor Pledge, repeating each line after the school's first sergeant.

"These recruits are entrusted to my care.

"I will train them to the best of my ability.

"I will develop them into smartly disciplined, physically fit, basically trained Marines, thoroughly indoctrinated in love of corps and country.

"I will demand of them, and demonstrate by my own example, the highest standards of personal conduct, morality, and professional skill."

It's a pledge they would repeat before each platoon of new recruits in the squad bay.

"Damn," Amy said, taking one more look in the mirror. "I actually made it."

Now came the hard part. It was time to hit the streets.

CHAPTER 9
Brotherhood Revisited

Angie: March 2008. MCRD, San Diego

 "I just can't believe you're leaving," Angie said, as she took a seat in Sergeant Major Woods's office, which he planned to pack up over the weekend. "What am I going to do without you?"

Angie wasn't one to be overly emotional, but now she had to fight back tears.

The sergeant major was heading into uncharted territory for his most anticipated assignment yet: retirement.

At age forty-nine, and after thirty years of serving corps and country, it was time to move on. Except that the sergeant major, like most sergeants major, wasn't sure he was ready to leave, and the general definitely wasn't ready to let him go.

Sergeants major must retire after three decades, unless they are approved for an extension at the three-star level. Angie had offered to ask for the extension, and the possibility piqued the sergeant major's interest. But RhodaAnn Woods, faithful Marine wife of twenty-six years, was determined to have her husband home, a place he had rarely been. And that was that.

"It's time," Sergeant Major Woods told Angie. At least Woods and his family would stay in San Diego, which eased Angie's sadness somewhat.

I'm still going to see him, thought Angie. *He's not really, truly leaving.*

She'd been trying to convince herself of that for weeks. But in reality everything would change. In fact, it already had, in ways unprecedented.

Commanders and sergeants major work closely together, and the success of the command often relies on their chemistry and communication. In the corps' world of men, not many would have embraced being professionally partnered with a woman, let alone one as a superior. But the sergeant major had a different view.

As a high-level and high-visibility command team, the two had broken new ground in the Marine Corps not only because they were paired together, but also because their bond transcended gender at one of the highest tiers in the corps. Their success served as an example and laid the groundwork for the next generation of command teams at every level in the corps.

Saying good-bye wouldn't be easy.

The following week, on Thursday afternoon, March 13, friends and family, including Woods's relatives, who were making their first trip to California for their first military ceremony, filled the VIP reviewing area, while others sat in the bleachers.

Dressed in his service Charlies and campaign cover, and standing on the parade deck he had marched across hundreds of times as a drill instructor, thousands of miles from where his journey had begun at Parris Island, Sergeant Major Woods faced Angie, as the adjutant read the Legion of Merit citation.

The medal is awarded to senior officers "for exceptionally meritorious conduct in the performance of outstanding services and achievements," and sometimes the medal is given to a senior noncommissioned officer. Angie had only ever submitted the Legion of Merit for one enlisted Marine, and that was Bobby Woods. Of all the sergeants major who had ever worked for her, he was number one.

It was a real honor, and it meant a great deal to Woods to have the Marine Corps appreciate his three decades of leadership and service.

Now Angie attempted to make light of the moment, as she often did in emotional situations.

"I know the moment you get out of that uniform you're gonna start growing that stinkin' mustache," she said with her back to the crowd.

"You know I'm growing it back starting tomorrow, ma'am," Woods responded.

"Don't come back to see me looking like a used-car salesman," she said. It was her last direct order to him.

And with that, Angie took the gold medallion with five white flares, centered with thirteen tiny white stars and hanging from a crimson ribbon, and pinned it to Woods's left breast pocket.

A year and a half earlier she and Sergeant Major Woods had been total strangers. Now they were the best of friends. They would have been an unlikely match even in the civilian world—a pint-size, smart-alecky, middle-aged Hispanic woman and a quiet, observant, square-shouldered African-American man. They certainly were avant-garde for the Marine Corps' brotherhood.

But what had started off as a public show of solidarity had over time grown into admiration and respect and finally into true friendship, absolute trust, and confidence. Such friendships hadn't been easy for Angie to find in the corps, and she and the sergeant major shared family occasions as well, which was not an area where officers and enlisted usually crossed lanes. But military bonds of this nature didn't come on a first-name basis.

He called her "General" or "ma'am."

She called him "Sergeant Major."

For Woods, the initial inquiries he'd fielded—"Why is she here?"—had shifted to, "What is it like to work for her?" That question followed the sergeant major like the San Diego sunshine. In the eyes of Bobby Woods, Angie Salinas was no longer a woman in a man's Marine Corps.

"I'll tell you the truth," he'd say to the questioner. "It is an honor to work with her. I've learned so much. It's the first time I've ever worked for a female Marine in all my thirty years. The lesson is, it doesn't matter. We've all earned the title. We are all Marines."

CHAPTER 10
The Lieutenant

Bergan: May 10, 2008. Norwich University

 As they had on their wedding day nine months earlier, Bergan and Tom faced each other before family members and peered into each other's eyes. This time for a vow of another kind.

"Please raise your right hand and repeat after me," instructed Tom, who was dressed in his green Class As. He had flown up the day before from Fort Stewart, Georgia, where he served as an MP platoon leader in the 385th Military Police Battalion.

Bergan wore her hair slicked back into a tight bun. She, too, was dressed in Class As and wore the gold crossed-pistols insignia of the Military Police Corps on her lapels. She'd found out the previous fall that she had gotten her first choice of service branch.

Today was the first time Bergan had ever worn a skirt as part of her uniform ensemble. Norwich didn't issue skirts in the school's vast inventory of uniform components, but female cadets were authorized to purchase one at their own expense after their freshman year. Bergan never did.

Now she wore a uniform specifically designed for a woman—a green jacket fitted at the waist, a matching knee-length skirt, and a blouse with a black neck tab. The rows of ribbons she had earned as a cadet were gone; her Army uniform was bare, except for her nameplate and silver jump wings.

She was a walking, breathing blank green canvas. No one in the Army would care that she had been a cadet drill instructor, a cadet company commander, an honor graduate, a high performer at Advanced Camp and on the A Team in the Ranger Club. Any advantage that she may have had over her peers because of her performance at Norwich was gone. What mattered now was performing with real soldiers. She would have to earn her bona fides.

Tom raised his right hand, and Bergan did the same as they stood in Shapiro Field House before a massive American flag secured to the wall. Its size rivaled the iconic flag in the movie *Patton*. The field house was the same place where Bergan got her start as a rook four years before, when she had a tear-filled parting with her parents and sister. The good-bye then had been tough, but she had been more anxious to get things going than anything else. Today she was saying good-bye to cadet life, and once again her eyes looked forward.

Tom: "'I,' state your name, 'having been appointed a second lieutenant in the United States Army . . .'"

Bergan: "I, Bergan Flannigan, having been appointed a second lieutenant in the United States Army . . . "

Tom: "'Do solemnly swear that I will support and defend the Constitution of the United States against all enemies, foreign and domestic.'"

Bergan: "Do solemnly swear that I will support and defend the Constitution of the United States against all enemies, foreign and domestic."

While some officers read the oath of office from an index card when administering it, for fear of mucking up a line, Tom had the oath memorized, as was Norwich's standard. On his wedding day he had been overcome with emotion and had difficulty reciting his vows; today, though, Tom was collected and all business. As for Bergan, she was as calm today as she had been at the altar.

Tom: "'That I will bear true faith and allegiance to the same; that I take this obligation freely . . .'"

Bergan: "That I will bear true faith and allegiance to the same; that I take this obligation freely . . . "

Tom: "'Without any mental reservation or purpose of evasion . . .'"

Bergan: "Without any mental reservation or purpose of evasion . . ."

Tom: "'And that I will well and faithfully discharge the office upon which I am about to enter. So help me God.'"

Bergan: "And that I will well and faithfully discharge the office upon which I am about to enter. So help me God."

Tom's and Bergan's eyes softened, and smiles spread across their faces. With the appropriate military bearing they shook hands, and then Tom stole a kiss.

Like Tom, Bergan was a Distinguished Military Graduate (DMG), which meant she ranked in the top 20 percent of ROTC cadets in the nation, who have excelled above their peers in academics, military skills, and leadership potential.

Nearby, other cadets, including her rook sister Meghan, surrounded by their families and friends, took their commissioning oaths. Next came the moment Bergan had been waiting four years for. Her parents stepped forward, ready to pin the gold bars of a second lieutenant, long nicknamed "butter bars" because of their resemblance to a stick of butter, on their daughter's shoulders.

Billy and Amy Arsenault had practiced the procedure beforehand under the close direction of Bergan, who wanted her rank to be straight and properly aligned on her uniform.

"Mom, do it right!" Bergan had said during a practice run.

Now Amy ably secured the two-pronged bar (actually about the size and shape of a piece of Trident gum) and hugged her daughter. She couldn't have been prouder.

Years before, Amy's older sister had insisted, "Don't encourage her to do this!" when she heard Bergan was showing an interest in attending a military college.

But Amy's response was definite. "I respect her, and this is who she is," she told her sister at the time. "I have two choices: I can support her or not." That had always been Amy's approach, whether Bergan was jumping out of an airplane or qualifying with an M4 carbine.

Soon after Tom administered the oath, Bergan was again struck by the import of it all when Marine General James "Hoss" Cartwright, a four-star general and the vice chairman of the Joint Chiefs of Staff, with thirty-seven years in the military, again administered the oath to the ninety-one cadets assembled before him—fifty-two Army second lieutenants, seventeen Marine Corps second lieutenants, fifteen Air Force second lieutenants, and seven Navy ensigns—during Norwich's joint service commissioning ceremony.

This is amazing, thought Bergan, her rank now fastened to the tops of her shoulders. *Is this really happening?* The past three days had been a whirl of activities, including a senior class dinner, graduation rehearsal, commissioning practice, an awards ceremony, a reception for new graduates and family, and tomorrow—finally—graduation.

Next the new officers received their "first salute" as commissioned officers from an enlisted person of their choosing. Bergan picked her nineteen-year-old cousin, Carter.

"Second Lieutenant Bergan Flannigan, an Army ROTC distinguished graduate, will receive her first salute from Seaman Apprentice Carter Bierwirth, United States Navy," announced an officer in the Army ROTC department from the podium.

Bergan stood below the dais and waited for Carter to approach. As the cousins faced each other, Carter saluted and Bergan returned the gesture. After they shook hands, Bergan reached into her left pocket and placed a silver dollar in Carter's palm, following a longtime military tradition with origins in nineteenth-century British military practice: The first salute an officer receives is bought; all others afterward must be earned.

★

The next morning, bushy-browed General John Abizaid, dressed in a black doctoral gown and yellow academic hood, compliments of the honorary doctor of military science degree bestowed on him by Norwich, stood on the dais in front of the *Patton* flag and addressed the class of 2008.

The former commander of the U.S. Central Command had overseen operations in the Middle East until his retirement from the Army the previous May. With thirty-five years of military service behind him, he was a man who knew too much.

Now the eager eyes of those who knew too little watched him intently.

"Your challenge will be to serve well," he said, "to lead others to repair the damage not of your making, to live the values of your university and your nation, and to make a difference in a world so much in need of people who can make a difference. My confidence in your future is boundless. I trust you to make a world a better place for my grandchildren. I'm willing to bet that the class of 2008 will leave this planet a better place than they found it. I'm willing to bet that you will be our greatest generation."

As college commencement addresses unfolded across the country, speakers imparted life lessons and advice, or talked about themselves, or plugged political agendas. Those such as Abizaid, who addressed young men and women graduating from the service academies and military colleges, had to find the right tone for an audience whose members would undoubtedly deploy to an unpopular war in Iraq or a little-understood one in Afghanistan.

Bergan sat upright in her seat and listened. For the last time she was wearing her cadet dress blues, a uniform that dated back to the school's founding—white trousers, white hat, white gloves, and gray jacket. It felt odd, though, to be back in her cadet uniform, since she was now one of the Army's newly minted second lieutenants. Bethany, who sat in a separate section for civilian students, was dressed in a traditional cap and gown.

In his follow-on remarks, Norwich president Dr. Richard Schneider, himself a retired reserve Coast Guard rear admiral and Vietnam veteran known for his intensity, encouraged the students to be courageous enough to make tough and ethical decisions, and to use their leadership to make the world better. "I know you're going to make us proud as we watch you in your lives yet to be," he said to the 4,500 people gathered in front of him. On this Mother's Day, it was probably a bittersweet message for most moms of graduates in the audience.

The war games are over, Bergan's mother thought, as she smoothed out the commencement program on her lap. *It's real.* She had spent four years hearing all about Bergan's training exercises and cadet adventures, much of it fun for Bergan. Amy always knew that they would lead to commissioning into the real Army. Four years ago at Shapiro Field House, Amy had been fearful for Bergan as a female at a military school. She was fearful again, but also immensely proud of her daughter's accomplishments, a dichotomy that came with being a military parent.

Across the room, Bergan was anxious to start the next chapter in her life. She planned to stay in the Army four years, the time required to fulfill her ROTC scholarship commitment. Then after that perhaps grad school. She'd have little time to reflect on graduation. Unlike Tom, who hadn't been needed for active duty until five months after commissioning, Bergan had to report in a week for five months of duty at Fort Knox, Kentucky. Then she'd go on to schools at Fort Benning and Fort Leonard Wood. The good news? She found out earlier in the week that she'd be assigned to Fort Stewart, where Tom was stationed. But that was nine months away.

Meanwhile, outside the building, two blasts from a cannon reverberated in the field house and jolted everyone in it to attention. In a display that looked like popcorn popping, on cue Bergan and her classmates tossed their hats high into the arched rafters, a boisterous farewell to adolescence and a symbolic transition from pupil to practitioner.

CHAPTER 11
Paradise Lost

Candice: June 5, 2008. Schofield Barracks, Hawaii

 In the early hours of the morning, hungry eight-week-old Tom O'Brien awoke like a kitchen timer in his portable crib provided by the Inn at Schofield Barracks. That afternoon his mother had checked into the maroon-carpeted room with its dated multicolored bedspreads and pastel ocean scenes in shiny gold frames. With the exception of the white furniture and seashell prints, it was typical Army lodging. On Candice's last night in Hawaii she shared the room with her children and father, who had come from Muscatine, Iowa, to help her pack and move back to the mainland.

The weather had been beautiful all week, and the storm that had ravaged the island the previous winter, when Candice was pregnant, was a distant memory.

The baby rarely cried at feeding time, preferring to hum and sing. On Tom's first night home from the hospital, he kept Candice awake for hours with his serenades. She was convinced Tom's mellow and agreeable manner was a result of her mostly stress-free pregnancy and delivery, even though her husband, Will, had missed part of the pregnancy and experienced his son's April 2 birth over the telephone at Camp Victory, Iraq.

Candice pulled her hair back in a ponytail and reached for her glasses on the bedside table. The clock read two a.m. Just before Tom was born, she had started growing her hair out to donate for cancer patients' wigs. She'd always wanted to donate her hair to a good cause. The combination of being on six weeks' maternity leave and heading to a school environment at Fort Leavenworth, Kansas, provided the perfect opportunity to experiment with her coiffure. She discovered that the ease of caring for pulled-back hair was one reason a number of Army women chose to wear their hair long, twisted into a tight bun during the duty day.

"Come here, handsome." Candice lifted Tom out of his crib. "That's a boy." He was a hefty baby with a thin fringe of blond hair. Almost ten pounds at birth, he was already outgrowing his baby carrier. The streetlights streaming through a crack in the drapes provided just enough light for Candice to prepare Tom's formula in the room's small kitchenette. She had tried nursing him his first week, but with his large size and rapid growth she couldn't keep up.

Except for the hum of the air conditioner and Kate's deep breathing, the room was silent. In the next bed was Candice's father. Since Will's deployment to Iraq in January, Candice's parents, both retired special education teachers, had been arriving in shifts, each making the long trip from Iowa every three to four weeks, to help their pregnant daughter and later trade off child-care duties. Candice paid for most of their flights, and her parents used frequent-flier miles collected from their credit card to cover the rest.

"It's worth every penny!" Candice told friends.

But the help came with logistical hurdles. Candice had to have a memorandum approved and signed by Schofield's commanding general allowing her parents to live with her on post. Simple tasks such as buying milk at the commissary meant the Frosts had to take their granddaughter Kate along to show her ID card before they could make any purchases. This six-month arrangement also meant Don and Shelley Frost saw each other only once every few weeks. The Frosts pined for each other and talked on the phone every night. It was the longest they'd been apart in their thirty-five-year marriage. Will and Candice chuckled at how much her parents missed each other, since by Army standards the separation was short.

But as Candice stared out the hotel window, she realized she wanted a marriage like that. When she and Will were apart, she wanted him to long to see her. She wanted him to ache for her and not to see their conversations as a burden or requirement.

If Candice's parents hadn't made such a big commitment, Candice didn't know what she would have done. There was no plan B. She was fortunate to have such devoted parents, because in the Army world, the Army came first. Male soldiers who were husbands and fathers relied on their wives to keep the family and household going when duty called. Women like Candice didn't have that assurance.

"Family is first. You have to do what you can to help your family," was Don Frost's motto. Her parents had always been there for Candice and her younger brother. They coached her softball team, never missed a cross-country meet, and, since the school district Candice attended employed them both, always had immediate feedback on everything Candice did, something she now viewed as a blessing.

And while the politically liberal Frosts didn't always favor the military's operations overseas, they were Candice's rock and did everything they could to support their daughter as she struggled to balance children, career, and a military marriage. Along the way, the Frosts experienced a human side of military life that they never were exposed to in Iowa. During his stays on Millet Street, between diaper changes and bottle feedings, Don Frost walked the neighborhood to see who needed a helping hand. Half the families on Millet had a husband and father deployed, so he changed light-bulbs, waxed cars, and put together jungle gyms. Everyone on Millet Street knew him.

"America doesn't see this!" he'd often tell his daughter. "How hard it is for women to raise children alone—all on one block."

And in Candice's case, that meant raising children alone while serving in the Army. The O'Briens were the only dual military couple on their street.

By now Tom had finished his bottle but was still wide-eyed. Candice stepped away from the window and slipped into a pair of loose shorts and a T-shirt and strapped on Teva sandals, the off-duty footwear she'd lived in for seven and a half years. She had gained forty-five pounds during her pregnancy and was working to lose the weight.

"Okay, let's go for a walk, BT."

BT stood for Baby Tom. Candice bundled him up and, as her father and daughter continued to sleep, softly slipped out of the room. Hawaii had two seasons—rainy and dry. June was in the dry season, and the island air cooled her cheeks as she walked down the steps. Under a moonless sky Candice could just make out the outline of the Waianae Mountains. She used to stare at the mountains often; from one angle they looked like a woman lying on her back.

Few cars sat in the hotel's parking lot. Like other military hotels, the Schofield Inn wasn't a vacation destination but lodging for people in transition, moving either to or from the island. And like all Army lodging, hospitality took second place to Army regulations, which were prominently posted. Children had to be supervised at all times, no babysitters allowed. Older children had a curfew, and no privately owned weapons were allowed on the property, "including war trophies," which had to be registered at the provost marshal's office within three days. There was a reminder about the 120-day quarantine in Honolulu for all family pets entering Hawaii, and all POVs (Privately Owned Vehicles) had to be registered within ten days of arrival. If anyone wanted to question the regs, they should contact the MPs, not the front desk. Aloha.

Candice held Tom close as she crossed Kolekole Avenue in front of the Nehelani Club and made her way along a dirt path. Like the inn, the former officers' club had a distinctive green, Hawaii plantation–style sloped roof. Back in the old Army days, O-clubs were the center of officers' social lives. But in the last decade, many Army O-clubs had gone the way of the tommy gun. Often money losers, the clubs couldn't compete with off-post competition that offered better food and service. Most were combined into all-ranks clubs, which took away the exclusivity but helped them break even. Candice ate at the Nehelani occasionally for lunch, but it had typical club system food, which wasn't saying much.

Rarely was Candice out at this hour. She wasn't used to the silence. It was odd not to hear the birds that were always caroling in the foliage. But the soft air still smelled of flowers, and Candice breathed in deeply on her last Hawaiian night.

Military families either loved or hated Hawaii; rarely did they harbor an in-between sentiment. Those who hated Hawaii discovered that living there and vacationing there were two different things. The high cost of living, the terrible public school system, cockroach-infested quarters, and traffic worse than the metro Washington, D.C., area were significant reasons to dislike the place. If you favored long road trips, four seasons, and seeing grandparents once a month, Hawaii was not the place for you. For these folks the excitement of living in paradise wore off by month three.

Others adored Hawaii's endless summer, the fresh air, the beaches, and the warm, easygoing people. There were less desirable duty stations, after all—Korea, for one, and some would add Fort Irwin, Fort Polk, and Fort Drum to the list. But military life is about blooming where you are planted.

When the O'Briens received orders for Hawaii in 2001, Lieutenant Candice O'Brien had just one request: "Wherever we go, let's live on the beach!" She was determined to learn to surf as well as enjoy her new living arrangements. Even though she and Will had married a year earlier, Army schools had kept them geographically separated the entire time. Hawaii would be their first time actually living under the same roof.

Will, who arrived on the island first, found an eight-hundred-square-foot bungalow across from Sunset Beach on the North Shore through the "For Rent" section of the *Honolulu Observer*. The wooden cottage, painted white and trimmed in blue, looked like it would collapse in a windstorm. It sat on a half acre of an old farm, with mango, macadamia nut, and banana trees in the front yard.

But the telltale cracks of the Hawaiian military myth presented their fissures early, even before Candice moved in. A month before her arrival, she received news that her new unit would be deploying to Bosnia. After 9/11, orders to Afghanistan and then Iraq would follow for the O'Briens. For all of Hawaii's beauty, it couldn't erase the ugliness going on in other parts of the world.

Now, after more than seven years, Candice was excited to start a new chapter.

Later that day she'd fly to Iowa and spend six weeks there on the military leave she'd accumulated.

"Paradise is relative," she'd always tell people.

Hawaii was nice, but Iowa was paradise. It was the rolling hills and sunrise above the cornfields. It was the beauty of a sunset on the Mississippi River, seen from her family's summer cabin. Iowa was where her family and her heart remained, wherever the Army sent her.

Candice was never one to look back. She rarely had a "coulda, woulda, shoulda" moment. Like a tank commander, she looked forward and drove toward the objective.

This had been evident even when she was eighteen years old, when her parents said good-bye to her inside West Point's Arvin Gym, possibly the only gymnasium in America to resemble a Gothic castle. An officer announced it was time to say good-bye and begin Reception Day, the first day of Beast, West Point's version of basic training. Candice turned to her father and gave him a hug.

He looked her in the eyes. "I love you, Candey."

"I love you, too, Dad. I'll miss you. I'll call when I can." Then she turned to her mother.

"Go conquer the world," her mother said. "We love you to bits." Candice hugged her, then walked swiftly up the stairs. She failed to look around and notice how everyone else was clinging to lengthy embraces.

Candice was the first cadet of the Class of '98 to report for duty.

It was comforting for Candice to look ahead to the rest of 2008. She always had a chart, a pattern, and a plan. Despite giving birth without her husband present and facing an overseas move and a new duty station alone, with two little ones, she had everything lined up: her parents' help, and her orders to attend the Command and General Staff College (CGSC) at Fort Leavenworth, Kansas. She also had her goal of staying on a second year to attend the highly competitive School of Advanced Military Studies (SAMS) for a second master's in military arts and science. That would allow her to be a strategic planner at the highest tactical and operational levels with war-fighting units.

It was an ambitious plan, with only one hitch: The infantry branch did not allow Will to attend CGSC the same year as Candice, even though he had been selected into the program. It seemed like a no-brainer that the Army would allow the O'Briens, who were in the same year group, to attend school together. Instead, once again, their marriage and family were "professionally desynchronized."

Will's deployment to Iraq was what Candice called a nice Army curveball. The Army was a major league pro of the curveball.

The dirt path Candice had been following finally brought her to the 25th Infantry Division's war memorial. Surprised by a sudden welling of emotion, Candice felt tears in her eyes.

The memorial consisted of four life-size soldiers united in sacrifice. Three men, cast in gray metal, represented World War II, Korea, and Vietnam. They walked toward a fourth, cast in bronze, representing the War on Terrorism. This soldier held his helmet and stood before a deceased soldier's field cross—the dead soldier's rifle positioned vertically inside his boots and topped with his helmet. In a place surrounded by so much beauty, here was a tangible tribute to the kind of pain no amount of sunshine, sand, and surf could ever fix. And the pain was still going on. June 2008 would be the deadliest month in Afghanistan for U.S. and coalition forces since the 2001 invasion.

"BT," she said, "I want to tell you all about the wonderful men this memorial represents. It's a reminder of the ultimate sacrifice paid by so many great men."

She held Tom tightly to her and told him about the loss of Lieutenant Colonel Mike McMahon, her boss in the aviation brigade, who, along with Chief Warrant Officer Travis Grogan and Specialist Harley Miller, had died in a helicopter crash in Afghanistan on November 27, 2004, while Candice was a company commander. The three men ranged in age from twenty-one to forty-one, with Lieutenant Colonel McMahon the oldest. Before the deployment the O'Briens had attended a pool party at the home of the McMahons, whose youngest son was three at the time. His parents had said, "No, Ricky!" so much that she and Will joked that the boy thought his name was No Ricky!

As those memories flooded back, Candice let her tears flow. Most of the time military women aren't allowed to show emotion, so when they do break down, it's significant. Candice rarely got to the emotional threshold where she expressed extreme joy or sadness with tears. Typically it was when no one else could see.

Staring at the field cross, Candice remembered Will calling her on August 22, 2007, and telling her that a helicopter crash in Iraq had taken the lives of eleven young men in his unit. She had gasped after hearing that awful news.

Here, on this spot in 2001, long before the memorial had been built, Lieutenant Colonel Pugliese, the intelligence officer for the 25th Infantry Division, had promoted Candice from first lieutenant to captain. Now, as a major, she was leaving the island inexorably changed. She had become a mother in Hawaii to her two precious children, made it through two deployments of her own, and knew what it felt like to be the spouse of a deployed soldier. Tomorrow she'd start another phase of her life, one that included further development of her tactical and operational skills as a field-grade officer.

The Army needed "iron majors" like Candice now more than ever. Due to repeat deployments and high operational tempos, midcareer officers with families were leaving the Army, resulting in a shortage of majors, a critical rank. Majors are the military workhorses who run tactical units by serving in key staff positions in battalions, brigades, and divisions—the very units deployed overseas—doing the bulk of the planning and logistics for operations. Candice had no intention of leaving. She had much to accomplish.

Candice noticed Tom had fallen asleep. She needed to get back to the room. She turned and took the long way back.

CHAPTER 12
Nicky the New Hat

Amy: July 2008. Parris Island, South Carolina

★ "Good morning, ladies!"

"Good morning, ladies!"

"Good morning, ladies!" squawked each recruit, voicing the greeting of the day inside the 4th Recruit Training Battalion's chow hall.

Never mind that it was half past noon. Down the Parris Island rabbit hole it wasn't officially afternoon until after the recruits ate lunch. Recruits weren't authorized to wear watches, and it was mealtime that marked the passage of time, with evening chow greatly anticipated, since the recruits knew then that they were almost finished for the day.

The 4th Recruit Training Battalion dining hall, like the battalion itself, was for women recruits only, and there were dozens of them lined up there at the moment.

"Good morning, ladies!" echoed eighteen-year-old Samantha Finley, a redheaded recruit from Crooksville, Ohio, as she carried a tan plastic tray with her forearms parallel to the deck. She was addressing Amy and

Sergeant Elisa Gaines. Amy had been on the drill field for a month; Elisa, a twenty-seven-year-old Hispanic from Los Angeles, already had one cycle under her belt, and she tried to help Amy any way she could. With three or four DIs assigned to each platoon, Amy and Elisa were both "fourth hats"—in the same company but in separate platoons. Their job was to instill discipline.

"Eyeballs forward, Finley! Who do you think you are, lookin' me in the eyes?" Amy blasted, with her hands along the green web belt cinched tight around her waist in the DI power stance. Making eye contact with a drill instructor was a big no-no that Recruit Finley kept flubbing.

"Aye, ma'am."

"Moooove! Go away!" It was as if the devil himself catapulted from Amy's mouth before recoiling back into her larynx to await the next hapless recruit.

"Aye, ma'am." And with that the recruit scurried to the second food station, which held salads, fruit, and chocolate pudding. The pudding was the only sweet item offered, and recruits were limited to one scoop.

"Blasting" is a DI specialty, more powerful than a yell and heavier than a scream. Volume was a sign of confidence in a DI, and Amy's goal was to be the loudest. It was all about pride, and it had the practical purpose of making a DI heard on the drill field. The back of the formation had to hear a DI call the drill movements.

When Amy screamed, she screamed as hard as she could, using her diaphragm, as she'd been taught. A scream of this magnitude spring-loads from the lower ribs and thrusts the DI's upper body forward, much like a beast attacking its prey. Amy didn't want anybody moving faster or blasting louder than she did. Marines were competitive by nature, drill instructors even more so.

If a recruit didn't "open her face"—shout—loud enough, the DIs took it as a sign of disrespect. Amy wanted her recruits to have confidence when they spoke.

The sixty recruits in Platoon 4027 knew Amy was fresh out of DI School. It was easy for them to tell. She'd started off the cycle the previous month somewhat quiet and in the background, trying to fit in with the experienced DIs in the company. But she was a quick learner, and she now had a reputation in the platoon for being as mean as any of them.

It was the best compliment a new hat could receive. Making a recruit cry was like winning the lottery. It meant Amy was doing her job. Being mean—which was different from being demeaning—was expected of a green belter, and every one of them wanted to put pain into the recruits' bodies.

"How many recruits did *you* take to the pits today?" the DIs would ask while sizing one another up.

"The pits" stood for sandpits. If Satan had a sandbox, this would be it. Infested with sand fleas and edged with telephone poles, the sandpits were large enough to hold a platoon of sweaty bodies grinding out push-ups, sit-ups, and flutter kicks as disciplinary punishments, known as "incentive training." At Parris Island what the mind failed to comprehend, the body would pay for, and females were no exception.

If a woman wants to enlist in the Marines, she'll come through Parris Island for thirteen weeks of boot camp. The island graduates 21,000 recruits annually, of which about 2,400 are women.

Males and females have trained separately at Parris Island ever since the first group of women Marines graduated from the island in 1949, the year after females were integrated into the regular corps from the women's reserve.

And though they're separate, the females receive the same instruction and training as the males—which includes close-order drill, bayonet, pugil sticks, martial arts, gas mask, rappelling, marksmanship, obstacle courses, and combat water survival. Not to mention Marine Corps history, values, and traditions.

Along with all that, the DIs teach self-discipline, military bearing, physical fitness, and esprit de corps.

The senior DI's job is to be a tough-love mother figure to the recruits, but the goal of the most junior hats is to instill discipline and, yes, put pain in the recruits. This is accomplished by making constant "corrections" on how they stand, walk, talk, run, eat, and breathe. And in Recruit Finley's case, where she focused her eyeballs.

At the beginning of each recruit cycle, there was no shortage of corrections; the instructors were, after all, dealing with females who knew nothing about recruit training. Amy and Elisa corrected the women on not moving unless they were told to do so, sounding off, not scratching, how to stand at the right position of attention (fingers curled, feet at forty-five degrees, not looking around), speaking in the third person, learning commands and the rules in the squad bay, how to carry a rifle, how to wear their uniform, how to eat, and on and on.

The magnitude of corrections at the beginning of a cycle was overwhelming, not only for the recruits, but also for Amy and Elisa. In the eyes of their senior DI, Gunnery Sergeant Martinez, and her experienced DIs, Amy and Elisa were never fast or loud enough with corrections. Often it seemed they were whispering, because their voices were shot. Calling commands during drill was especially painful. The other hats would tell them, in front of the recruits in a "you suck" kind of tone, "Get louder; the recruits can't hear you."

It was embarrassing, but Amy and Elisa knew their only option was to improve. They would get in trouble—someone was always watching—if they walked past three recruits without making a correction, which meant screaming as loudly as possible.

"Recruits are never right," was the daily refrain.

The last thing DIs wanted were complacent eighteen-year-olds. That was a trait that could get them killed in war. The screaming and stress of boot camp were meant to simulate chaos on the battlefield. Female recruits tended to break down more often than their male counterparts, because they took the criticism more personally. But almost everyone, male or female, cried at some point. And those tears incited a DI like gas on an already raging fire.

Crying meant recruits had given up on themselves. Blasting them for it meant the DI still believed in the recruits, even those who had given up on themselves. If a DI wasn't screaming her head off, she was failing her recruits. So went the ideology of Marine boot camp.

So each morning at three thirty, as Amy drove to work, she readied her voice for the day by cranking up the radio as high as the volume would go and screaming over it. The technique had been passed on to her at DI School. Then she'd flip on the windshield wipers, whose rhythmic motion mimicked the "left, right, left" of drill, and she'd shout out the cadence. By the time she arrived at the squad bay, her voice was revved up and ready for action.

Now inside the chow hall, Amy strutted by and observed her recruits shoulder-to-shoulder, tan trays touching, side-shuffling down the food line, calling out requests to the servers.

"Chicken, sir!" Plop.

"Rice, ma'am !" Plop.

"Green beans, ma'am!" Plop.

No one dared stop moving as they sidestepped like showgirls exiting stage right. Amy followed them into the eating area, where the decor evoked a fast-food restaurant with plastic maroon seats with a stencil cutout of the Marine anchor-and-globe emblem, lest anyone forget where they were.

Amy stood over the recruits and kept an eye out.

The sixty recruits, hurried, hungry, and tense, sat on the edge of their chairs with their feet cemented to the deck at a forty-five-degree angle, backs straight and mouths shut except when inserting food. One hand, when not in use, remained flat on the knee, palm extended, fingers and thumb together atop their napkin. The recruits stared at their food and ate like automatons in silence.

Within a year many would be deployed overseas. Almost all of the female drill instructors knew what that was like. They had been to a combat zone, and now it was their job to turn these young women into Marines.

"Sit up straight right now!" Amy barked, hands still on hips. The recruits, eyes wide, bobbed their heads in a sweeping up-and-down motion several times in midchew. To ensure they don't choke, the recruits cannot shout out a response during meals, but acknowledge the DIs with a dramatic head bob.

Meals were for surviving, not savoring. The females were authorized to have less food than male recruits. The senior DI decided on just how much, but typically each young recruit could have one of everything, but just half a glass of beverage, which they held with their thumb and forefinger. It was an unnatural way to grasp a cup, but it was the same position used when pulling the bolt on a rifle to the rear for the inspection arms drill command and made good practice.

Amy and Elisa exchanged glances, and Amy slipped away into the bathroom. She locked the stall behind her, leaned over, and threw up, though it was mostly dry heaving, since her stomach was empty. She was coming down with something, and the stress didn't help. She figured she was getting sick due to the way recruits spit on her when they screamed. In the Parris Island universe, everything was always the recruits' fault.

Amy sat on the toilet and closed her eyes for two minutes, a ritual she and Elisa practiced during most meals. Striving to be perfect had its side effects. Her body hurt in ways she had never felt, and there were never breaks, because "somewhere there is a recruit scratching."

Not eating or sleeping and charging forward like a rodeo bull for eighteen hours a day, seven days a week, in an unwrinkled uniform, with a hair bun as smooth as butter, was part of the mystique of being a drill instructor.

But being "Nicky the New Hat," as female DIs fresh out of DI School were called—males were Nick the New Hat—was the hardest job of all, because they spent the most time with the recruits. To be effective, Amy knew she had to be where the recruits were, and she didn't want to be labeled lazy. She pushed through the pain and tiredness, because training the recruits came first. She didn't go into the DI hut for breaks. If she needed a sip of water while running around the squad bay, she'd slip into the laundry room unnoticed, cup her hands, and drink out of the deep sink. The recruits never noticed she was gone.

Other times, she and Elisa were purposely locked out of the DI hut and told to "stay on the girls" in the squad bay.

Though some called this training, it still felt an awful lot like "hat hazing." Every time an errand had to be run or there was a shitty task, Amy and Elisa would have to do it. Once, as punishment for screwing up, Amy and Elisa had to "pick up all the brass" after a series of recruits shot on the rifle range. That meant two people picking up hundreds of bullet casings on a time limit, while the other hats went home.

"This treatment isn't normal," Elisa often told Amy.

If the recruits left anything behind during a training event, it was Amy and Elisa's fault, and they would have to run back to get it. Not drive, run. If the EDI, experienced drill instructor, who is second in command, didn't have time to make the recruits clean the squad bay, Amy and Elisa would have to stay back and do it. And the experienced hats would constantly correct them, telling them they were not screaming loud enough, or moving fast enough, or making good enough corrections.

But Amy put up with it all. *It sucks and it's painful,* she told herself, *but because of us being put through hell, recruits are properly trained, and that saves lives in combat. I truly believe that.*

Besides, she wasn't one to back down from a challenge—even if she didn't always win. Once when she was in Iraq, an armored turret needed to be put on top of a gun truck in order for the weapons to be mounted.

"Can you gimme a hand?" Amy asked a Marine standing nearby.

"What, you can't do it?" he said. The guy wasn't exactly one of the top-notch Marines in the unit, just another lance corporal like herself.

Hell, no! she thought. Those things were so heavy. She had seen males have trouble putting them on top of a truck. It was really a two-person job.

But she kept those thoughts to herself as she climbed onto the truck's roof. Amy figured she should at least try, and if she struggled she assumed the Marine would jump up and help her out. But that didn't happen. As the Marine watched her lift the turret, it was clear he just wanted to see her struggle. Amy managed to get it to the top of the truck, but she couldn't hold it in place and put the bolts in at the same time. The turret ended up crashing down onto her head.

The Marine gave her a sheepish look.

"Thanks a lot for your help," Amy said.

———————————————— ★ ————————————————

Amy returned from the bathroom, and Elisa exited for her own few minutes of rest.

"Bring your chow to your face, not your face to your chow!" Amy said, picking up where she had left off, which was followed by a wave of head bobs.

Following lunch, back outside in the sweltering heat, the recruits lined up in formation at the position of attention as the DIs left the chow hall.

"Roll yer thumbs back to yer trouser seams!"

"Forward!" Amy said. "Stand tall, lean back! March!"

The recruits stepped off with their left feet and marched back to the squad bay.

It was officially the afternoon.

Eight and a half hours later

Roaches the size of hotel bar soap skittered across the cement catwalks, the outdoor suspension walkways on stilts that connected the 4th Recruit Training Battalion buildings, as Amy finally headed home. Now, at nine thirty p.m., the temperature had slumped to eighty-three degrees, making it a typical Parris Island summer night, where days sizzled in the nineties and nights were left on simmer. Stepping outside was like walking into a dark, dank closet. The humidity clung to the air like the island's Spanish moss on live oak trees.

Amy worked from "lights to lights." She was there before the recruits woke up at four a.m. and remained long after they went to bed.

She got into her car, turned on her headlights, blasted the air-conditioning, and left the depot. For the first time in eighteen hours she was sitting down. Her head throbbed. Like most DIs and recruits she suffered from pounding headaches from round-the-clock screaming.

"Hey, Mom, how's it goin'?" Amy asked in a raspy whisper, placing her mom on speakerphone. It was the first nice thing she'd said all day.

Calling her mother or her sister, Shay, while she drove kept her awake.

"Hi," Diana said. "You on your way home?"

She could tell her daughter was totally exhausted.

"Yeah, finally," Amy said. "How're my girls today?" Amy always asked about her two nieces.

"Amy Gail, I can't understand a word you are saying." Amy's voice was as rough as scorched earth.

Her stomach muscles ached, too, from all the screaming. Amy rolled into a McDonald's drive-through and lowered her window.

"Hold on, Mom," she said. "I'd like a number six with a bottle of water."

A six-piece Chicken McNuggets and fries were Amy's staple and her only meal of the day. Amy didn't eat with or in front of the recruits. By regulation she could, but there wasn't time. Some experienced DIs even believed a hungry drill instructor was an effective drill instructor, because hunger made them more irritable and meaner. In any case, Amy didn't want the recruits to see her eating.

Marines aren't permitted to wear their cammies in public places such as restaurants, shops, or while pumping gas. Since it was too late to cook, she usually stopped at McDonald's, one of the few places still open when she drove home. But Amy had also found a late-hours Mexican restaurant that would bring her order—a bean and cheese burrito, no onion or sauce—out to her car.

Diana worried about Amy eating only once a day. But Amy didn't complain.

She guzzled down her water. She tried to stay hydrated because she thought it helped, but having time to drink enough fluids sometimes was hard.

"All right, Mom, I'm home," she said, as she pulled into the apartment parking lot. "I'll talk to you tomorrow night. I love you."

"I love you, too. Good night."

Against her better judgment, Amy had moved into Saleem's apartment. He, too, was a drill instructor, and though Amy knew they weren't meant to be together forever, at least they were used to each other. In any case, they were like hands on a clock, crossing paths only briefly each day. She was glad to be home. That didn't happen every night. Since the recruits could never be left alone, even asleep, every third evening Amy and another DI slept inside the DI hut.

She made herself a cup of tea with lemon and honey to soothe her vocal cords. Her smoking certainly didn't help things. Then she ate and went straight to bed. A shower would have to wait until morning, which would arrive in exactly four hours, when her alarm went off at three fifteen a.m.

She lay down. Recruits screamed in her head, and she broke out in a sweat.

★

The next morning

It wasn't yet dawn, but Amy was dressed and ready to go as she entered the darkened squad bay with the other DIs.

"Turn on my freakin' lightssssss," a drill instructor blasted, which was the cue for the recruit on fire watch to snap on the overhead lights. It was four a.m.

"Lights, aye, ma'am!" the recruits said, scrambling from their beds and lining up their heels with their footlockers.

"Good morning, ladies!"

CHAPTER 13
Exhaustion

"Mommy, I don't feel good. My tummy hurts," a small voice moaned from the side of the bed.

It was two a.m. Candice opened her eyes and saw Kate peering up at her.

"Come here, honey." Candice hoisted her daughter up into bed. As if on cue, vomit coated Candice's chest and the bedsheets; then Kate started to cry.

"It'll be okay," Candice said, as much to herself as to Kate. "Just calm down."

Candice and her kids had arrived in Kansas that summer and were still getting settled.

After changing Kate's soiled pajama top, her own clothes, and the sheets, Candice laid Kate on a blanket on her bed. The little girl had complained of an upset stomach earlier that evening, and Candice hoped it was just something she ate. She had a six thirty a.m. PT test, a biannual Army physical fitness test, which meant she would have to drop the kids off early at day care. At two thirty, with Kate beside her, Candice finally lay back down for a few more precious hours of sleep.

But half an hour later the sound of wailing filled the bedroom. Tom, now six months old, was demanding to be fed.

A few hours later she was roused again with the abruptness of a cannonade. Beep . . . beep . . . beep . . .

It was five thirty. Candice shut off her alarm and quickly got into her Army PT uniform: black nylon running shorts and a gray T-shirt with "Army" stamped across the chest in black letters. She woke her groggy children, changed their diapers, and got them dressed and bundled for the car ride. Candice washed down a slice of wheat bread with a glass of milk, and, with coffee in her hand, out the door the three went, swallowed by October's early morning darkness.

Active-duty military parents everywhere played out similar routines, only Candice was doing it solo, and on this particular morning she'd be depositing a sick child in day care, but she had little choice.

Half an hour later, Candice arrived at the gate. Fort Leavenworth is an old frontier post, dating back to pre–Civil War days, which makes it one of the Army's oldest active-duty installations. When Candice had time, she loved to jog past the historic brick colonels' quarters that lined the bluffs above the Missouri River. The view from the residences' deep porches was testament to the old Army saying that rank has its privileges.

The genteel post, which schools many of the Army's finest young officers, is neighbored by the military's ne'er-do-wells, who are kept locked up and out of sight at the U.S. Disciplinary Barracks (USDB). In business since 1875, the USDB is the military's only maximum-security prison and the country's oldest federal prison still in use. Within its walls are prisoners from all service branches, half of them incarcerated for sex crimes.

The prisoners are curiously linked to the Fort Leavenworth officers' wives, who like to shop at the USDB store, where it's best to focus on the craftsmanship and not the criminal craftsmen. The place is filled with everything from wooden toy chests and picnic tables to iron lamps and wall shelves fashioned by inmates skilled in carpentry and ironwork. Wives have to sign up on a waiting list for the popular Leavenworth baker's racks. According to local scuttlebutt, the most skilled craftsman is an Army obstetrician. What exactly he is serving time for, no one knows, but the wives' eyes often sparkle with speculation.

Candice pulled her tan Jeep Grand Cherokee into the post day care center parking lot and told the woman in charge that Kate had been sick the night before but did not have a fever.

"I think it's something she ate," Candice said, wanting desperately to believe that was all it was. But deep down she had a sinking feeling. *I'm the mom who is taking the sick kid to the day care center, great person that I am.*

Over at Harney Gym, Candice stepped on a hospital scale for a mandatory weigh-in.

"Oh, my God." She stared at the arrow that pointed like an accusatory finger to 118, a dozen pounds under her normal weight range. *This is not good*, Candice said to herself. *This is not healthy. This is kind of sickly.*

She hadn't weighed herself in so long. Had she really lost fifty pounds since giving birth six months ago? Diapering two children and eating on the go had whittled her athletic shape into a stick. Candice once caught her reflection in a window and thought she was model skinny, a look she thought was gross.

Most days Candice ate whatever she could grab. A peanut butter and jelly sandwich, leftover mac and cheese, or a hot dog with Kate were her staples.

That eating regimen was quite different from how she'd dined as a cadet at West Point's Washington Hall, the academy's grand dining hall, where General Douglas MacArthur had given his famous "Duty, Honor, Country" speech to the Corps of Cadets following lunch on a sunny Saturday on the twelfth of May in 1962.

Washington Hall was the kind of place where King Arthur and the Knights of the Round Table would have felt right at home. In this cathedral-like setting where the worshippers paid homage to war, battles raged in arched stained-glass windows, flags and battle murals awakened the walls, and chandeliers illuminated the plates of the 4,400 cadets who all ate together each morning and noon.

These days cereal often sufficed for dinner.

After the weigh-in, Candice started her warm-up stretches. She'd take the test with the other eighteen students in her Intermediate Level Education (ILE) "small group." The students would grade one another, but Candice wasn't really worried. She usually maxed the test, officially called the Army Physical Fitness Test (APFT), with a perfect score of three hundred points.

There were three timed events: sit-ups, push-ups, and a two-mile run, each accounting for one hundred points. A passing score was 180, with at least sixty points needed in each of the three events. Candice was always amazed by how stressful the test was for so many women, a number of whom had to be "taped"—that is, had their neck, waist, and hips measured—because they were over their weight limit for their height and age. For those soldiers the PT test was an embarrassment and a public acknowledgment that they couldn't meet the standard the Army had set. (In 2011 the Army announced it was overhauling its PT test to better measure strength, endurance, and mobility; reduce injury; and enhance combat readiness.)

That standard differed based on gender and age. Men and women had the same required number of sit-ups, but the push-ups and run times varied, since men and women are built differently. That didn't mean Candice couldn't outrun males. Whenever Candice arrived at an infantry unit, much like a spider beckoning a newbie fly, there would be a male peer, senior NCO, or superior to welcome her by wanting to go on a run—always a long one—in an effort to smoke her.

Good luck, she always thought. Running was Candice's secret weapon. She especially loved trail running and being out in nature, where the only sounds were the birds and the pounding of her feet on the path. PT was exceptionally important to Candice. Not only was it a stress reliever, but it was also an opportunity for team building and camaraderie in a way not offered in civilian work environments. Candice found that daily PT reduced the formality of being in the Army and offered an opportunity to learn a lot about a person. In her case, it was also an instant résumé-worthy qualifier, an easy way to show "I'm in your league; I can do what you can do."

She was convinced that as a lieutenant she had landed her platoon leader job in the 82nd Airborne Division solely because she ran well. In those high-speed units soldiers are judged by their physical fitness. But Candice also learned that as you progress through the ranks beyond the tactical level—where lieutenants and captains predominate—to the operational and strategic levels, leadership is based on different skill sets. What becomes important is how well you can condense a three-hundred-page document into two double-spaced pages. By the time you're a major, your production is judged on what you can do mentally, rather than physically.

Except when it came to the APFT.

While some personal weaknesses could be hidden in the Army, this test put strengths and weaknesses on display. First came the push-ups, which Candice considered her weakest event. Women in her thirty-two-to-thirty-six age category needed to do forty-five push-ups in two minutes for a perfect score, and fifteen to pass. Candice cranked out fifty-two. She sat on the floor and exhaled. "I didn't realize how much lifting my kids did for my upper body," she said to her friend Major Brian Memoli, a stocky logistics officer, who was keeping count.

Next came the sit-ups, seventy-six for a perfect score and forty-two to pass. Two minutes later, Candice had finished with seventy-five, one point from perfection, dammit.

"Candice, you look exhausted," Brian said, after letting go of her feet.

In fact, Candice was seeing stars. "Yeah, dude, I was up all night. Kate projectile-vomited on me. She was sick."

Brian extended a hand, and Candice got up, still light-headed and close to passing out. "Here, drink some water," he said, handing her a bottle. He knew that the rigors of academics and the stress of trying to maintain her family had altered her eating habits severely, as was evident from her weight loss. Brian often packed extra snacks for Candice in his lunch as a way to entice her to eat more.

She took a deep breath, walked around the gym with hands planted on hips, drank the water, and felt better. *I need sleep. I need to eat more,* she lectured herself.

On the way to the track for the two-mile run, Candice rode with Brian and fellow classmate Navy Lieutenant Commander Jason Schwarzkopf in Brian's truck. As Jimmy Buffett played on the radio, the music transported Candice back to some better days in Hawaii, where she and Brian first served together.

"You know what I miss most? More than food, more than sex?" Candice asked from her perch in the pickup, between her two friends. The guys in her ILE small group were pretty much the only adult human contact she had had for these few months. At her remark, the men started to crack up, and Jason's ears perked up, as they always did when a woman mentioned either food or sex. He was a bachelor, and the most energetic of the three that morning not only because he was filled with caffeine, but also because, as a Navy man, he didn't have to take the Army PT test. He helped out holding feet and counting push-ups and sit-ups, and would time the run.

"This should be good," Jason said. "What?"

"Sleep. I long for sleep," she said. "That deep, completely Zen feeling of sleep and not having someone wake you up or disturb you."

Brian and Jason started laughing again.

"Really? What are you saying? You miss sleep *that* much?" Jason said.

"You don't understand," Candice said. "You're single. But, Brian, you've got two kids. You know what I'm talking about. Now imagine how exhausting it is being a single parent because Will is away in Iraq and how it impacts your life. You're on autopilot charging ahead. I miss and long for sleep."

"More than sex?" the guys said in unison.

It was the only time Jason had ever seen Candice let her guard down. She never shared difficulties in her personal life. Of course, they all bitched about parking, class scheduling, being a no-notice audience for every guest speaker that showed up at CGSC, and the ILE curriculum. But to hear her talk about something personal, Jason and Brian knew Candice must have been pretty tired and stressed. They also realized their friend was tougher than hell to be able to handle kids while being utterly *driven* to crush the proverbial class curve. They respected her dedication to family and nation,

and suspected that, as exhausting as it was for her, she'd do it all over again
to get the mission done.

It felt good for Candice to be able to joke about her hardships. But back
at her Jeep after the run, her waiting cell phone blinked with what could
only be bad news. A message from the day care center said Kate had thrown
up on the provider's shoes. It was now eight thirty a.m. Candice quickly
changed her clothes at the gym and called her instructor to let him know
she wouldn't be in class.

She'd championed the two-mile run at fourteen minutes and thirty
seconds, a bit slower than her usual pace, but still better than the fifteen
minutes and fifty-four seconds for a perfect score, and twenty-one minutes and forty-two seconds to pass. Despite the rough night, she had mastered the PT test, well above the passing standard for females—and even
males, for that matter—in her age group. But at the moment that meant
little. As Candice drove to the day care center, the sheepish feeling from
earlier that morning returned: *I'm that parent who takes her sick kid to
day care.*

★

Child care had been a problem since Candice arrived at Fort Leavenworth
that summer, and she had to make do with the post day care center. But
every time her kids had a runny nose or upset tummy, she'd have to leave
class to get them. There was no alternative. Since cell phone reception was
poor in the classroom building, a secretary had to come alert Candice.
These interruptions were always heart-stopping moments for her. With her
husband deployed to Iraq, the last thing she wanted was someone to pull
her from class for an emergency. Yet she'd get calls from day care about
once a week.

Every afternoon after class, before picking the kids up, Candice paused
at the door of her Jeep. She took a deep breath and said to herself, *I can do
this.* Then she'd change from being an Army officer to being a mother, and
her night shift, as she called it, began. After dinner and baths she'd put the
kids in a double stroller for her daily PT workout and sing "You Are My

Sunshine" and "Danny Boy." Tom often fell asleep on the walk, which allowed her to get Kate into bed, read her two books, and then snuggle for a few minutes. She'd pray Tom wouldn't wake up until his sister was asleep. Then, if all went right, Candice had thirty minutes or so to herself before his nine or ten p.m. feeding. She prayed he'd sleep through his two a.m. feeding and wake up at five. Most nights he wouldn't. Then the day would start again.

Candice's routine differed greatly from that of most of her classmates at ILE, which provided graduate-level education to Army majors in the "uses of military power at the operational and tactical levels." The ILE curriculum was new, replacing the selective Command and General Staff College, for which the Army had chosen only the top 50 percent of each year group's majors. The CGSC program had stunted the careers of the young officers not picked to attend and denied them the leadership, academic, and skill development provided by the school. Now, under ILE, all majors attended—which included mediocre majors—and the program became deridingly known by some as "No Major Left Behind." In September 2012, the Secretary of the Army changed the name back to CGSC and directed the education to return to competitive residency selection.

Alumni from the old CGSC days included Bradley, Patton, Eisenhower, and MacArthur, men who, like Madonna, Cher, Prince, and Oprah, need only one name for identification. When David Petraeus graduated from CGSC in 1983, he was the Marshall Award recipient, nicknamed the "white briefcase" winner, for being first in his class of more than 1,000 students.

At this point in their careers, many of the ILE majors, who were in their early to mid-thirties, were either bachelors or married with young children. Their wives tended to be homemakers and volunteers, since it was difficult for spouses who wanted to work outside the home to find employment during a one-year assignment. Many simply lived on post and stayed home with their kids.

Meanwhile, their husbands focused on studying and enjoying CGSC/ILE's well-known "family time" and "downtime," terms of distinction in the Army, since there was usually so little of it. Students' days revolved around lectures, small group projects, reading coursework, and being with family. For those who lived on post, it also meant barbecuing and drinking with classmates in the neighborhood. ILE was student life Army-style, a relaxing year of short hours (by Army standards) on a picturesque post, with a reprieve from deployments and troop units where workdays and stress always ran long.

Candice never compared her situation with anyone else's or measured herself against them. She often thought how blessed she was to have two children and a job she loved. To have both as a female field-grade officer was not the norm. Often an officer had to make difficult choices—leave the Army to raise her children, have someone else raise her children, or not have children at all. With demanding schedules, commands, and deployments, there was rarely an opportune time to have or raise babies, which may explain why so many successful female Army officers in their forties and fifties are childless.

"There's never a good time to get pregnant when you're in the Army. You try to plan it out. It won't work," was the blunt advice Candice had received years ago. She had experienced that truth during her first pregnancy. As a company commander returning from Afghanistan in 2005, Candice decided it was the perfect time to start a family. Years earlier, her consummate first sergeant, Chris Raines, an airborne trooper who loved jumping from planes, gave Candice a warning: "Don't ever get pregnant in command."

She took his advice to heart. So as always, Candice had a meticulously thought-out plan: a baby-making time line. She'd try to get pregnant while on postdeployment leave; if she succeeded, since she'd be scheduled to change command within three months, she'd be in a different position before anyone knew she was pregnant.

The first half of the plan was flawless. Candice got pregnant a month after she returned to Hawaii.

But then . . . an Army curveball. Candice's twelve-month company command was extended by an additional six months due to reorganization, and she went to a new unit. Doing the math, Candice realized she would spend her entire pregnancy as a commander.

Don't ever get pregnant in command. . . .

And so the challenges began. Being in command in an infantry division while pregnant was hard and frustrating. It wasn't like Candice held a desk job in the Pentagon, surrounded by more civilians than green suiters.

At first, she told only her first sergeant, whom she referred to as her "day husband" because they spent so much time together. Candice continued to do daily PT runs with her soldiers and marched in field ceremonies until, one day in her fourth month, she felt sick after standing for hours in the sun on the parade field. Her first sergeant told her the jig was up, and she'd have to let her command know. By her third trimester she did unit PT walking with soldiers who had medical restrictions, a humbling experience for sure, but Candice had already proven herself as a commander in combat and took it in stride.

Still, she was disappointed when her company went on a field exercise in the Kahuku Training Area in the Koolau Mountains on Oahu and she couldn't make the trip. The only way to get there was by Humvee on unpaved roads. Due to excessive vibrations, that was a no-go for pregnant soldiers.

When she would visit her soldiers working on their trucks in the motor pool, Candice, visibly pregnant, always broke the awkwardness with a joke. "I'm growing an American citizen in here," she said. "What are you doing for your country today?"

A pregnant soldier in her twenty-eighth week is mandated to work no more than eight hours a day, forty hours a week, and to take a fifteen-minute break every two hours. That is, if she has a supportive chain of command that enforces the rule.

Candice continued to work long hours, pushing through her exhaustion and grateful that Will, who was worn out by his own company command, would often take her boots off at the end of the day and rub her feet.

As her change-of-command date approached, Candice let everyone know she might go into early labor, which could affect the ceremony date. That fell on deaf ears: A superior told her, "It's like when a soldier breaks his arm; you still go on with the ceremony."

Candice wanted to respond, *No, going into labor is nothing like breaking my arm.*

But, at her change-of-command ceremony, as others looked on from the viewing stands, Candice formally handed off the guidon. As she passed the flag from one side of her body to the other, in front of her belly, she said to herself, *Kate, stay in there.*

In her farewell speech Candice shed some tears, and her face turned bright red, as it always did when she cried. A commander's farewell is one place where it is acceptable to show such emotion in the Army. She acknowledged her soldiers, their missions, and their bravery in Afghanistan, which inspired her. And she noted the obvious—that she was adding to her family.

The next day Candice gave birth to Kate.

Children always pose challenges to a woman's military career, but at ILE, for the first time, Candice realized she had to limit herself because of her children. She knew her boundaries and committed only to the bare bones, which wasn't like her, but she had to do it to survive. She had wanted to get another master's degree while in ILE. But she had earned a master's in public administration when she was stationed in Hawaii. And she was aiming for acceptance to the prestigious and competitive School of Advanced Military Studies (SAMS), an intense graduate-level program for the Army's brightest majors, who study operational planning in war tactics and strategy. If she got in, she'd graduate with a master of military arts and science.

Candice realized she didn't need three master's and instead put her kids first. But that didn't mean she let up on her coursework. This was a year the Army gave her, and paid her well, to study her profession. While some people were at ILE to "check the block" and just make it through, Candice had never been a merely present person. In a group setting, she couldn't simply attend a meeting. At some point she'd move to the front and lead.

She certainly didn't fade into the background at ILE, where classes were broken into small groups of eighteen to twenty-one, each meticulously structured to get just the right cross section of Army personnel, from the infantry, armor, artillery, military intelligence, signal, psychological operators, chaplains, engineers, and logisticians.

One of the instructors, Bruce Stanley, a retired infantry lieutenant colonel who had served with the 10th Mountain Division in Afghanistan in 2002, noticed something special about his redheaded student. He saw a highly motivated officer who had great potential. She was an instant informal leader in the class, and it was clear she not only had high standards for herself but also expected others to meet them. Her educational background made her stand out from the average Army officer, and he was impressed with her background in tactical intelligence, rare for the intelligence community. She understood the intelligence information operational commanders needed in combat. "Candice has more time in the infantry than most infantrymen," Stanley told the class, after each student had given a brief autobiography on the first day of class. He encouraged Candice to apply for SAMS and challenged her with additional readings to prepare her for the course.

Efficiency was Candice's watchword. She read for class whenever she had a free minute—during class breaks, after class, before going to bed, if she woke up before her alarm. She thought it was pitiful that some classmates would say it was only a lot of reading if you did it all. Candice believed that everything you do in life, you should do completely. She wouldn't half-ass her classes and was always ready for them, even when she struggled with readings on logistics.

She also studied for entrance into SAMS, which would keep her at Leavenworth for a second year. As usual, Candice was disciplined in preparing for the written test and the oral interview. Often she'd read in bed, surrounded by field manuals, with her study notes fanned out on the Hawaiian quilt, while a Kansas breeze blew through the open windows and filled her spacious bedroom.

It felt good to be back in the Midwest. This was the closest to home she could ever be stationed. Candice had rented a five-bedroom 1980s-era house in a subdivision populated by retirees a few miles off post in the town of Leavenworth. Sparse, mismatched furniture dotted her bedroom. Candice felt dwarfed by so much space, such a contrast to their Hawaiian quarters. She often wished she lived on post, where the kids would be around children their age. But living off post would make it easier for Will's family to visit. And the large house could support an au pair, which Candice had planned to hire but never did, thanks to an Iowa flood that had threatened a riverside cabin the O'Briens purchased a few years ago, and kept her from turning in the au pair forms on time.

The flood served as a reminder of how much Candice loved her family and Iowa. The cabin—a modest structure with white siding and black shutters—sat just feet from the Mississippi, whose floodwaters on June 22 had reached 23.31 feet in Muscatine, more than seven feet past the flood stage. A week earlier, on Father's Day, Candice joined her family and friends as they sandbagged at a furious pace. In the days that followed they built a knee-high wall around the cabin. It was the only thing separating the cabin from the rising river. And it paid off . . . until the river rose again.

With two sump pumps going nonstop, her father had said, "We have to do more."

So they kept sandbagging from sunup until sundown. No day in the Army had ever been this exhausting. Candice had never worked so physically hard in her life. But that was balanced by a sense of pulling together to fight Mother Nature, everyone rowing in the same direction, giving the same effort to save that little cabin that was Candice's piece of paradise. It was exhausting but exhilarating, as they hoped and prayed that their efforts would succeed.

The next morning the river crested, and the cabin survived.

Candice struggled to impress on Will what saving the cabin had entailed and how much it meant to her. But Will hadn't been there, and he didn't really have anything at stake. Their deployment phone calls, which had been daily while Candice was in Hawaii, dropped off significantly during the flood, and did not pick up afterward. The flood represented a monumental milepost in Candice's life, and she didn't think Will realized, at the time, what it was like for her to take care of a baby and a two-year-old and save the cabin. Though Will didn't demand much of her time, he didn't display much sympathy either, and that bothered her greatly. At the same time, Candice, perpetually busy, wasn't particularly empathetic to Will's situation in Iraq. The couple Skyped occasionally after Candice moved to Kansas. But for moral support she mostly relied on her mother, whom she called every night.

Life would get easier when Will returned, Candice reasoned. Shortly after Tom's birth, Will had dropped a verbal bombshell over the phone from Iraq.

He was working on his master's in military history during his free time, and Candice had repeatedly asked him to apply for tuition assistance through the Army. For months Will had put off filing the paperwork, and Candice couldn't understand why. During one conversation, she brought the topic up again.

"Will, why are you dragging your feet on this? This is money out of our pocket that doesn't have to be."

"I'm getting out, Candice. I'm leaving the Army."

"Yeah, right. Come on, please get off that kick again." Will would often say this out of frustration, but she never put a lot of weight into it.

"No, I'm really getting out. I'm going to drop my resignation papers."

"And do what?"

"I want to be a stay-at-home dad."

"Will, oh, stop complaining. You don't really mean that."

"Candice, I'm serious. I'm getting out. If I take the money from the Army, I'll incur additional years of service."

Candice held the phone in stunned disbelief. They were Team O'Brien, both of them defined by their jobs. Will was such a dedicated infantryman.

But military people say, "You know when it's time to go." And Will knew. Seeing the war and its impact from the home front in Hawaii had partly influenced his decision. Will had always considered himself a blind patriot, a good quality for a warrior, he thought. He was a foreign policy implementer, not a foreign policymaker. He was an "ours is not to question why" and "march until the man says stop" infantryman. But when those eleven young soldiers from the scout platoon in Will's unit died in that August 22, 2007, chopper crash, Will realized he might have to convince troops to do something he no longer believed in.

Only one of the eleven was married: Twenty-one-year-old Specialist Jeremy Bouffard had a wife, Mandy. On the day of the helicopter crash, Will had just gotten off the phone with her about some paperwork when, fifteen minutes later, he got word that her husband had been killed. Will went home to get his dress uniform. Technically another officer would do Mandy's death notification, but Will was always there right away, since a familiar face was needed and Will had a relationship with the wives.

As he was putting on his uniform, the TV showed a story about Congress passing a resolution on the status of the war, with a sound bite by President Bush along the lines of, "Congress doesn't decide when we're at war; I decide when we're at war." In other words, "Because I said so."

Will remembers thinking that there he was, ready to knock on Mandy Bouffard's door, and he'd have to tell her that her husband was dead, "Because the president said, 'I said so.'" That used to be enough for Will, but suddenly it wasn't.

After he deployed to Iraq, Will tried to convince himself that though he'd never be a cheerleader again, that was okay; he could still be a good infantry officer and fight the war. But it didn't turn out that way. Like many of his peers, Will was burned out.

"Candice, you and I always said if it got too hard with both of us being in, which it has, then one of us would get out and take care of the kids," Will told his wife. "I'm doing that willingly."

Balancing chaos was their theme. Something had to give. By now, Candice realized it was a relatively easy decision for Will to leave the service, and it would free them of so much stress. For dual military couples it was close to impossible to keep everything functioning. Most couples reached a point of seriously looking at their priorities before having more children while the responsibility of work increased. If officers decided to leave the Army, they usually made the decision around their tenth year of service. Cross the ten-year mark, and conventional wisdom says to stay in for the long haul, since officers are eligible to retire with a pension after twenty years. Will was approaching the twelve-year mark.

In most cases, it was the wife who sacrificed her Army career for the sake of her family. But unlike Will, Candice still had the fire in the belly to serve in an Army that she loved and believed in. She had too many goals to reach. She enjoyed the daily challenges of life as an intelligence officer, especially when working with maneuver units, and she aspired to someday command a battalion. She'd loved her time as a company commander in

Afghanistan, being around soldiers and feeding off their energy. For her, getting out wasn't an option, no matter that having and doing it all was becoming increasingly more difficult.

Candice was determined to stick it out, even though the long-ago comment from a mentor echoed in her head: A happy military marriage, a successful career, and well-adjusted kids—you can only have two of the three. . . .

CHAPTER 14
The Fight

Candice: November 1, 2008. Kansas City International Airport

Candice wobbled through the airport wearing a cocktail dress and black patent-leather high heels, with one child planted on her hip and the other at her knee. Still, she felt as if she were walking on air. It had seemed as if this day would never arrive, though she'd planned this very moment for weeks.

She had completely covered the house in yellow ribbons and red, white, and blue streamers. "Welcome home, Daddy!" scrawled in sidewalk chalk covered the driveway. But first there was the airport reunion. A friend's husband was going to take pictures at the airport from an unobtrusive distance.

Candice wasn't used to wearing so much makeup, and it weighed on her face like a mask. Her hair was now past her shoulders, and she curled the ends in such a way that the locks flipped this way and that like sea anchors. Would Will recognize her?

She'd carefully prepared the kids' outfits, too: a velvet red dress, white tights, and black Mary Janes for Kate, and a blue denim jumper with matching shoes for Tom. Candice wore the same black-and-white dress she'd worn last month for her ten-year class reunion at West Point. She was anything but a clotheshorse, but she felt fabulous in that dress, with its swirls of stemmed white flowers on black. A number of her classmates hadn't recognized her.

"You look different with long hair, a dress, and heels," was the response she heard several times. She'd had a wonderful time catching up with old friends and classmates. A decade after their graduation from the academy, members of the Class of '98 were comfortable in their own skins. Everyone's face showed signs of age, sure, but at least outwardly they were much more mellow, refined, and grown-up—attributes not usually attached to your typical cadet.

Although Candice took great pride in her alma mater and had enjoyed much of her time at the academy, she'd have a hard time if Kate wanted to go. Her son was another matter, but it was different for a woman. The Cadet Honor Code, etched in granite, as well as in the brains and hearts of generations of cadets, reads: "A cadet will not lie, cheat, steal or tolerate those who do." But some cadets didn't feel the honor code applied to badboy behavior.

"You're either a whore or a lesbian by the rumor mill," Candice's female tactical NCO had warned her during plebe year. The male cadets watched everything Candice and her female classmates ate, made constant comments on the women's weight, and let the women know what they couldn't do. Every female cadet had something said about her that wasn't true.

But the real Army, Candice found out after graduation, had little to do with the negative aspects of West Point, and that was one reason she decided to make the Army a career. By her tenth reunion, only about 25 percent of her class was still in the service. Thirty years ago that percentage would have been reversed. Her gung ho classmates, the real "hooah" guys who were part of the infantry tactics team in school, were most likely to have left the Army, while many people were surprised at those from the class, such as Candice, who had stayed in. Why it was that way was anyone's guess, but interests and goals can change. Health, marriages, opportunities, and other life circumstances also play a role.

Candice's path to West Point was certainly unconventional. Growing up, she knew nothing about Army culture, and later at the academy found it offensive when people asked her whether she was an Army brat, an endearing term for children of career soldiers. She had never watched or known about the storied Army–Navy football game, which is televised nationally each December, and she never would have expected that many of her future classmates would have fathers and grandfathers who attended the academy and, in fact, had been groomed for West Point since they wore diapers and "Future West Point Cadet" onesies.

She'd applied to West Point because her high school guidance counselor, Mr. Pogemiller, had encouraged her to do so. Though West Point accepts less than 15 percent of applicants, he thought a female from Muscatine should go to a service academy and that Candice would be the perfect candidate. For Candice, West Point was just a prestigious school she'd go to, then complete her five-year service commitment to the Army, get out, and go to law school.

But she did like the glossy West Point pamphlet with its wintry photo of Washington Monument, a massive bronze-green statue of General Washington sitting on horseback, on West Point's parade field, known as the Plain, with the caption: "Much of the History We Teach Was Made by People We Taught." Candice kept the photo taped to the back of her bedroom door during her junior and senior years of high school. She found the application process and the hype completely challenging, though she was taken aback when, during an interview for the West Point nomination—which had to be supported by her senator, Chuck Grassley—a staffer asked Candice, "What does your boyfriend think of you wanting to go to West Point?" The question stunned the eighteen-year-old. First of all, she didn't have a boyfriend, and if she did, why would his opinion matter? Were male high school students who wanted to attend West Point asked the same question about their girlfriends? Nevertheless, Candice pursued acceptance to the academy, and in the end welcomed the challenges at the school.

She quickly learned that the ways of West Point were very different from life in Iowa, where everyone worked together to build a barn. The academy was exceptionally competitive, a collection of hyper, type-A people.

The Army runs on type-A personalities; it wouldn't be able to function otherwise. Officers and NCOs who don't fit that mold tend not to do as well professionally. Transitioning to civilian life, however, where different standards apply, can be difficult for many, and explains why stories abound of command sergeants major who keel over dead soon after retiring.

Will was type-A, and Candice certainly was, too. Both were headstrong, ambitious, and driven, and Candice liked to be in control. They were typical Army officers, who just happened to be married to each other.

And finally, after nine months of being apart, without even the break of a midtour leave, they would be reunited. At least for a few weeks. Will was still assigned to duty at Fort Belvoir, Virginia, outside the nation's capital. He would return there after Thanksgiving and remain until he transitioned out of the Army in February. And until then it looked like the next few months would present familiar challenges. Candice's child care provider, who watched the kids in her home (after the day care center hadn't worked out), had recently informed Candice that she could no longer care for Kate and Tom. After visiting another center in town, Candice realized she would again have to ask her parents for help until Will returned for good.

I just want it to be us again, she thought. *Beginning right away.*

Candice had asked Will's parents and brothers, who all lived nearby, not to come to the airport. She knew Will's identical twin, Mike, felt put out, but this was the first time Will would meet Tom, now seven months old. Like many military spouses, Candice viewed this special introduction as an important private moment for her immediate family.

She was so excited she could hardly breathe. It was exactly how she felt eight years ago on her wedding day, as she waited to walk down the red-carpeted aisle of the 82nd Airborne Division Memorial Chapel at Fort Bragg, with its stained-glass windows depicting paratroopers dropping from the sky with rifles at the ready.

She had daydreamed about the moment Will would see Tom for the first time. And she thought about how wonderful it would be to get to sleep through the night. Will would take over Tom's nighttime feedings, she assumed. They were "Team O'Brien," after all.

• • •

A few hours earlier and a thousand miles to the east, Will had boarded his plane at Reagan National Airport, which was a madhouse due to the imminent presidential election. He chose to dress in civilian clothes; he didn't see a valid reason not to. He'd deployed before with units to Bosnia and Afghanistan and had done what he called the "homecoming thing" in his uniform. But deploying and coming home as an individual, rather than with comrades, robbed him of any feeling of mission accomplishment. As he saw it, he went, did his job to the best of his ability, and came home. Any pride or sense of being part of something for the history books was hard to perceive when you did it alone.

Holy cow, this is what Vietnam veterans must have felt like, Will thought on the flight to Kansas City. *We ran the whole war as individual replacements for the most part. No wonder so many ended up with issues.*

As Will's airplane landed in Kansas City and taxied on the runway, he lacked that mix of excitement and apprehension—normal emotions for a returning soldier. He felt something else: that his family reunion was merely routine. He and Candice had so many deployments between them that a part of him felt this was no big deal. Just another work trip. Not worthy of any special notice.

Except that it was. He'd meet his baby son for the first time, see how much his daughter had grown, and, of course, see Candice after he'd spent nine months in a war zone. He knew this should be a momentous and emotionally stirring event. But it wasn't. Will felt no surge of anticipation or excitement as the plane lumbered to a stop at the gate, even though his previous experiences told him that he should. As he gathered his duffel from the overhead bin, he didn't feel anything at all, good *or* bad. Instead he ran through a checklist in his mind: *What is my mission today? Return home, check. Homecoming with wife and children, check. Be happy and excited to see them, check. Begin reintegration, check.*

As Will walked down the tunnel that linked him to the rest of his life, Candice squeezed Tom, who was still on her hip. She tried to balance herself in her heels as she and Kate waved and walked toward Will. Even in civilian clothes, Will was a dead ringer for an Army officer. He walked erect, with purpose, and kept his coal black hair shorn on the sides, just long enough on top to be parted.

"Daddy!" Kate, now two and a half, ran to him with arms wide and one hand holding a box of animal crackers.

Will couldn't get over her vocabulary as she chattered excitedly in his arms. When he'd left, her conversation had consisted mostly of "Daddy! Elmo!"

Next, Will perfunctorily moved to Candice.

"Welcome back, honey!" Candice said. Hefting Tom, she gave Will, who was still holding Kate, a one-armed hug and felt happiness wash over her as her family was sandwiched together.

"You look beautiful," Will said. "I've never seen your hair this long."

He knew she hated wearing heels and that much makeup, but had gone out of her way to "do herself up" to look special just for him. He knew they were significant accomplishments for a woman who had essentially been a single parent to two children for the last year while trying to manage the duties of an Army officer.

"You look great, too, honey," Candice said. "It looks like you've lost some weight. You're really fit. Somebody wants to meet you."

Will put Kate down, and Candice handed him Tom, who was spilling out of his jumpsuit.

"Here's your daddy!" Candice said. While the baby eyed the stranger in front of him, Will carefully took his son from Candice and hoped the little guy didn't reject him, every returning soldier's worst fear.

"Hey, buddy, I'm your daddy." Will was amazed at how big Tom was. At seven months he looked like a one-year-old or older. Will took in Tom's blue eyes, so much lighter than his own brown ones but shaped like his.

Even now, Will felt absolutely nothing. It was as if a stranger at the airport had asked him to hold her baby while she reached into her purse for a minute. Rationally, he knew how he was supposed to act, though, and he did his best to fake some semblance of joy.

Candice was so happy to finally see Will. *All of us, together,* she thought. *It's the start of the rest of our lives. We're finally together.*

★

Three days later

On Tuesday, November 4, the O'Briens put the kids to bed after dinner, and Candice immediately went downstairs to watch election coverage on TV. Like many service members Candice had voted a month ago, casting her absentee ballot for the Obama/Biden ticket. Will did not vote, because he believed professional officers should remain apolitical. General David Petraeus hadn't voted in the presidential election either, as a way to maintain his political independence. But those views weren't shared by the majority of service members, who have the same right to vote as any American. It's a right they sacrifice for. Their livelihood, as well as their very lives, can hinge on who is in office.

Candice was determined to see the results through to the finish. Her liberal views provided for lively political discussions at ILE at Fort Leavenworth. She savored a good debate, though she was careful not to break Uniform Code of Military Justice rules, which limit service members' political speech and activities: It is a crime for an officer to use "contemptuous words" against the president, Congress, the defense secretary, and so on, down the line to state legislatures.

Growing up in Iowa, she'd worked on Democratic presidential campaigns as a kid; the political process was a big part of Candice's life. She was just nine when she helped her parents with the '84 Mondale/Ferraro campaign. The Iowa Caucus had a huge influence on her upbringing and her interest in politics. She even majored in American political science at West Point.

Candice went to the kitchen to get a Diet Coke, which had become her staple drink. Anything was doable in the Army with Diet Coke and chocolate, she surmised. She was barefoot, in jeans, a T-shirt, and a cardigan sweater, her usual after-work outfit. Magnets secured her birthday cards to the refrigerator door. Two days earlier, Candice had turned thirty-three. On Friday, just as class was ending, her classmates sang "Happy Birthday" and surprised her with a vending-machine pastry topped with a candle. It was touching, and really the only celebration she had. Birthdays weren't a big deal for her. While her parents had mailed her a box of presents, having all of the light shine on her for the day of her birth wasn't superimportant. She'd rather receive praise for a wonderful job briefing or share special moments with her kids.

Candice turned out the family room lights and settled in on the couch. After Barack Obama won the critical swing states such as Ohio and Pennsylvania, it was clear that he would be the forty-fourth president of the United States. In fact, he would beat John McCain in an electoral college landslide.

An hour later, Will, whose plans for his first week back from deployment did not include election coverage, walked into the family room.

"Candice, why the hell can't we go to our room?"

Candice looked up from the TV. "Will, I have to watch this. We're making history. This is monumental."

"What about me?"

Candice looked up again. "Don't you understand how much hope I've put into this race and what it means to me? This man is going to end the war in Iraq. Our friends will stop dying, and we'll get to be together as a family. He'll focus on Afghanistan. You know, the real threat to our country."

"You love Obama more than you love me!"

"What? That's preposterous!"

Will wasn't about to back down. He clenched his fists. He was letting his beard grow out, and his stubbled jaw became rigid. "You'd rather be here with him than with me."

"Will, don't you understand how important this is to me? Please, come and watch the results with me."

"Fuck you." Will then ranted about extremist views.

Candice's blue eyes widened, as if she were witnessing an accident. "What? What are you saying?"

Will's face was now flushed with anger, and Candice could see the veins on his temples popping and pulsing like blue worms. Who was this person?

"You are talking like a crazy person," Candice yelled. "Listen to yourself."

Ever since Will had been in Northern Virginia, after returning from Iraq, he had observed the large numbers of people of Middle Eastern descent living there. Rationally, he knew most were probably U.S. citizens, but he had developed such a fear and hatred of Arabs while he was deployed that he perceived each of them as a potential terrorist.

"Will, you are really scaring me right now," Candice said. "What in the hell is wrong with you?" This was a side of her husband she had never seen.

"I'm fine, but you care more about the next president than you do about sleeping with your husband, who has been in Iraq for a year."

"Will, that is not true. I just don't want to be around you in this state right now."

"Fine! I'll go to bed alone. Have fun sleeping with your future president."

"Will, that's not fair!"

"I don't care. I just want to have everything back."

"Back to what?"

"Back to normal."

"What is normal?" Candice said.

"Just me and *my* family."

"We are your family; we are here now."

"No, you're not here with me in my bed."

Unbeknownst to Candice, Will had started "clearing" the house, checking every room and corner a few times a night, and sleeping on the downstairs couch. It was the best place to interdict any intruders and protect his family.

"Will, please just go to bed; I'll join you later." Like a schoolteacher at the end of the day, Candice had no more energy. "I want to watch his acceptance speech. It's really important to me; don't you understand?"

"Yes, I get it. You love him more than me!"

And with that, Will stormed upstairs. Candice's mind raced. *What the hell just happened here? Who just took over my husband's body? He sounds like an insane person. What in the world just happened?*

This was supposed to be one of the happiest times of her life. It was all supposed to be aligned: Will would come home. They'd be reunited. A new president would be elected. The United States would get out of Iraq. No more worries about day care. Candice would get to be herself again. The pressure to do it all, all of the time, would disappear.

Instead, it was like a nuclear bomb had just gone off in her family room. She sat there in the dark, with just the glow of the TV. But Candice didn't hear the sound. Tears streamed down her face. She pulled the blanket tighter around herself. As forty-seven-year-old Barack Obama strode across a presidential blue–carpeted stage at Grant Park in Chicago, illuminated by floodlights like a rock star at a concert, she leaned over and rested her head on a quilted Hawaiian pillow. The cheers from more than 150,000 people, many of them waving American flags, were ecstatic. Flashbulbs from their cameras lit up the night sky. Through her own blurred vision, Candice watched others crying.

This was supposed to be wonderful, and instead it was horrible. Obama's victory was supposed to be everything she'd hoped for, waited for, and wanted, but this exceptionally joyous event had been destroyed by the man she'd married. Candice felt as alone again as she had been during the deployment.

"If there is anyone out there who still doubts that America is a place where all things are possible . . ."

Candice didn't hear the rest of Obama's historic speech. She closed her eyes and drifted off to sleep.

The next morning Candice sat in her kitchen with a mug of coffee as if enveloped in a haze. In a matter of days she'd gone from the joy of watching Will see his son for the first time, the happiness of having her husband in her arms, to crushing verbal blows. What happened last night was completely foreign to her. *How do I react?* she asked herself. *What should I say or do?*

Moments later Kate came downstairs in her pajamas and with wide eyes announced to her mother, "There's a monster in the house, Mommy! I heard a monster last night."

Kate heard Will ranting, Candice realized. The last thing Candice wanted was for her kids to pick up on that kind of rage. Would she have to kick Will out of the house if it got worse? *If I have to do a divorce, I will raise the two kids. I can't live like this*, she told herself. Later that week, Chaplain Scott Brown, one of Candice's classmates, asked, with a big grin on his face, "How's it going with your husband back?"

Candice paused and sighed. Should she tell the truth?

"It's okay."

Chaplain Brown's face fell. "Whoa, that's not okay. When your husband's been gone so long, you should be excited to have him back. What's wrong?"

"Will's having some problems adjusting," Candice said. "It's like he has a filter around him. He's just not completely there."

In fact, Will had started sleeping in the guest room. Neither of them felt any passion for the other, and Will was completely consumed by hate and anger, unable to reciprocate his family's affection. Candice couldn't bear to touch someone who apparently had no love within him.

"This can't continue," she told Will. "You need to get help; you need to fix this."

That was her normal reaction. As a captain in intelligence, Candice was known as a "fix-it" officer. She rarely got top-shelf lieutenants, because of her reputation for turning substandard officers into professionals. It was what she did best.

But this was different. Throughout the week friends called and e-mailed, eager to connect with Will. Yet the last thing Candice wanted was for anyone to see him in this condition, with such crazy and erratic behavior. Will seemed to go off into a dark place in his mind, filled with radical and extremist thoughts, completely consumed with himself. Despite their problems, she felt protective of Will and wanted to shelter him.

I have to face this. I can deal with this. We're going to take care of this, she told herself, with the same determination she used when assigned officers who needed extra leadership, mentorship, and guidance. *I can fix this. We're going to fix this.*

CHAPTER 15
A Christmas Farewell

Angie: December 2008. Quarters One, MCRD, San Diego

The holiday season in San Diego is filled with Christmas parades, festivals, theater performances, elaborate neighborhood lights displays, and a boat parade of lights in the harbor. All of it takes place during one of the sunniest times of the year, which makes for a Southern California–style Christmas.

Likewise, the social calendar aboard the depot is full. With so many generals and admirals in the area hosting their own holiday bashes, Angie scheduled hers at Quarters One on the Sunday afternoon of December 14. Two hundred people had attended the first year; by this, her third Christmas, word had spread, and the invite-only guest list had to be cut off at 450.

Angie greeted each guest at the front door.

"What did Janie do this year?" people wondered, and as lieutenants and captains escorted guests through the house they found out. For starters, Janie had put a tree in every room. The dining room featured a black-

and-white theme, with a white tree decorated in black boas. The Kennedy Room was decked out in leopard print. Fuzzy and furry balls covered that tree. The living room was done up in the color teal and peacock feathers. Nothing was traditional, yet it all had a Christmas feel. In the three years of parties, Janie had done fifteen different themes. The one consistent theme year after year was the "Patriotic Tree," a reminder to all that the nation was at war, with a peak of 188,000 young men and women serving in Iraq and Afghanistan, far from their loved ones during the festive season. Stateside, recruits on the depot, most away from home for the first time, spent their holidays training.

★

After the tour, guests were escorted outside to Butler Gardens for a reception with music by a jazz combo. Later, everyone strolled over to Pendleton Hall for a holiday concert in the courtyard, which Angie had opened to the community. A few thousand people attended, including seven hundred lucky soon-to-graduate recruits. It was probably one of the few Christmas concerts that opened with "The Star-Spangled Banner."

As the sky darkened, Angie, surrounded by children, flipped a switch, and a three-story artificial Christmas tree sparkled with green and "scarlet-and-gold" lights.

While the band prepared for the finale, the narrator announced, "Two key musicians have been called off the stage, and the band can't play the closing song without them." Spotlights came on, and the search began for someone in the audience to step up. The lights focused on Angie and Sergeant Major Brian Jackson, who had replaced Bobby Woods.

"Ma'am," the narrator said, "rumor has it you and the sergeant major are musicians. Will you join us?"

Both promptly moved to the stage. A musician handed Sergeant Major Jackson a trumpet and Angie a clarinet.

"Do you need a warm-up?" asked the band officer of Marine Band San Diego. Angie, who had learned to play the instrument in grade school, took a few deep breaths and gave a hearty rendition of "Twinkle, Twinkle, Little

Star," at which the crowd broke into thunderous applause and laughter. She then joined the band in the finale of "Here Comes Santa Claus."

A few days later Angie spotted Vic Krulak, a retired Navy chaplain and the oldest of General Brute Krulak's three sons, running on the base.

"How's your dad doing?" she asked.

"Not too well," said Vic, who also lived in San Diego. "He's worn-out."

"I'm sorry to hear that," Angie said. "I've got some great photos from the cake-cutting ceremony I can bring by."

"That'd be great," Vic said. "It might perk him up."

Angie had last seen Brute Krulak a month earlier, during a ceremonial cake cutting at the depot to mark the Marine Corps' 233rd birthday. The attendants rolled out a large four-foot-wide wooden cake for such ceremonies, with a cutout that fit a real four-by-six-inch piece of cake. Angie, wearing white gloves and dressed in her most formal dress blue uniform with a Sam Browne belt, sliced through the piece with the Mameluke sword.

As is the custom, the first piece went to the guest of honor, followed by the oldest and youngest Marines present.

"Sir, happy birthday, Marine," Angie said as she leaned forward and presented the slice to Krulak, who wore sunglasses and was dressed in a coat and tie with a white handkerchief in his breast pocket. Chuck Krulak, who was sitting next to his father, kept a tight grip around his shoulder, while Vic sat next to his brother.

"Not too much, Dad," Vic cautioned, concerned about his father's sugar intake.

Such ceremonies were held throughout the Corps on November 10, and General James Conway, commandant of the Marine Corps, had noted in his official birthday message: "Lieutenant General Victor H. 'Brute' Krulak said it best when he wrote, 'The United States does not need a Marine Corps; the United States wants a Marine Corps.'"

That month Angie had attended three birthday balls with Jim—the Sergeants and Below Ball, the Staff NCO Ball, and the MCRD Officer Ball. If she had time between traveling, she'd paint her nails red, the sanctioned polish color for the female dress uniform, but often she was lucky if she just got to the hairdresser.

In years past at the San Diego balls, Lieutenant General Krulak had taken pride in preparing the "grog," a centuries-old tradition throughout the military that featured rum, brandy, lemon juice, water, and sugar in the concoction. Brute prepared his own special recipe, known as Fish House Punch. But Angie had never tasted the general's legendary potent brew; she'd just heard about it.

Now, just after eleven a.m., as she had done more than two years ago, Angie checked in at the Wesley Palms, and an attendant drove her in a golf cart to the general's house.

The general was sitting in his recliner with a blanket draped over his legs, and he had his hearing aids in. He had deteriorated a great deal in the month since Angie had last seen him, but today was evidently a good day for him.

Both sons and his assistant, Judy, were there.

"Hi, sir, I just wanted to stop by and see how you're doing," Angie said. "I've got some photos for you."

The general recognized Angie as she handed him a handful of eight-by-ten and four-by-six photos taken by the public affairs office.

"Judy, give me my glasses," Krulak said. "I need to see. Get the light."

He seemed excited to see the pictures.

"Judy, get me my pen. I'm going to sign this."

And without asking, the general autographed a photo for Angie.

Since she knew she would be leaving command that summer, Angie seized her opportunity. "I just want to thank you for your tremendous support, sir," she said. "Thank you for tolerating my being here."

Brute looked up from the photos, leaned forward, and zeroed in on Angie.

"No! Not true! I did not!" he shouted. "You are wrong!"

The color drained from Angie's face.

"When I found out you were coming here, I wrote a letter to the commandant asking him, 'What the hell are you thinking?'" the general said.

Angie sat stunned on the edge of the couch. She had always met angry responses with humor or a smart-ass comment. Now she was unable to form a sentence.

The general's sons, standing nearby, were aghast.

"Dad . . . " Vic said.

"But," the general continued, "I could not have been more wrong. You were the right general. You were the absolute best decision. You did a great job."

All the tension drained from the room, like air easing out of a balloon that had been about to pop.

Angie's eyes started to well up. Her own father had never seen her in uniform, and Krulak's approval meant more than he could ever know.

A few minutes later, Angie said her good-byes and headed to the door.

"My dad's never said anything like that to any of us," Vic said, referring to his father's compliment, as he ushered her out.

Two weeks later, on December 30, Angie picked up the phone at Pendleton Hall. Vic was on the line.

"My dad died yesterday," he said. Brute had passed away in his sleep.

"Oh, I'm so sorry to hear that," Angie said. The general would have turned ninety-six in nine days.

Two decades' worth of depot generals had worried that Krulak would die on their watch. And just as newspapers keep prewritten obituaries of elderly celebrities, plans had been in place for years on how to memorialize and honor the general. A huge event on the parade deck had been expected.

But as Krulak aged, and then aged some more, his wishes grew simpler. He did not want pomp and ceremony. He would have a private interment.

Brute's wish, though, was to be buried at Fort Rosecrans National Cemetery in San Diego, a glorious final resting place of white stone markers sitting atop the greenest grass overlooking San Diego Bay. But there was a problem. The 182-year-old cemetery, established when California was still a territory, was full. It had more than 100,000 graves and was now closed to casket burials.

"We need an exception," Angie said, when she called cemetery officials. "Not only for the general's military accomplishments but for all he has done for the San Diego community."

Both generals got their wish.

In the end, admitting he was wrong said something about the old general's character—and much more about Angie's ability to effectively command Marines.

PART III
IN THE TRENCHES

--- ★ ---

"You gain strength, experience and confidence by every experience where you really stop to look fear in the face. You must do the thing you cannot do."

—Eleanor Roosevelt

2009

Barack Obama is sworn into office.

A month later, the United States announces most troops will be out of Iraq by the summer of 2010, with 50,000 troops remaining to train Iraqi soldiers until December 2011.

At the end of June U.S. troops pull out of Iraqi cities and security is turned over to Iraqi forces.

In November, Major Nidal Malik Hasan, an Army psychiatrist, kills thirteen and injures twenty-nine at Fort Hood, Texas.

On December 1, Obama announces the United States will send 30,000 more troops to Afghanistan, beginning in January 2010, to improve the security environment. The surge will bring the total number of U.S. troops in Afghanistan to 100,000.

CHAPTER 16
Winds of War

Bergan: February 14, 2009. Fort Stewart, Georgia

"I have some news," Bergan told her mother. "And it's not good news. I'm deploying."

Clunk. Bergan always delivered difficult news like a barbell crashing to the floor.

On the other end of the phone, Amy's heart sank.

Bergan had arrived at Fort Stewart only two weeks earlier, and after a year and a half of marriage she and Tom were finally under the same roof in Richmond Hill, a sleepy southern town separated from Fort Stewart by twenty-five miles of pine forest and swamps.

"I'm deploying to Afghanistan, Mama, at the end of July."

"Wait, I thought you were going next January . . . to Iraq."

The Flannigans had been looking forward to spending a year together before deploying. But the second lieutenants learned right away that the Army's welcome wagon often arrived with a door kick instead of a knock.

"The deployment order got changed and moved up six months."

"For how long?" Amy asked.

"A year."

There was silence, the inevitable silence that always follows such news.

The deployment was part of President Obama's 30,000-troop surge to Afghanistan in an effort to bring stability to that country. And so the countdown to July began.

Bergan had to quickly focus on training her soldiers and be ready to head out the door in less than 180 days. By the end of February the battalion commander had moved Tom into Bergan's company, the 293rd Military Police Company, as executive officer, so the two would be on the same deployment cycle. The Flannigans didn't ask for the switch, but they welcomed it. Now they would deploy together, something they didn't think would happen, since there were only five officers in the company, and conflict of interest prevented a married couple from being in the same supervisory chain of command. As the XO, though, Tom did not rate the platoon leaders.

It was a welcome development following a rough six weeks. A few weeks before Bergan's arrival at Fort Stewart, someone broke into their newly built home. Tom, who had been camped out in an apartment for a year, waiting for the three-bedroom house to be finished, had been living in it only two months, though he'd kept a close eye on every step, from laying the foundation to applying the blue siding. Bergan had loved the idea of starting off married life in a new house, although now it was one they would not get to live in for long.

One evening Tom arrived home after work to find tire tracks leading to the back, where a window on the door was smashed in. The thieves had hauled out flat-screen TVs and stolen Tom's Norwich class ring and Bergan's jewelry box, the one Tom carved by hand, which contained her wedding jewelry and Tom's letter. Just like that, when no one was looking, evil had slithered in through the back door. The crime went unsolved.

With less than six months to "train up" soldiers, however, Bergan and Tom had little time to focus on the loss. Individual tasks—weapons qualification; training in nuclear, biological, and chemical warfare; first aid; and cultural awareness—all had to be completed, as did administrative updates covering shots, emergency contact data, life insurance, wills, and powers of attorney.

Then there was training at the team, section, and platoon level with convoy live fires, "advise, train, and assist" scenarios, and mounted and dismounted patrolling. Precombat checks and inspections of personal equipment and company vehicles and many other details had to be attended to before the soldiers were granted block leave. As the company XO, Tom was now responsible for the logistics of the deployment. Their days were intense and grueling. Workdays stretched from four thirty in the morning until seven thirty at night.

In the middle of it all, Bergan was invited to a battalion coffee for the wives. She found it funny that she, who like her husband was active-duty, was always the one invited to functions for spouses, because she was a woman.

Meanwhile, she felt she still had a lot to learn. The Basic Officer Leadership Course that she had attended before transferring to Fort Stewart provides a new lieutenant with an academic foundation of leadership principles, but it can't fully prepare one for the multitude of new challenges facing an Army officer. Much of that insight can be gained only through experience.

There was something else, too. In predeployment preparation the expectations now were even greater for every leader. All eyes were on Bergan. Her superiors and subordinates wanted a sense of whether this young, untested leader had the capability to lead soldiers in combat. Her superiors watched, one question ever-present in their minds: *Can this officer accomplish the missions I'm going to give her in combat?*

Her soldiers wondered, too: *Is this a person who can lead me in combat?*

Bergan was scared, nervous, and anxious—emotions she masked well behind her focused manner and drive to get things accomplished. She knew everyone was counting on her. Leading real soldiers for the first time was difficult. All lieutenants have to prove themselves. Bergan knew the soldiers would respect her rank, but, as a leader and person, she would have to earn their respect and trust.

Though most soldiers expect new lieutenants to come in thinking they know everything, the sergeants in 2nd Platoon—nicknamed Spartans, after the ancient Greek fighters—sensed that this small woman with the pink cheeks and calm demeanor had a different attitude. She was eager to learn, do her job, and get to know her soldiers.

She asked questions. That was something twenty-year-old Private First Class Paul Torres wouldn't dare do—ask Lieutenant Flannigan a question, that is. Though few officers realized it, in the world of Army privates, there was an unspoken rule: You don't speak to an officer unless you're addressed.

So Private First Class Torres, who was a driver, observed Bergan from afar and kept his megawatt smile to himself. The first-ever person he was going to drive for was the lieutenant.

She's going to be my leader when I go to Afghanistan, and she's as new to the Army as I am . . . he couldn't help thinking. Preparing for the deployment had him so stressed, he started smoking as soon as the news hit in February.

"When it rains, it pours," he said. "I might as well start smoking now."

It made perfect private first class logic.

Another private first class was nineteen-year-old Jacob Beebe, and this was his first duty station, too. He'd had it hammered into him during basic training that officers and NCOs are the leaders and discipline figures and nothing else.

When Bergan first arrived, she added camaraderie to the list. She wanted everyone in the platoon to greet her with "Spartans" when they saw her. A common practice, it was a way for her to identify her soldiers and build team spirit.

Bergan spent every day with her forty-two troops. As a platoon leader, she spot-checked equipment, including soldiers' gear and vehicles, with Sergeant First Class Arnaldo Colon by her side. A six-foot-four Puerto Rican with a square jaw and a deep voice, Sergeant First Class Colon, nicknamed "the Terminator," seemed like he was seven feet tall to platoon members, and he scared the hell out of some of them. He was known to be by the book and took no easy shortcuts. And in a platoon where ages ranged from nineteen to twenty-four, Sergeant First Class Colon, at forty-five, was ancient.

Bergan found him to be a very manual-oriented type of guy, authoritative where she was more easygoing. He had never deployed in his twenty-plus years in the Army, a disadvantage for a new lieutenant, who usually relies on a platoon sergeant for insights based on experience.

About ten soldiers in the platoon *had* deployed before, including Doc Newman, a plainspoken medic with a Southern drawl and a penchant for smoking. Doc, whose real name was Jeremy, looked older than his thirty-six years. He certainly was old for the baby-faced rank of corporal. A married man and Navy brat, he'd had military friends die overseas. So he'd stepped out of his comfort zone as a firefighter and joined the Army three years earlier with a calling to be a medic, never mind the low rank and pay.

Two months into his first deployment with the 10th Mountain Division, roadside IEDs struck two trucks in his convoy, injuring the only other medic present. Doc treated eight severely wounded infantrymen, among them a paralyzed soldier, some with severe head injuries, and others with burns that would lead to amputations. A ninth soldier died instantly from the blast.

As far as he was concerned, an MP unit with females—notably two out of three platoon leaders—was different, since he had come from an infantry unit, but he was going to "take it as it comes."

Sergeant Aaron Thomas, one of Bergan's team leaders, had also deployed before. An amiable black twenty-four-year-old, he had been a star wide receiver back in high school in Enterprise, Alabama, but he had been unable to find a job after graduation and joined the Army. He had just re-enlisted for another three years when Bergan came aboard.

Getting to understand what enlisted soldiers like Thomas wanted and needed was part of her learning curve.

There was no doubt, though, that Bergan would have to prove she could do the toughest missions with her soldiers. She had all the training she could get, but she lacked the actual experience—and that was what made her nervous. It didn't matter to most of her soldiers that she was a woman. What mattered was whether she could do her job as the platoon leader. And that remained to be seen.

CHAPTER 17
Jedi Knight

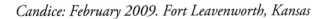

Candice: February 2009. Fort Leavenworth, Kansas

The General George S. Patton Jr. Master Tactician Award competition was among Candice's highest priorities that winter, and as a result her kitchen on a gray afternoon looked like a Tactical Operations Center, a TOC in military parlance, where battlefield operations are commanded and controlled.

Surrounded by maps, stencils, and a box of alcohol markers from battalion intel days, Candice focused on the task at hand: planning a brigade air assault from her table. This was a test of the last ten years of her work as an Army intelligence officer. She carefully stenciled in an enemy weapons cache on an acetate-covered map that draped over the table like an Andy Warhol version of a vinyl tablecloth.

In late November, Bruce Stanley, Candice's instructor at ILE, had nominated her to try for the award, which "recognizes that the intricacies of modern warfare have reinforced the Army's need for exceptionally competent tacticians at all levels." The contest also provided "a challenging academic forum for students demonstrating a special aptitude for tactics."

To Candice, tactics was like a massive game of chess on a three-dimensional board. It fascinated her to attempt to understand the actions, reactions, and counteractions of a military force. She enjoyed analyzing how both friendly and enemy sides reacted to different environmental factors.

But competing for the award was a time-consuming and demanding extracurricular endeavor on top of Candice's regular ILE coursework. The Master Tactician Exam was divided into several parts. Before Christmas, Candice and the ninety-nine other nominees had taken a four-hour written exam on tactics that covered rapid decision making, mission command, and issuing a battalion operations order. Candice scored in the top four and moved forward to the final round, an oral defense of her operations plan before a panel of experts. The winner would be crowned "Distinguished Master Tactician" and, upon ILE graduation that June, receive an M-1902 officer's saber with his or her name etched on the scabbard. The honor followed an officer throughout his or her career.

Friends encouraged her when she studied in the library, and she felt lifted up by her peers. Although it was one of the other competitors who would go on to win the Patton Master Tactician Award, Candice's classmates generally recognized her as their valedictorian type: supersmart and absolutely driven to excel.

She'd been noticed by her superiors, too. On the Friday before winter break, during a massive snowstorm, Candice found out she'd been accepted into SAMS, the competitive postgraduate program for the Army's brightest majors.

Candice basked in this wildly successful side of her life—her career. But like a draft invading a cozy room on a winter's day, the words of her West Point mentor chilled her. *You can only have two out of the three. . . .*

And Will, in his anger, would tell Candice, "We're just lines on your officer record brief. We're just a bolster for your career."

Exceptionally successful officers are often accused by envious peers and subordinates of putting their careers before their families. It is a convenient, albeit potshot way to explain away another's success. But having that accusation come from a spouse was especially stinging. It hurt Candice to hear that her family felt like mere window dressing.

For the moment, though, she was free to focus on competing for the award and not the fact that her kids were in Iowa. Her child care options had dried up again when a new provider informed her before Thanksgiving that she would no longer be able to watch the kids. Candice's parents agreed to take care of the children in Iowa for two weeks in December and from January 4 through February 14, when Will would out-process from the Army and return from Fort Belvoir for good.

As Candice focused on her maps, outside the kitchen's bay window rain pelted snow into slicks of glazed ice. January and February tended to be the coldest and snowiest months of the year in Kansas. Snow almost always covered the ground when she drove to her parents' to visit the kids each weekend, a routine of Friday-night drives and Sunday-night returns. One time she turned from I-35 north onto I-80 in Des Moines to head for Muscatine and ran into a huge snowstorm. That trip took eight hours.

Those long drives and the pressure of child care would melt away like the snow outside her kitchen window once Will returned on Saturday—Valentine's Day. Despite their rocky postdeployment reunion several months ago, Candice and Will had a great deal of hope for the future.

For one thing, they now had a medical diagnosis for his volatile behavior: PTSD.

———————————————————— ★ ————————————————————

"I'm going to do everything I can to get better as fast as possible," Will had told Candice over the phone that night in December when he'd first been flagged for PTSD during a physical at Fort Belvoir.

Candice was supportive, although she was of the opinion that her husband had potentially serious anxiety and anger issues going on, more than PTSD specifically. Will had shared with her something the doctor had said: "Your wife is an active-duty officer. Why didn't she diagnose you with PTSD?"

Candice immediately got defensive. "I just thought you were being a dick," she said. She knew she was a good officer, and to have a doctor state that she was lax in her duties deeply offended her.

This medical officer has no clue what I've lived through, she thought.

Will's diagnosis had almost slipped through the Army's medical system, too.

With some wrangling to get a separation physical, he secured an early morning appointment and met with a doctor at Fort Belvoir's DeWitt Army Community Hospital, a typical tired-looking Army hospital built in the 1950s after the Korean War.

After a flight surgeon, a petite captain with pale skin and dark hair pulled into a tight bun, finished going through his physical status, Will asked for a referral for a sleep study. Tired and rarely sleeping more than two hours at a time, Will thought he might have sleep apnea.

The doctor looked at Will. "Well, I'll put in the referral, but what you're describing sounds a lot like PTSD symptoms."

One in five Iraq and Afghanistan veterans—both men and women—has PTSD, though women with combat-related PTSD are a relatively new area of study, with the potential to benefit from diagnosis and treatment. According to various studies, civilian and military women's PTSD is often connected to sexual trauma. Women with PTSD have more depression than men, while men have more anger issues and drug and alcohol addiction.

The thought that he might have PTSD had crossed Will's mind, but it certainly wasn't something he was ready to commit to. He'd never been diagnosed with any sort of behavioral health issue. If anything was going on, maybe he had a little depression following the deployment. His homecoming with Candice had been kind of rough, he conceded, but he chalked that up to their both being in survival mode for so long and having been apart.

The referral eventually got Will to the behavioral health clinic, where the Army doctor, a tall colonel wearing ACUs, his Army Combat Uniform, needed only minutes to make his initial diagnosis.

"I'm going to give you a comprehensive battery of tests to confirm PTSD and rule out other disorders," said Colonel Donahue.

Will shifted uncomfortably in his chair. Was it possible this guy had him figured out in five minutes? But Will respected the doctor's no-nonsense approach. The man knew how to talk to and reach infantrymen and how to get them to listen and respond.

"Tell me what you've been doing since September eleventh," Colonel Donahue said.

"Well, I went to Bosnia, came back, went to Afghanistan, came back, served as a rear-detachment commander while my battalion was in Iraq, went to Iraq myself, and just got back," Will said. "And somehow managed to have two children along the way as well."

"So what you're telling me is that you've been either going or gone pretty much continuously since September eleventh?" Colonel Donahue said. "You don't think existing in a high-stress environment for eight years has some sort of effect on your brain chemistry?"

"Well, I guess if you put it that way," Will said.

★

May 2009. Kansas City

Candice pulled into a parking spot on the top floor of the Vet Center parking garage and hurried inside before the doors locked at seven p.m. The Vet Center sat next to public housing near the corner of Main Street and Westport Road in a sketchy section of Kansas City. The forty-five-minute drive there on the first Monday evening of each month always made Candice feel uneasy.

But once she was inside the Vet Center, it was like coming in from a thunderstorm. Women, many of them old enough to be Candice's mother, greeted her warmly. They were your average Midwestern women, a bit on the frumpy side, dressed in jeans and basic blouses.

"Candice! You made it!"

"How are the babies?"

"Oh, you brought some of those yummy cheeses again. There's a place for them right here. . . ."

Candice said her hellos and squeezed in her dish of favorite goat cheeses and Port du Salut on the table next to an array of homemade dishes. The savory Midwestern food was always a treat for Candice. And she was grateful for the fellowship of these wonderful women, who could help her understand what she was facing. She was as determined as ever to fix things in her marriage.

Each meeting commenced with these potluck suppers, and the ladies spent the first thirty minutes complimenting one another's dishes. Looking at these women, no one would ever suspect the hardships and horrors they had endured for decades. There was Betty, whose Korean War vet husband slept with a loaded gun under his pillow; Barb, whose Vietnam vet husband self-medicated with sleeping pills and alcohol; Gina, whose spouse, another Vietnam vet, finally left their basement and ventured out to a shopping mall for the first time in years; and Gloria, whose Vietnam vet husband often slapped her. The support group was the saving grace for so many of them. They were all victims of problems caused by someone else, impacted by something they didn't do.

When the food was put aside and talk of potato salad and the weather ceased, the women gathered around a conference table dotted with Styrofoam cups filled with coffee. Vintage recruiting posters hung on the walls behind them, and clipped to easels were five-by-eight-inch oil paintings of pastoral scenes and bowls of fruit painted by the vets as part of their therapy. Meanwhile, the women spoke about difficult, dark things, such as addiction, abuse, and fear of their husbands.

The O'Briens had to travel to Kansas City for these sessions, since there was no PTSD support group at Fort Leavenworth. Knowing there was something mechanical or chemical going on with his brain that could be directly attacked instead of his just being considered "weak minded" made it more acceptable to Will that something was wrong. While he didn't want PTSD to be an excuse for things he'd done, he could look back and realize he'd had issues for four or more years before he was diagnosed.

He knew Candice had had to learn to live with him during that period; she'd gotten used to dealing with his quick temper and the hurtful things he said during minor disagreements or major fights. Among the worst was his comment when Candice was four months pregnant with Kate in

Hawaii in 2005. One day while coming out of Costco, out of the blue, Will said, "I don't even know if the child you're pregnant with is mine."

"Are you shitting me?" Candice said. "Fuck you, Will!"

And with that she walked away from the car and started walking home, numb. It was the middle of the afternoon and hot as all get-out, but Candice would be damned if she was going to stay with a man who accused her of adultery. She made it a good mile toward the house before Will drove up and begged her to get into the car.

Four years later, Candice had attended her first meeting with Will in a couples' group session. That spring they had waited in a small room as others arrived. One by one, Vietnam veteran couples lumbered through the door, followed by a Gulf War vet, and a handful of Iraq and Afghanistan veterans.

Candice felt completely out of place. She was peering into something she didn't want to see; and while it was good to hear about other people's journey through the PTSD maze, she didn't like being this exposed. She also thought, *At least Will isn't that bad*, though she realized that in that setting Will could also delude himself with, *Oh, I'm not so bad; look at that guy*, instead of really confronting his own issues.

As for herself, Candice thought the real culprit lay in that part of her personality that believed she could fix Will and her marriage without getting help from anyone else. Nevertheless, it became obvious that the solution wasn't here, among people who were of a different generation and had different problems. So Candice tried the spouses-only group instead.

The first time Candice attended, she was very nervous. While she could charge into a room full of generals and knock out a speech without breaking a sweat, this was different: These were women she was expected to open up to and display emotions that she was not at all comfortable with.

Will attended his group sessions every Thursday night and almost always came back better, a bit stronger. Candice almost always drove home from hers perplexed.

How does Will get beyond this? Where is the finish line? she wondered.

PTSD had no cure, only treatment. It involved the rewiring of the brain. Yes, some of those wires could be reconnected. But the military focuses on mission accomplishment, and how that applied to PTSD therapy was never really clear to Candice.

The room was warm, but Candice sucked down coffee to stay awake and alert. At the head of the table sat the social worker, an attractive woman in her fifties with a head of black curls. The woman knew her job well and was there to ask the wives questions when needed and comfort them continually. She passed compliments out like candy on Halloween.

The women often told stories of how their husbands were alcoholics, or mixed alcohol with antianxiety or depression medication, which caused serious mood problems. When Betty talked about how her husband slept with a loaded pistol, all the women nodded. Then the social worker went into one-on-one mode with Betty to explain why she was in danger and had to move to safety.

Will doesn't sleep with weapons under his pillow, or hit me, and can at least leave the house and go out in public, thought Candice. But there was still plenty of common ground.

And the other wives were curious and inquisitive about this modern-day woman warrior from Fort Leavenworth. At one meeting the conversation turned to Candice's role as an Army officer and how she dealt with the current generation of soldiers.

"What's it really like going to war and then coming back to deal with PTSD in your own house?" one of the Vietnam vets' wives asked.

"It's like building a house one brick at a time," Candice said. "You just deal with the resources you have and mix the mortar and haul the bricks and face the task at hand incrementally."

Then one of the younger spouses chimed in, "But doesn't your job in the Army, as this tough woman, simply emasculate your husband? He's at home with the kids, and you're doing a man's job?"

Candice's blue eyes widened. She hoped her face wasn't turning red. No one had ever said that to her. She sat stunned. *Emasculate my husband? It's my job, and I love the Army. How would that emasculate him?* she thought.

She'd never felt she pushed Will into anything he didn't want to do. She knew it was different to have a husband who cared for the kids, but that was his decision, and as a family they were working through it.

Candice put on her game face. "I've never thought of that before," she said to the woman. "I have no tricks up my sleeve. I've always been pretty straightforward. I'm a woman who loves my job, and that just happens to be in a hypermasculine environment.

"I've been in the Army since 1994 and know no other profession than the profession of arms, where you're in a community, a real family," she continued. "It's a brotherhood, a fraternity of sorts, where people take care of one another. That's what we're all trying to do here, take care of each other, right?"

On the drive home that night Candice thought of all the reading she had to do before class the next morning. But the woman's question—a challenge, really—seared through her mind. Emasculate her husband? She'd never considered that angle of thinking.

★

One week later. Fort Leavenworth, Kansas

As Kate pedaled her tricycle across the driveway, which was covered with her pastel chalk scribbles, Candice noticed budding daffodils and purple irises popping up in places where she didn't even know they were planted. Perennials were always a wonderful surprise for military families.

That spring, Candice's hair, which had grown past her shoulders, had finally gotten long enough to be cut and donated for a cancer wig. She welcomed back her chin-length bob like an old friend. She didn't miss constantly pulling her hair into a tight bun when she wore her uniform each day. Now she could literally let her hair down.

At home, too, the O'Briens were experiencing something they hadn't in a number of years—normality, or a new normal, at least. It was like a nagging pain had finally eased, and life was calm.

Candice enjoyed the simple things most. She discovered happiness in her own backyard. She loved spending hours with the kids, digging for worms in the garden and playing in the sandbox. A day earlier she'd taken the kids to the Fort Leavenworth library and then to the dock overlooking the lake on post.

With Will home, the stress of shuffling the kids from one day care spot to the next was gone. She hadn't realized how much pressure there had been until the problem no longer existed.

Will and Candice communicated more, and Will stopped picking fights over small things. His group therapy and medication helped control his drastic mood swings, which now weren't as evident or prevalent.

He loved his new role as a stay-at-home dad. And despite having PTSD, Will was a wonderful father. He loved the kids, and as a caregiver he did a good job of managing them. But providing emotional support required some real learning on his part, Candice knew.

Meanwhile, Will tried to control his PTSD triggers. He avoided crowds and long car drives and gave up alcohol, switching to Excalibur, the nonalcoholic version of Guinness. Will was choosing a path to get better. *He is getting better; we are getting better*, thought Candice.

But like a fresh coat of paint on a crumbling wall, plenty of chips reappeared in the O'Brien household. Candice was only quasi-comfortable with Will in public. She always felt like a monitor of sorts. Gone were the days when they could go to an event and walk around separately and meet again later. Now she was never more than a couple of arms' lengths away.

About once a week, Candice still received child care–related phone calls during class. Frantic calls. Only now they were from her husband. The calls all had a similar theme: Will was exhausted and needed Candice to come home right away. At every opportunity Candice checked her cell phone for messages, knowing that none of them were good.

"Honey, what's wrong?" Candice asked during a break between classes.

"The kids are going nuts," Will said. "They're just bouncing off the wall. Tom's had three huge dumps, and Kate won't take her nap."

"Kate's like me," Candice said. "We just don't nap. Sorry, it isn't going to happen."

"Well, she needs to, because I've gotta have a break, too," Will said.

"Please just calm down, and I'll be home as soon as class is over," Candice said.

"How much longer are you going to take?" Will asked. "Do you really need to be there that late?"

"Will, it's just two o'clock, and class will probably end at three thirty. I'll race home, and you can take a break."

"Fine, get here as fast as you can." *Click.*

I never got a break, Candice thought, as she hit the red hang-up button on her phone. *I never had anyone at my beck and call to come to my rescue.*

Six weeks later

With about an hour left to drive on July 4, Candice turned onto Interstate 36 West in Missouri, and her windshield view transformed from darkness into colors that sparkled and popped against the night sky. It was that mystical moment on a summer evening just after twilight when dusk turns to darkness. And when, on this holiday night, the show finally began. All along Route 36, little towns' fireworks displays lit up the horizon. Candice thought of the families around America enjoying the celebration with their loved ones, while here she was in a car listening to Will rant, complain, and gripe for six hours. About her family. About her mother. About Iowa. About Iraq. About growing up in a trailer park. About every negative thing that had ever happened in his past and present life he could think to bitch about.

It was like being in a car with a loud, agitated monkey.

As often was the case on car trips, Candice was driving. She was prone to air- and carsickness and couldn't read in the auto. Plus, she liked to be the driver, the one in control. Will, who liked to read books on a trip, didn't mind.

She kept the TV going for the kids in the back to at least try to filter out some of what was going on in front.

Hour after hour, Will picked, picked, and picked. Finally, just fifteen minutes from home, Candice turned off Highway 92 onto 45 and pulled into a corner car dealer's lot in Tracy, Missouri.

"Stop! Stop! Stop! No more! You are making me crazy now, Will!" Candice shook her clenched fists in the air. "This is too much. I cannot live with the constant bitching. I know you are crazy, but you're taking me there with you—and I don't want to go."

Still physically shaking, Candice pulled out of the parking lot. The children were fast asleep. Will sat in stunned silence, and they drove the rest of the way home without another word.

They had left Muscatine, Iowa, earlier that day, after watching Candice's niece walk with her Girl Scout troop in the local Fourth of July parade. The plan had been to drive home on July 5, but Will wanted to avoid any traffic. He didn't see what the big deal was; Candice had just spent the last three weeks, between graduation from ILE and the start of the SAMS program, with her family, while he had been back east at Norwich University, finishing the residency portion of his master's degree in military history.

When Will joined her for the long holiday weekend in Iowa, the tension kept mounting. After three days, he had to get out of Iowa and back home. That was a theme with him: just to get back home to "us" as a family.

She knew he'd had enough. But why couldn't he accept that her family loved him? Why did he always try to pit them against her? Will couldn't see how much Candice loved being with her parents, or maybe he did, and that brought out a jealousy that overtook his rationality, she thought.

During the three weeks she and the kids were in Iowa, they went swimming, toured children's sights, and visited the cabin, all the things Candice loved doing. She especially enjoyed the cabin. It was hard to believe that just a year earlier floodwaters had almost destroyed her little piece of paradise. Now she didn't feel threatened there; she simply savored the beauty of the muddy Mississippi. It was wonderful and comforting to be back with her family in Iowa.

And that was the problem.

She came to the unsettling realization that she loved those summer weeks alone with the kids and her parents. It was a nagging feeling she kept to herself.

Two months later

After bedtime stories and snuggles with Kate and Tom, Candice headed to the kitchen for a second glass of red wine, which had become a nightly ritual—a glass with dinner, followed by another after the kids were in bed. It helped her get through the nights.

It was now September, and she was fully immersed in SAMS, reading up to two hundred pages daily. She'd wake up at four or five in the morning some days to finish reading because she was too exhausted after putting the kids to bed.

SAMS was not only academically stimulating, but Candice also loved the challenge of using critical and creative thinking to find solutions for operational problems at the tactical and strategic level. She was in her zone and often drew upon her experiences in infantry divisions that gave her the background knowledge for SAMS. Her school year had begun with strategic explorations of how countries relate to one another. For her monograph—a forty-page paper similar to a thesis—Candice chose problem reframing, a subject, she realized, with some correlations to her marriage.

It seemed as if their relationship were on cruise control, or as if they were merely existing, even stagnating. For their ninth wedding anniversary on the ninth of September, the couple had planned to visit San Francisco for Labor Day, but the trip fell through because Will had to finish his military thesis.

Then, on a breezy autumn day in the middle of September, Candice was sitting in Fort Leavenworth's Eisenhower Hall when one of her classmates announced, "The list is out!"

Throughout the year, at designated times, the Army releases its life-changing lists—promotions, commands, schools—that control an officer's professional destiny. Everyone in the room knew this particular roster would affect their lives and their families' future. It was the one they'd been clamoring to see: the Army G-3's (operations) list of possible follow-on assignments for SAMS graduates. Each of the 118 students, nicknamed "Jedi

Knights," after the warrior heroes in *Star Wars*, had a one-year requirement to fulfill a SAMS-coded billet as an operational planner at the division or corps level. For Candice that meant an intelligence post.

As a paper copy made its way around the room, she and her classmates punched in keys on their laptops, searching for the list on AKO, Army Knowledge Online. Finally Candice located the list and scrolled down the page. All of the major Army divisions had one or two slots available for an intel planner—Fort Drum, New York; Fort Carson, Colorado; Fort Lewis, Washington; Fort Hood, Texas; and Fort Bragg, North Carolina, to name a few.

All around her, Candice's classmates discussed their possibilities.

"What's it like in Hawaii?"

"What do you think about Carson or Korea?"

They would go home to discuss their options with their spouses and note their top ten preferences in order.

But to Candice, the point was moot. She'd already thought it through long before she saw the list. Despite the number of great spots available to her, in her mind she had no options.

Except one.

On her computer screen Candice zeroed in on a single assignment.

Afghanistan.

CHAPTER 18
Into the Desert of Death

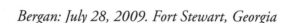

Bergan: July 28, 2009. Fort Stewart, Georgia

 On a blisteringly hot afternoon, the Arsenault clan and hundreds of others milled about like penguins in the parking lot behind the 293rd Military Police Company area off Gulick Avenue at Fort Stewart.

Despite the danger of encountering fire ants, Amy braved a seat on the curb, as she had done on and off throughout the day, and took a sip from her water bottle. It was almost six p.m. Families had been waiting outside since eleven that morning to say good-bye and see their soldiers off. But the call to depart never came, so everyone waited in parking lot purgatory. Pregnant women paced, babies got heat rash, and families clustered around their soldiers.

By six, the temperature had dropped to ninety-three degrees, but the parking lot was still a baking sheet. By now everyone knew what the Army meant by "hurry up and wait." Bergan's parents, her brother Timmy, and his wife were on hand, but sister Brooke, who was pregnant, had left a day earlier, and twin sister Bethany was working as a summer camp director back home.

Tom, who had been promoted to first lieutenant in April, had already departed for Afghanistan as part of the advance party.

It had been a difficult summer. Bergan and Tom were renting their house out for the next year, which meant it had to be emptied of all its contents. Tom loaded up the furniture and put it into storage before he deployed. But Bergan's mind was elsewhere. Meticulous in packing her personal gear, she floundered over house stuff.

And when she finally went on leave, it hit her hard that she was actually going to Afghanistan.

I don't want to let my platoon down or lose anyone, was the thought that kept filtering through her brain. Almost eight years after the United States–led invasion of Afghanistan that crippled the Taliban, like a vampire its insurgency, supported by al-Qaeda, had come back to life stronger than ever.

"I don't want to get there and screw anything up and put my soldiers in unnecessarily dangerous situations," she told her mother. Bergan wasn't one to open up, but Amy, sensing something was troubling her daughter, encouraged her to share.

"I think something's going to happen to me, Mama," Bergan finally said. "This is going to be it. . . ."

It took many more such conversations for Bergan to come to grips with her fears and nervousness. Under her uniform, about where the American flag patch rests on a soldier's right shoulder, Bergan got a new tattoo, hoping it would help keep her strong and brave: "In you, O Lord, I trust. I let go all of my fears."

Amy had always been against her children's having tattoos and wouldn't talk to them for days after their latest additions. But it was a losing battle. When the family went with Bergan to the tattoo parlor this time, Amy finally gave in. To everyone's shock, she announced, "Maybe I'll just get a small cross on my ankle."

It was her way of bonding with her daughter during a difficult time. But as the tattoo artist worked on her, she screamed, "Ow! Ow! Ow! This hurts!" Brooke, Bergan, and their dad, Billy, couldn't stop laughing. Amy unwittingly had chosen one of the most painful places to get a tattoo.

But she did it, thought Bergan. Now, while she was stuck in the parking lot, the thought of it made her smile.

By nine p.m., the soldiers still hadn't left. Heat lightning flashed through the night sky, offering some distraction.

"Two Ninety-three! Get in formation!"

The 140 soldiers lined up as a company and then got their gear.

The moment everyone dreaded was quickly approaching.

"Time to get on the buses!" someone yelled.

A deployment good-bye is like no other. No words seem adequate or appropriate. *Take care . . . stay safe . . . see you soon . . .* go down like flat soda. And hovering over everything was news no one liked to think about: The month had been the deadliest yet for American troops in Afghanistan, with thirty-nine dead.

"I love you. Keep in contact with me," Amy said, hugging Bergan, who had her helmet on.

Bergan wore a size "small, short" ACU top, which could be problematic for little people with long nameplates. The letters in her last name almost ran off the side of her chest.

Tears were welling behind her Army-issued shatterproof glasses, and her gear weighed more than Bergan's 120 pounds.

Billy, who also had tears in his eyes, just hugged his daughter.

As the buses pulled away, some family members waved; others stood like statues. Amy broke down, sobbing.

But Bergan kept her emotions under control. Like so many before her she was following the call of the bugle, and where it would lead her she would soon find out.

★

One month later, Kandahar, Afghanistan

"Ah, fuuuck!" yelled Private First Class Torres as the armored Mine Resistant Ambush Protected (MRAP) truck he was driving started to roll onto its side into a sewage hole the size of a swimming pool. He'd seen the hole, which was in the middle of a narrow dirt road in an alleyway leading to a market, and tried to avoid it. But in doing so he hit it anyway, causing the truck to almost tip completely and scaring the hell out of Torres.

The private turned the wheel in the direction of the roll, as he'd been taught, and the vehicle righted itself in three feet of muck.

"Oh, man. Fuck this shit!"

"Everybody okay?" asked Bergan, who was in the troop commander seat, which is the passenger seat in military vehicles.

"Other than its smelling like a toilet, Ma!" said Sergeant Thomas from the back.

He had anointed Bergan with the nickname after he was sick beyond sick, and the squad was getting ready for a mission the next day.

When Bergan saw him, her response was definite: "Thomas, you look like crap; you're not going on mission."

"I'm fine, ma'am," he said.

"Are you talkin' back?" Bergan said. "Go to bed."

It was like something Sergeant Thomas's real mom would say.

Only a few soldiers called her Ma—Bergan was about the same age as her soldiers—but when Bergan was talking to her squad out on patrol, or leaders from other platoons were around, Thomas and the others knew to give her the courtesy of her rank and called her by her official title, "Ma'am."

Bergan could come off as quiet and standoffish, even to her own family, but as she had in Norwich's military setting, Bergan found her niche in the platoon. It was a place she could shine. She had a compassionate side, and she extended that to her soldiers, which gave her a connection to them.

They had discovered that she was the type of leader they wanted to do right for, not someone who made them afraid to do something wrong. They saw that she gave it her all when she was on mission, and the four women in the platoon thought it was great that they had a strong female officer whom the males also looked up to.

After they had found out she was approachable, her soldiers regularly went to Bergan for advice—about college, about being an officer, and especially about romantic troubles. Once mute, Private First Class Torres now talked with Bergan any chance he got, in the trucks, at chow, and after night missions while eating MREs.

"No one really wants to put a lot of work into a guy who is deployed for a year, ma'am," he told Bergan, complaining about the difficulty of finding a girlfriend. He had joined the Army because he wanted to do the right thing. He wanted to be "that guy" whom friends and family looked up to. But it was complicating his love life. He took to heart Bergan's advice and was grateful that the lieutenant always made him feel comfortable and good about himself.

But right now he was feeling neither.

"Torres, get us outta here, man! We're literally in shit! I can't breathe!" someone from the back of the MRAP yelled, as the soldiers started laughing and gagging from the stench.

The design of the hulking MRAPs made them more resistant to bombs than the up-armored Humvees. But their weight and high center of gravity made them vulnerable to rolling on the crumbling roads in Iraq and Afghanistan, causing injury and in some instances drowning when the trucks flipped into canal ditches.

Still, Torres loved driving, especially MRAPs, which each cost about the price of two Lamborghinis. It was fun, and it made him feel as important as being a gunner or team leader.

"Torres, calm down," Bergan said. "It's gonna be okay. Just steer the vehicle."

He laid on the throttle, stepped on the gas, and finally the nineteen-ton truck lumbered out of the cesspool like an elephant emerging from a mud bath.

Hoots and cheers filled the truck.

Torres looked over at his lieutenant like a kid at the principal's office.

"It's okay; it happens," she said. "Just be more careful."

Bergan always kept her cool in dicey situations, including the time the platoon was patrolling on foot and spotted two Afghans digging up a metal pot in an orchard. The men ran off into the village, and the soldiers found the pot, which turned out to hold bomb material. The squad went from alley to alley and house to house looking for the men but never found them. It wasn't until later that Torres realized how dangerous the situation was. He hadn't been afraid, because Bergan was there, calming them, giving them confidence, showing concern, just like a mother would. A mother with a grenade launcher.

The 293rd Military Police Company had a combat advisory mission in Kandahar. MPs traditionally provide combat support in war, which includes detaining enemy prisoners of war and overseeing detention centers. But years of fighting in Iraq and Afghanistan had expanded their role, and though the branch was made up of 25 percent women, it was based in the most dangerous regions of Iraq and Afghanistan.

Bergan patrolled Kandahar with one of her squads almost daily, sometimes on foot, sometimes in a vehicle, constantly changing their patrolling times—night and day—for safety. They also manned checkpoints, protected roads, and performed route reconnaissance.

The weapons her MPs carried left no doubt as to the types of dangers they faced. Bergan toted an M4 carbine with an M203 grenade launcher, and a nine-millimeter pistol strapped to her right thigh. Private First Class Torres had an M249 squad automatic weapon (SAW), as did the gunners, and Sergeant Thomas also carried an M4 with an M203 grenade launcher. Their truck was outfitted with machine guns.

The platoon performed missions similar to the infantry, but what separated the MPs was that they trained the Afghan National Police (ANP), a ragtag group of mostly illiterate men, who patrolled with them. The goal was for the ANP to take over the responsibility when coalition forces left.

For the most part, Bergan thought the ANP were all good guys, but she wasn't sure she would trust them with her life. Their culture was completely different, and their lack of discipline with their weapons meant they were constantly accidently shooting one another. Doc Newman treated a number of the men for old bullet wound infections. Although the MPs on paper were supporting the ANP's missions, it was really the other way around.

And the ANP found the female lieutenant a curiosity as well. It took time for them to understand that she was the leader, and if they wanted anything they were going to have to go through her.

The same went for the local village elders, who often didn't want to work with the platoon because Bergan was the leader. Under Taliban rule, women and girls had been deprived of even the most basic of human rights. They could not work, go to school, seek medical care, or leave their homes without a male relative escort. And when they went out, they had to wear the burqa, a head-to-foot cloak with only a rectangular mesh area around the eyes. While women's rights had improved since the fall of the Taliban in 2001, they were still treated as second-class citizens.

The elders, however, had no choice but to work with the MPs, since the soldiers were helping train the Afghan police who "tried" to provide stability and security in each of their districts. If the village elders attended meetings it was because they were asking for help or supplies—wood, barriers, sandbags, fuel, and concertina wire for the village checkpoints, for example. Usually the MPs acted as middlemen when the village needed something by setting up and paying for contracts and hiring people to do the work.

And if the elders wanted those things, they had to accept that a woman was in charge. But they would push the limits by not acknowledging Bergan. Instead, they listened to the interpreter and never looked her way. It wasn't hard to read their body language. When they saw her and found out who she was, they passed furtive looks to one another and muttered things under their breath.

★

September 30, 2009. Kandahar Airfield

On the last day of September, following a mission, Bergan got wind that the company commander's squad had been in an IED attack. She made a beeline to find Tom.

"Did you hear the commander's squad was hit?" she said.

"Yeah, it was. I was there," Tom added, anticipating Bergan's next question. "I didn't tell you right away because I didn't want you to be worried."

Tom had been walking in front of his truck when the IED went off two vehicles behind him. Thirty minutes later another one exploded in front of the truck, but no one was near it. Then, as the squad was leaving the area, several more mortars blew up around them, and a firefight ensued to their rear.

Bergan started turning red.

"The commander *promised* me he was going to keep you safe," said Bergan, who had turned twenty-four five days earlier.

"Bergan, I am safe," Tom said. "I'm here. No one was hurt."

"We're less than two months into the deployment, Thomas," Bergan said. "You've gotta stay safe."

"I will. That goes for you, too."

Tom didn't really worry about Bergan, though. He looked at it from a practical standpoint. This was part of their job, and he knew her squad leaders were looking out for her. As for Bergan, she realized she'd have to get over her worry quick, or else she'd be a wreck.

Later, she realized she'd probably overreacted because she was scared. She knew that, in reality, just as her duty was to be with her platoon, the company commander's place was out with his soldiers. And some commanders took their executive officers with them, wanting their lieutenants to have that experience.

Where Tom was concerned, though, it was hard for her to think like a soldier and not a spouse.

A month earlier the couple had marked their second wedding anniversary, August 18, just as they did the night they got engaged at Norwich: They went to Pizza Hut. In this case the Pizza Hut was a wheeled trailer with an outdoor walk-up counter, complete with sliding windows and just a few selections.

"This is so romantic," Bergan joked. But at least they were together, if only for an hour.

The Flannigans lived on separate FOBs, forty-five minutes apart, and saw each other about once a week for a few hours, depending on how busy Tom was when Bergan brought a squad back to Kandahar Airfield, known as KAF, the NATO base in southern Afghanistan. The sprawling desert base, outside Kandahar, is surrounded by bare mountains that look like heaps of gray ash, while the base itself is a mix of air-conditioned tents and buildings and sand or gravel roads. Everything is a single shade—tan.

KAF's covered wooden boardwalk was a dusty quadrangle of shops and restaurants serving the 20,000-plus NATO troops stationed there. An oblong gravel pit in the center was used for concerts and volleyball matches. It was like being on an island surrounded by shark-infested waters, except that these sharks often bombarded the base with rockets and mortars.

Still, the boardwalk was a great getaway, especially since Bergan's quarters were a simple tent. She posted an anniversary photo of her and Tom on Facebook, both of them unsmiling and sunburned.

Not everyone approved of the Flannigans' spending time together. An officer outside their company spotted them eating lunch together on the boardwalk, took issue with it, and complained to their commander, Captain Michael Thurman, saying other soldiers couldn't see their spouses.

Captain Thurman told them not to go to the boardwalk together.

"You have to be more careful when and where you see Tom," Captain Thurman said to Bergan. "Just be aware of who is around." At least he didn't say they couldn't see each other, she thought.

No one in the company cared that they were married. They were one of three sets of spouses in the unit, and the only officers. Sergeant Thomas and a few other soldiers had a running joke that they were "the couple of the decade," because it was obvious they loved each other so much, even though they kept it professional in front of the soldiers. Others thought of them as a power couple, the two perfect officers. And Tom had his nickname, too—Pa.

October 16, 2009. Kandahar Airfield

Tom and Bergan didn't dare embrace. They walked away to compose themselves and cried in silence, arms crossed, consoling each other with their words and eyes.

Bergan had been with one of her squads on KAF, performing maintenance on the vehicles, when news came that a squad in 3rd Platoon was hit.

"We'd better get back," Tom said after a few minutes, his blue eyes lined in red. They would have to start answering questions from their soldiers and making arrangements at the company tactical operations center.

One of the first soldiers Bergan saw was Private First Class Beebe, who had been working on the vehicles with her.

"I've got some bad news," she said. "Sergeant Ski's been killed."

"Oh, my God, what happened?" he asked.

By the sound of Bergan's voice, Private First Class Beebe could tell she was trying as hard as she could to control her emotions.

Everyone knew and liked Sergeant Christopher Rudzinski, a twenty-eight-year-old squad leader from Rantoul, Illinois. "Sergeant Ski" was on his fourth deployment. But this time was different. He had a blond-haired, blue-eyed baby boy back home, who had just turned a year old. He'd told Sergeant Thomas the previous week that he couldn't wait to get back to little Ryan and his wife, Caroline.

But early that afternoon, Sergeant Rudzinski had died when an IED hit his vehicle.

By nightfall, Kandahar's noisy flight line was silenced out of respect for the fallen. Balls of light glowed from the airfield lamps, making them look like electrified lollipops.

This was Bergan's first "ramp ceremony," and she hoped it would be her last. The military strives to have fallen soldiers returned to their family within twenty-four hours, so the troops were still in shock over Sergeant Ski's death as they stood shoulder-to-shoulder to give one final farewell salute.

The glow, the dust, and the tan-and-green uniforms produced a sepia-toned scene reminiscent of an old frontier photograph. Into the frame rolled an MRAP truck, which this night served as a hearse. Protruding out of its back end was a metal box, known as a transfer case, with an American flag secured around it like wrapping paper. Soldiers in Sergeant Ski's squad—his "kids," he'd called them—performed their last duty for their squad leader. Carefully, struggling, they lifted his coffin, hoisting it upon their shoulders.

Two rows of soldiers flanked both sides of the back of the C-17 plane.

"Present arms!"

Bergan held her salute and tried to keep her composure as the casket went up the ramp and into the belly of the plane. During the twenty-one-gun salute and the playing of taps, she could hear muffled cries. Sergeant Thomas sobbed, his big shoulders heaving. He cried for Sergeant Ski. He cried for his best friend who died in an IED attack during his first deployment to Iraq. He cried for all the fallen. His tears came tumbling out of him like a Southern rainstorm, suddenly and with force.

By month's end, twenty-five Americans would be dead in Afghanistan.

The tears were mixed with anger and smack talk of revenge. One soldier ripped a bracelet inscribed with a Bible verse from his wrist and threw it on the ground near Private First Class Torres.

"How could He let this shit happen?" the soldier said. "How could God let this happen to him?"

That night in her tent Bergan tried to sleep.

I hope this isn't the beginning of many deaths, she thought. *We've only been in country two and a half months . . . we still have a long way to go. . . . I hope it's not me next. . . .*

The next morning she and her platoon carried on with their mission, as usual.

CHAPTER 19
Looking Back, Moving Forward

Angie: August 28, 2009. MCRD, San Diego

On her last day as commanding general, before she took on the challenges of a new assignment, Angie rose before the sun, pulled on her "CG MCRD" PT shirt for the last time, and slipped out the door of the "the Q," the Temporary Officer Quarters on Neville Road, where she had been staying in a suite with Janie and their mother for the past two weeks.

It was four a.m. and a balmy seventy-two degrees. Inside the yellow barracks lining the depot's parade deck, three floors' worth of lights snapped on simultaneously, as drill instructors blasted the blinded out of their racks. MCRD San Diego didn't simply stir awake; it bulldozed into each new day.

Six elated platoons would graduate on the parade deck in the late morning, and Angie would be the reviewing officer for the ceremony. Before that, at the flagpole outside Pendleton Hall, she would speak to the new Marines' parents at morning colors. Then, in the afternoon, she'd speak again at her change-of-command ceremony, which would be followed by a reception.

For a last day it was a hell of a full day. But at four p.m., when she passed the regimental colors to the incoming commander, Brigadier General Ronald Bailey, the one-star flag atop Pendleton Hall would fly for someone else. *Snap!* Like a burned-out lightbulb . . . out with the old, replaced with the new.

There is no hanging on, hanging around, or hiding out when one relinquishes command. Jim would pick up the Salinas family early Saturday morning and take them to the airport for a flight back east. For Angie and Jim, it was never "Good-bye," only "See you soon."

Angie had received her new orders in April, when the Marines released the slate for general officer assignments. She would become the director of the manpower management division, Manpower and Reserve Affairs, at Marine headquarters in Quantico, Virginia. In that role, she would be responsible for everything from assignments, awards, and promotions to retirements and records for the 202,000 Marines stationed across the globe.

Angie continued north on Neville Road, which bordered the back of Butler Gardens. Her knees were holding up well on this day, but this run—more a jog, really—was less about physical exercise than about thinking, absorbing, and letting go. There was plenty to think about after all this time . . . her staff, the young men who had graduated from boot camp, and the Marine veteran whom she presented with the Silver Star in the spring, forty-two years after his heroic acts in Vietnam.

On her left, overlooking the marina, was the Bay View Restaurant. "The club" was a 1920s-era Spanish colonial building, where the previous night hundreds of people from various commands and their spouses had attended Angie's farewell, which included a Mexican-themed buffet. The commands and organizations on the depot each presented her with farewell gifts, which ranged from plaques and T-shirts to a fishbowl-size ceramic margarita glass engraved with her name. Marine Corps Community Services (MCCS) had surprised Angie by instituting the General Angela Salinas Character Leadership Award, a scholarship for kids to attend camps on the depot. When Angie had arrived, no such camps existed, so she initiated them for soccer, Little League, and families with special needs.

"This means more to me than my military awards," she said. "Because it tells me that my message that we don't just make Marines here, that we take care of our families and invest in our future, will carry on to those who will come here long after we're all gone. Years from now some kid will remember what you've done for them. Thank you, thank you, thank you."

The farewell party had been just one of many in a summer of long good-byes that started in June with a sunset concert and farewell party at Quarters One, followed by more events in downtown San Diego. Every group, commission, and organization—from the Girl Scouts to the chamber of commerce—wanted to bid Angie farewell.

"Please come back to San Diego" was the common refrain.

Her staff NCOs said good-bye on a harbor boat dinner cruise. They went all out and came dressed in coats and ties for the occasion. It was an unforgettable sight: Angie out on the water surrounded by more than two hundred buzz-cut men in their Sunday best.

The R & A Society crowd said their good-byes, too, at its annual ladies' night at the Hotel del Coronado. With Scotch and martinis in hand, they'd given a "We'll miss you . . . you were a great addition to the group" toast. The theme for the evening was favorite sports teams, so Jim put on San Diego Padres attire, while Angie came dressed as an MCRD San Diego football player. The depot had its own intramural team.

Themes and costumes were an R & A tradition. The previous August, for ladies' night, they'd invited members to "Get Gnarly on a Harley." Jim arrived at Quarters One decked out like a biker dude. Angie's mother, who was starting to show signs of dementia, looked at Jim and told her daughter, "You can do so much better!"

But in Angie he had met his match. She had borrowed an entire outfit from a niece who had gone through a Goth phase in high school, and was wearing tight jeans with a star on each cheek, knee-high lace-up leather boots with four-inch heels, flesh-colored sleeves with printed tattoos, a dog collar around her neck, a do-rag on her head, and a leather jacket.

Nobody recognized them. "We look like somebody you make your kids run from," Angie told Jim. They ended up winning second place for best-dressed couple.

As part of the farewells, earlier in the week Sergeant Major Woods, who was now the director of the Neil Ash USO Airport Center in San Diego, and his wife, RhodaAnn, took Angie to lunch at a seafood place in Point Loma. Over margaritas—the sergeant major had eventually acquired a taste for them—he pulled out a framed picture.

"We have some things for you," he said. "I got this at a USO auction. I bought it for myself, but in my heart of hearts I knew it was about you."

Angie held the sixteen-by-twenty-inch print of a bas-relief sculpture of Civil War generals.

"This reminds me of leadership," Sergeant Major Woods went on. "This print embodies your leadership, and I wanted you to have it."

Beneath the image an engraved plaque read:

Brigadier General Angela Salinas
Commanding General Marine Corps Recruit Depot San Diego/WRR

"The Essence of Leadership"
With the deepest of respect and appreciation
for your mentorship and friendship

Aug 2006–Aug 2009
Sgt. Maj. Bobby Woods and Family

The sergeant major—everyone still called him sergeant major—had been retired from the corps for more than a year, but he was still frequently asked one question by senior Marines: "Sergeant Major, what was it like to work for General Salinas?"

The answer he gave was always the same: "It was an honor, and we were a good match," he said. "For both of us."

Even Iron Mike Mervosh, the retired sergeant major, came around. He told Woods at a drill instructor association meeting, "You know, she's doing a great job."

Now RhodaAnn put another gift on the table.

"We have something else for you, too," she said.

Angie unwrapped the package to reveal a silver jewelry box dotted with rhinestones. Engraved on the top was:

General A. Salinas
True friends are never apart,
Maybe in distance, but not in heart.
Aloha, The Woods Family.

"This is your memory box," Sergeant Major Woods said. "But wait until you get home to open it. It's filled with memories and thoughts from people in your command."

On the sergeant major's fiftieth birthday, his USO volunteers had given him a surprise birthday party and presented him with a similar box. When he later opened it and read the notes, messages, and good wishes, he was absolutely touched. He wanted his former boss to have that same experience.

It was still two hours until sunrise when Angie turned onto Pendleton Avenue, near Quarters One. The house stood ready, like a theater on opening night, to receive its forty-ninth family, and the Baileys were in the process of moving in. Angie had moved out a couple of weeks before. As outgoing commander, she believed in exiting quarters in plenty of time to allow for cleaning and repairs so the new commander's family could get settled as soon as possible.

It had finally hit Angie that the end was in sight when she stood alone in Quarters One, surrounded by boxes piled high. She and Janie had been at the house all day with the packers, and the movers were due to arrive the following morning. Janie was pooped and had headed back to the suite.

It's that time again, Angie thought. *We're leaving*. Her gray shorts pockets held a box cutter, a role of tape, and a black marker, all the essentials for packing day. She couldn't wait to get a shower.

In past assignments she had always been ready to follow the bugle call to the next duty station when Uncle Sam gave the order to go. She had moved twenty-five times with the Marines. The three years at MCRD were the longest time she'd lived anywhere since she had joined the corps. But this was different. It felt as if she were leaving family.

Not that it had been easy. Despite the scrutiny of her every move, her packed calendar, the constant presence of aides, and a stream of people waiting to see her every day, being a woman at the general officer level was lonely. She had no female peers, which also meant no close military friends. Angie was one of only three female Marine generals, and to be friends invited rumors. So the women tended to stay away from one another.

Her position meant that junior women Marines often sought out Angie for advice for how to deal with getting pigeonholed.

"Ma'am, I have three paths," a female Marine would say. "I'm either a whore, gay, or a bitch."

"Well, if those are your choices, if you're going to be anything, be confident," Angie would tell them. "The person in the mirror is the one who matters."

At least San Diego provided a sense of normality. Through her community relations efforts, Angie met women professionals her age, many of whom were single or divorced and who knew what it was like to try to find a guy who was okay with a successful and powerful woman.

I'm not abnormal, she realized, as she was invited to power lunches with women who were CEOs, company presidents, business owners, and college presidents. Still, she noted that every time they saw her in town, they were wearing business suits and she was in nun shoes and a uniform. She got the feeling they were wondering, *Who are you, and why are you here? And even, Are you in our league?*

Angie's response was to invite them to what she billed as a "Woman's Night In" at Quarters One, a theme party that instructed: "Come as only your best friend would see you." For Angie that meant sweats and pink slippers.

On the designated night, seventeen women drove their Jaguars and Mercedeses to Quarters One, dressed in Juicy Couture sweat suits and puffy slippers.

Janie had elevated the formal dining room to five-star status with crystal, china, and silver and planned a seven-course meal of cilantro scallops salad, roasted garlic chicken, and dessert flambé, all prepared by Angie's enlisted chef. Marines volunteered as servers (and ate well on leftovers). Soon the room was filled with laughter and the high-pitched voices of the "alpha" women gathered around the table, quite a change from the baritone world Angie was used to. She had a headache by the time they left.

But the night was a fun one, and Angie was able to impart a different picture of military women who operate at the CEO level. When she held the event for a second year, she had nothing to prove, and it was a festive gathering of friends.

Now the grand dining room, host to several generations of parties, lay empty.

It went so fast, Angie thought. *We don't want to go.* But at the same time, the Marine in her knew she had done what she was supposed to do as a commander, and it was okay to leave. Much had been accomplished. She had firmly built up the relationships established by her predecessors between the depot and the community, and she had educated the community on the talent, resources, and economic impact of MCRD on the city.

She knew it was *time* to go.

Angie turned left onto Henderson Avenue and passed Pendleton Field, where the white chairs for this afternoon's ceremony were up and ready. Ronald Bailey and Angie had been classmates as captains twenty-six years ago at the Amphibious Warfare School, now the Expeditionary Warfare School, at Quantico, and Bailey's arrival hadn't sparked the slightest controversy or any headlines. She was being replaced with another tall, square-jawed, and graying general. Things were going back to the norm at the depot, Angie thought.

Or were they?

Did I make a difference? she wondered. *What will people remember me for?*

In the military you are only as good as your last fight, and Angie's mind quickly turned to what lay ahead: Quantico. Her new responsibilities were vast, and her leadership would impact every Marine in the corps. Darkness turned to light. Once again, the pressure was on.

In June, following a Rolling Stone *profile that included demeaning remarks about President Obama and his administration, Obama fires General Stanley McChrystal, the top commander in Afghanistan, and replaces him with General David Petraeus.*

A month later, WikiLeaks starts releasing 75,000 secret documents relating to the United States and the war in Afghanistan, followed by the release of Iraq War documents and diplomatic cables.

On August 31 the combat mission in Iraq officially ends.

In December, the "Don't Ask, Don't Tell" policy is officially repealed after a Pentagon review.

CHAPTER 20
Three Days

Bergan: February 24, 2010. Kandahar, Afghanistan

 "Three days, ma'am," Private First Class Jacob Beebe called out to Bergan as the squad moved along a gutter that reeked of sewage. "Only three more days."

In addition to his M4, Beebe had a large medical pouch slung over his shoulder. Every time the squad went on a dismounted patrol, one of the soldiers was chosen to wear it. Some complained about it, because extra weight was extra weight, but Private First Class Beebe didn't mind.

For the last couple of hours of the patrol, every time the squad came across something that smelled bad or looked disgusting, he had reminded Bergan that she'd be heading home for R & R in three days, after seven months in theater. It was turning out to be a constant refrain. In Kandahar the gutters were always filled with rotten food. Raw sewage stagnated in the streets and turned streams into black sludge littered with trash. It was common to see people carrying a dead animal. Some spots smelled so bad it was overwhelming. Burning trash and feces was the only means of disposal in

a country where most people didn't have running water and bathed in pol-
luted rivers.

"I can feel those heated floors under my feet already!" Bergan called
out as she kept both hands on her weapon and scanned the marketplace.
"Good-bye, sand; hello, snow slopes!"

Southern Afghanistan is desert flatlands with bare mountains along
the horizon. They are nothing like the lush, tree-covered heights back home
in the Adirondacks or the Dole and Paine mountains surrounding Norwich University, which Bergan had climbed more times than she could
count. But she liked mountains best when they were covered in snow. She
couldn't wait to go snowboarding during her leave, a sport she'd loved since
age ten.

Even with all her gear on—ballistic eye protection, helmet, body
armor, boots, and gloves—Bergan still resembled a young woman in the
softness of her cheeks and the curve of her nose. Afghan girls spotted
her right away and often trailed behind as if she were the Pied Piper of
Kandahar.

But as the afternoon wore on and most Afghans headed home for the
day, the streets emptied. Except for the motorcycles and rusty bicycles, it
was as if a time-travel machine had deposited the little band of soldiers into
a biblical landscape. Young boys, dressed in brimless round caps, vests,
sandals, and tapered, pajamalike pants, wore shy smiles. Bearded men in
tunics and either turbans or pancake-flat pukul caps tended to their sheep.
And women kept their heads covered, just as they have for thousands of
years. Except for the occasional splash of bright color from a young girl's
dress, everything was in grays and tans, as if the color had bled out of the
place centuries ago.

In three days Bergan and Tom would be on a flight headed home for
their midtour leave, two weeks of treasured R & R. Bergan's parents had
booked a ski cabin in Vermont just thirty minutes from Tom's parents, and
she looked forward to hanging out with her family.

And today's dismounted presence patrol on the outskirts of the city was
almost over. The squad and the Afghan police had been winding their way
on foot through shantytown markets and across fields, making a giant loop

through District 3 for the past three hours. But time always seemed longer on patrol. They covered about four miles, with security halts, and stops along the way to talk with locals.

By this point in the patrol, the soldiers' uniforms blended in with their surroundings. Everything—from the sky and storefront shacks to the roads and bicycle wheels—was covered in dust.

The "family-size" container of Tide back in Bergan's room that she'd bought at KAF came in handy. In December she had finally gotten a space to call her own. It wasn't much. She nicknamed it her jail cell, but at least it wasn't a tent. FOB Walton now had barracks buildings, a dining hall, and operations buildings, perhaps a sign of things to come. The additional 30,000 troops President Obama was sending into Afghanistan would be in place by the summer, with a third of those troops in Kandahar.

That same month the rest of the company, including Tom, had moved to the outpost, too. Married couples could not share rooms, but Tom and Bergan did get to see each other every day between missions, and on rare occasions they watched a movie together in one of their rooms.

It was a tight fit in Bergan's room. After patrols she'd practically shimmy between the plywood walls to get into her bottom bunk. Sometimes she got a full night's rest, other times as little as two or three hours. She used the upper bunk as a shelf to hold her duffel bag, books, and other items, such as a tin of cookies, a large Tootsie Roll tube filled with candy, and a care package of Laffy Taffy from her old Norwich roommate.

Minnie Mouse, in her polka-dotted red dress, sat perched on the bunk's metal ladder, yellow shoes dangling. Bergan had left Bum-Bum, another childhood stuffed animal, with Bethany. Except for Bergan's nine-millimeter pistol and M4, it could have been a teenage girl's room at camp.

During downtime, Bergan, like many soldiers, watched TV shows on her laptop, and she had turned her wall into a shrine to home, with a montage of postcards, snapshots, and a front-page *Tupper Lake Free Press* article about her and Tom. She also kept the framed certificate of her promotion to first lieutenant. The ceremony had taken place on the last day of November, with Tom and Captain Thurman pinning on her new rank.

Like most deployed soldiers, Bergan took satisfaction in crossing an X through each completed day on her wall calendar. She had compiled 210 Xs so far.

Now there were just three more days. Her mom was going to make her favorite, shepherd's pie. And she couldn't wait to have a good cup of coffee and a cold glass of milk. She wouldn't touch the milk in the chow hall, because it was always lukewarm, had no expiration date, and didn't come from the United States.

"Three-quarters of a mile left, ma'am," Private First Class Beebe called out. The squad had just passed through a field and was back on a paved street that would lead them to their trucks, which were parked at the Police Substation 3 parking lot. This patrol had been uneventful, unlike yesterday's, when one of the ANPs kept walking close to Bergan and tugging at her arm.

"Back off!" she kept telling him, to no avail. Finally she swung around and pulled her pistol out of its holster, but she didn't point it at the man. "I said back off! Your behavior is unacceptable!"

It was bad enough to have to be led by a foreign woman, but to be reprimanded by one greatly embarrassed and angered the Afghan police officer. Even so, the rest of the mission continued uneventfully.

Certainly the incident was history as far as Bergan was concerned, and today's patrol was almost finished, too. The soldiers remained in two staggered columns on the sides of the road and tried to keep five to ten meters apart. It was a classic tactical formation designed to avoid becoming clustered and to minimize possible loss.

Buildings and small fields lined the way. After a quarter of a mile the squad crossed over a small concrete section of road with a small car-washing station and a motorcycle parked in front. It was almost dusk. Staff Sergeant Armando Velez, the squad leader, walked first, followed by the Afghan interpreter, and then Bergan.

She was wondering whether the snowboarding suit she'd bought online had arrived yet at her parents' house. She'd have to ask her mom later, she thought, as she passed the motorcycle.

Suddenly everything went black, and a high-pitched noise from the netherworld enveloped Bergan. She lay in the dirt like a rag doll atop a blanket of blood, her arms extended and her legs forming the number four.

She knew instantly she was hit.

I can't believe it. I made it more than seven months without a scratch, and now all of a sudden I'm dying, she thought. She pictured her family, everyone she never got to say good-bye to, and prayed to God that they would be all right without her, especially Bethany, whom she knew would have the hardest time.

The blast blew Doc Newman, walking behind Bergan, off his feet. He smelled gas, his ears rang, and his head was abuzz as he tried to stand up.

Private First Class Beebe looked over his right shoulder and saw an enormous bright orange smudge surrounded by black smoke where the motorcycle had been. It was a dirty flame, the signature mark of a homemade bomb. Someone had remotely detonated an IED.

After ten seconds Bergan realized she was still alive and started screaming. Dust and debris kicked up from the blast made it impossible to see. Hearing her, Doc headed in the direction of the explosion.

She isn't where she's supposed to be, he thought, still trying to shake off the rattling within his head.

Private First Class Beebe took two steps toward Bergan, then remembered his training and dropped to the ground for cover. As the dust settled, he saw Doc Newman running toward the lieutenant, and Beebe scrambled to his feet and ran as fast as he could, taking off the aid bag he was carrying.

Meanwhile, soldiers spotted a man standing on top of a building videotaping, but he quickly vanished.

Doc peered down at Bergan. Over the course of many months he had come to view the Flannigans as the finest officers he'd ever served with. He always said he'd follow Bergan to the gates of hell. Now here he was.

Bergan's right thigh was a gaping hole, the leg attached by a piece of flesh the size of two thumbs to the rest of her leg.

I can't move her, he thought to himself. *I've got to treat her here.*

He set his rifle down, dropped to his knees, and applied pressure to stop the bleeding.

"Who's down? Who's down?" Staff Sergeant Velez called out.

"LT is down! LT is down!" Doc yelled, as he grabbed the first-aid kit attached to Bergan's body armor. "Urgent surgical evac! Urgent surgical evac!"

Private First Class Beebe ran up and looked at his platoon leader. He couldn't believe it: He could see right into Bergan's thigh. Her femur was broken and sticking out of the wound. Blood was already pooling in and around the wound, clotting in the sand like a ruby necklace. Bergan continued to scream.

"Bring me the bag!" Doc said.

"I'm here; I've got you, Bergan," he said, calling her by her first name for the first time.

"Am I gonna die?" she asked.

"You're not gonna die," Doc said. "You'll ruin my perfect record."

"Give me morphine! Please, morphine!" Bergan begged.

"I can't do that, Bergan," Doc said. If she had a brain injury, the drug could exacerbate the problem.

"Why? Please! I don't want to die!" Bergan wailed. *Not like this. Not here. Dear God, please let me pass out.*

Staff Sergeant Velez ordered everyone in the squad to seek cover and provide 360-degree security facing outward from the blast site. Then he got on the radio and tried to call the squad's trucks. The radio signals were blocked by the buildings, however, and couldn't get through.

Doc explained to Bergan exactly what he was doing as he wrapped a tourniquet—Velcro straps on a plastic stick—around her thigh. He used gauze to help control the bleeding and then reached into Bergan's thigh cavity to secure her femoral artery. He knew that if that huge blood vessel were not secured, blood pressure would pull it out of the tourniquet, and Bergan would bleed internally. To keep her from hemorrhaging to death, Doc had to keep his hand inside Bergan's thigh.

"Talk to me, ma'am," Private First Class Beebe said. "Let me know how you're doing." He helped take off her gear and propped her head up so it wasn't on the ground. It was hard for him to look Bergan in the eyes. He was terrified that she wouldn't make it.

"I hear you," Bergan said. "I hear you. My leg hurts so bad."

On this deployment Doc had treated soldiers for dehydration, diarrhea, dislocated fingers from playing basketball, and twisted ankles, the result of ill-fated truck exits. And he had done some "stitch work" with superglue, since getting supplies could be difficult.

Doc knew he had to keep Bergan conscious and talking.

"I don't want to die!" she pleaded over and over.

"I'm not going to let you die," Doc said in his gravelly drawl. She was also bleeding from shrapnel embedded in her chin, but she didn't notice that, since the pain in her leg was so intense.

"Please, I don't want to die. . . ."

"You're not gonna die on me," Doc repeated. "Stop talkin' like that."

Doc had to believe it. He knew Bergan had lost a lot of blood. But he also knew he was going to do everything he could—with the help of God—to keep the promise he'd made to Thomas Flannigan.

Months ago Doc had been the senior medic for the company commander's squad. At the time he had promised Bergan he'd do everything in his power to take care of Tom, should something happen. "The promise I made to her, I'm making to you," Doc told Tom, when he was assigned as medic to Bergan's platoon. Now he reiterated it to Bergan.

"I made the same promise to Thomas I made to you," he said. "Don't make a liar out of me."

★

FOB Walton

Tom Flannigan had just finished dinner at the chow hall and was walking back to the TOC when his cell phone rang.

"Lieutenant Flannigan," Tom said.

"Sir! Sir, it's Sergeant Radcliffe," said one of Bergan's team leaders.

Tom could tell by the urgency in his voice that something was wrong.

"We've been hit and need a medevac. It's urgent surgical," said Sergeant Daniel Radcliffe. "We're unable to reach the trucks with the radios."

"What's the grid?" Tom asked. "Sergeant Radcliffe . . . Sergeant Radcliffe . . ."

The phone went dead.

"Dammit!" Tom ran to the operations center of the unit's sister company and started to relay the information to the radio operator.

"Sir, we heard it on the battalion net," the soldier said.

Tom ran to his company TOC to get the unit to start gathering information on the attacked patrol. A squad from 1st Platoon was just leaving for patrol and asked to assist. Tom diverted it to the downed squad's location. Next he got his personnel clerk ready to fill out the casualty feeder card, which is the initial format for reporting casualties to higher headquarters.

Tom was so focused on getting support to the patrol, it never occurred to him it could be Bergan who was injured.

Meanwhile, back in District 3, Bergan's face was growing as pale as a funeral shroud, and she stopped responding to Doc, who looked up and saw her blank stare. As a firefighter, he had seen this look before . . . on the faces of car accident victims just before death.

"Goddammit! Wake the fuck up! Do not do this to me!"

As he said it, with his hand still inside her thigh, he squeezed her artery and the nerves surrounding it, knowing it would be excruciatingly painful.

Bergan's screams confirmed that.

"Quit falling asleep on me!" Doc said.

"I'm awake," Bergan said. "I'm awake."

Finally the trucks arrived. A soldier with a cell phone had reached a soldier on the truck. As soon as the first vehicle rolled to a stop, Private First Class Beebe ran over and grabbed the litter that was secured to the side with zip ties. Then he brought it back to Bergan.

"Jacob, secure her leg while we get her on the litter," Doc said.

Private First Class Beebe tried to hold her leg steady. Only the back portion of skin on her thigh was holding the lower half of her leg on. Beebe tried to be gentle as he grabbed behind her knee and her ankle.

Oh, my God, it's so stiff and light, he thought. It scared him. He didn't know what he was expecting, but that was definitely not it.

Bergan screamed. It was the first time she'd been lifted from where she'd fallen. It felt as if her leg were just hanging on by threads. The soldiers carried her over to a farmer's mud hut, under a makeshift awning that would cut down on the dust and wind when the helicopter arrived.

"Is that the bird?" Bergan asked. She could have sworn she heard the helicopter.

"No, not yet," Private First Class Beebe said. "It's on the way, ma'am." It seemed like it was taking an eternity. Almost an hour had passed since the explosion.

Doc wanted to take a look at Bergan's other leg. Her pants were already split, but he was concerned about keeping her dignity intact.

"You mind if I cut your pants?" he said. "You're gonna be down to your drawers."

"Do what ya gotta do," Bergan said.

He checked her abdomen and saw that her left leg was peppered with shrapnel, like her chin.

"Jacob, can you get me the gauze out of your med pack?" Doc said. "She's got shrapnel wounds."

Private First Class Beebe's hands were shaking so badly he couldn't pull open the gauze.

"Dammit!" he said.

"It's okay, Jacob," Doc said. "Calm down. You'll get it open."

Finally Private First Class Beebe managed to get out the square patch of gauze and handed it to Doc.

Just then the squad from 1st Platoon arrived with their medic, and within two minutes came the sound they'd been waiting for: rotor blades. A soldier threw smoke to signal their location.

The sun was setting, making it hard for the pilots to see, and the helicopter landed on the opposite side of the road, more than three football fields away. Trying to get Bergan there as fast as possible, Private First Class Beebe grabbed the litter's two front handles, and Doc and the other medic each grabbed a back handle, and they made the run of their lives across the road, over a ditch, through a gate, and across a field to the spot where the chopper had landed.

"Are you the medic?" the flight medic asked Beebe, who was in front.

Beebe could barely hear over the roar of the bird. He shook his head no and motioned over his shoulder to Doc. The pilot grabbed a litter handle and helped Beebe load Bergan onto the helicopter. Then the door closed, and like that, she was in the air. On the ground, Doc Newman looked dazed, and Private First Class Beebe felt as if he were going to pass out. He turned his gaze from the sky down to his gloved hands and sleeve cuffs, which were covered in blood. Dusk had faded into twilight.

What if I never see her again? Beebe thought. *What if she lost too much blood? What if the medevac was too late?*

The Flannigans were some of the best people he had ever met in his life. You could take away the Army, take away that they were officers, and they were still two of the best people he had ever known. A tuft of white caught Private First Class Beebe's eye. The bloody gauze from Bergan's chin had blown away and caught in some weeds.

Kandahar Airfield

Nurses wheeled Bergan into the combat support hospital at Kandahar Airfield.

This is where they brought me? Bergan thought. The walls were made of plywood. It reminded her of a field hospital in an old war movie. A beacon of light appeared in the form of a Navy doctor. He stood over Bergan and started asking questions.

Then everything went black.

FOB Walton

At the company TOC, Tom and the others monitored the situation by radio and knew the medevac had arrived and picked up the casualty. And by now they knew there was one soldier with severe leg injuries.

Tom picked up the phone. It was Sergeant First Class Lisa Peterson, his senior food service specialist, calling from Kandahar Airfield.

"Sir, is the commander or first sergeant there?"

"They're out at the site of the IED," Tom said.

"I'll call back later, sir," she said. "The medevac arrived, and I'm waiting for the doctors."

"Sir, the battalion commander is on the phone," said Master Sergeant Buck Shaul, the operations sergeant.

Tom hung up with Peterson and took the receiver. "Sir, this is First Lieutenant Flannigan."

The commander, Lieutenant Colonel David Chase, didn't hear Tom. He asked someone around him, "Does he know that it was his wife yet?"

Tom squatted down as he held the phone, waiting for the commander to realize he was on the line. His head started spinning as he tried to mesh his duties as executive officer with his overwhelming concern for Bergan.

"Sir, this is First Lieutenant Flannigan," he repeated.

"Tom, this is Lieutenant Colonel Chase. Your wife was hit. She's in surgery at Kandahar. She's getting the best possible care there. We don't have much information yet. I'm going to come pick you up and take you to Kandahar Airfield. Meet me at the landing zone."

When the conversation ended, Tom hung up the phone. Never one to let his guard down, he remained in soldier mode, relaying Bergan's battle roster number for verification purposes.

"Keep tracking the units on the ground," he added. Then he ran to his room, grabbed his rifle, body armor, and helmet, and returned to the TOC, so he'd know when to head to the landing zone.

Master Sergeant Shaul, a twenty-year Army veteran, watched Tom.

"Sir, can I talk with you outside?" he said.

The two walked out into the darkness.

"Sir, are you okay?" Master Sergeant Shaul said. "You can let it out. We got this."

"I'm good," Tom said, but his eyes told a different story.

Master Sergeant Shaul grabbed him as tears streamed down Tom's face.

"She's receiving the best care possible," Master Sergeant Shaul said. "The important thing is that she's still alive."

Tom wiped his eyes and took a moment to collect himself. Then the two went back inside. As the other soldiers watched Tom for his reaction, he carried on. That was what he thought his soldiers and Bergan would want and need him to do.

★

Kandahar Airfield

"She's still in surgery," a nurse told Tom. He had just arrived after a forty-five-minute ride from FOB Walton. "The doctors had to remove her right leg, which was severely damaged, and they're working on saving her left leg. Shrapnel severed her femoral artery."

"Is she going to be okay?" Tom asked.

"She lost a lot of blood. We're trying to stabilize her," the nurse said. "We'll know more later."

Tom's cousin, Captain Steve Flannigan, who happened to be assigned to KAF, was able to stay with Tom at the hospital. Captain Thurman arrived shortly after.

"Tom, you're being sent home with Bergan," he said. "Colonel Drinkwine signed your memo to release you from theater. Worry about Bergan and take care of her. That's your only job now."

★

FOB Walton

The rest of the platoon anxiously awaited more news and the return of the attacked squad. Specialist Paul Torres, who had been promoted earlier in the month, was overcome with anger and sadness.

"Why did it have to be her who got hurt?" he kept saying over and over.

They didn't know whether she was still alive. Everyone stood outside the motor pool, chain-smoking, pacing back and forth, and trying to calm down. Specialist Torres looked up at the stars. He had never seen such brilliant stars as in Afghanistan. He loved to look at them. It was a daily gift in a dismal place. But now he looked up at the stars and could feel only anger.

Finally the trucks rolled into camp. No one had uttered a word on the ride back. As the soldiers jumped out, the other platoon members pitched in to grab gear and weapons and refueled the trucks for them. It was hard for everyone to see the blood-covered items. Specialist Torres and Sergeant Thomas volunteered to soap down the back of the truck.

As soldiers gathered to talk, Private First Class Beebe got off the truck and, unnoticed, walked behind some large barriers. A civilian policeman from D.C., who was working as a contractor in Afghanistan, saw him and followed.

"Are you okay?" the older man asked. He had been attached to the platoon for just one week, and Private First Class Beebe knew him only as Officer Washington, an older black man with more salt than pepper in his once-black hair.

Private First Class Beebe couldn't talk. It was as if his body stopped working, and he shook uncontrollably.

"It's okay," Officer Washington said, as he wrapped the soldier in his arms. "It's okay. You did a good job."

Meanwhile, Doc Newman had lots of questions coming his way and situational reports to fill out. After making sure everybody drank water and Gatorade to replenish their electrolytes from the adrenaline rush, he made his way to an empty shower trailer. Still wearing his uniform, he turned on the hot water, entered the stall, and sat on the floor.

"Doc, you saved her," everyone had told him.

But it was hard to hear. *What could I have done better? Did I do everything I could have done?*

He tried to wipe Bergan's blood off his wedding band and from under his fingernails. There had been no time to put on medical gloves. Only then did Doc break down and sob, his tears mixing with the shower water.

He hoped he'd kept his promise.

L. P. Quinn Elementary School, Tupper Lake,
New York

Outside a light snow fell, as it had almost every day that month, coating the mountains surrounding Bergan's hometown. A group of six kindergartners gathered around Amy Arsenault as she showed the children alphabet letters and corresponding sounds. Amy was a teaching assistant at the same elementary school her four children had attended.

She had turned fifty-one five days earlier, and Bergan had sent yellow gerbera daisies for the occasion. The note read: "I miss you like crazy, Mama. We'll be home soon." The best birthday gift of all would be having Bergan and Tom come home. Her oldest daughter, Brooke, had been counting the days since January.

Just three more days, Amy thought. As always, she kept her cell phone on her desk, turned to vibrate in case Bergan called, as she usually did during Amy's morning break. Everyone at the school knew Bergan was deployed, and they "sponsored" her platoon. Each month a different classroom sent care packages, and Bergan kept a hand-sewn American flag, created by one of the classes, on her wall. She had her platoon take a group photo with it and sent the picture to the school.

At ten thirty Amy heard her phone, and another teaching assistant, her friend Mary Lalonde, covered for her.

"Hello," Amy said, expecting to hear Bergan's voice.

"Amy . . . Amy!"

It was Tom, and she could tell immediately that something had happened. Tom was always so calm and composed.

"What?" she said.

Tom was sobbing.

"What?" Amy said. She was now on her feet. "What? What, Tom?"

"I'm so sorry," he said. "I'm so sorry."

I've lost my daughter . . . thought Amy.

By now the children were looking at her. Mary began swooping the kids out of the room.

"Go get Bethany!" Amy told her. Bergan's twin was working at the school as a library teacher.

"Is she alive?" Amy asked. "Tom!" It was obvious to her from 7,000 miles away that her son-in-law was in shock.

"She lost her leg. She got hit by an IED."

"Is she alive?" Amy said.

"Yes, yes, she's in surgery," Tom said. "I haven't seen her yet. It's minute by minute. Her femoral artery was severed, and they're trying to save her other leg."

I have to hold it together, Amy told herself. *Tom is not doing well, and Bethany is on her way.*

Amy felt numb and cold. *She's still alive. She's still alive. She's coming home alive.*

That was all she cared about, and she clung to it. To Amy, Bergan was just a little girl in a big woman's job, leading troops.

Meanwhile, down the hall at the library, Bethany was teaching a class of first graders. She'd been so excited about Bergan's homecoming, she hadn't wanted to come to work all week, but that morning she had woken up feeling out of sorts.

"Bethany, may I see you for a minute?" Mary said. "There's been an accident. You need to see your mom."

Bethany could tell by the look on the woman's face that something was very wrong.

Something's happened to either Tom or Bergan, Bethany thought.

"Mom, what happened?" she asked as she entered the room.

"Bergan was hit by a roadside bomb," Amy said. "We think she lost her leg."

Bethany crumpled to the floor.

"Get your stuff, honey; we're going home," Amy said.

As soon as they arrived at the house, the phone started ringing. The news had spread. Amy had already called her husband, Billy, who was on his way home.

I'm just going to wait for Tom's next call, she told herself.

That afternoon a package arrived. It was Bergan's new snowboard outfit.

PART IV
DECISION POINT

"The best protection any woman can have . . . is courage."

—Elizabeth Cady Stanton

CHAPTER 21
The Purple Heart

Bergan: February 26, 2010. Kandahar Airfield, Afghanistan

 As a nurse led Tom back to see Bergan, it took everything in him to control his emotions. It was after two a.m., and Bergan had just come out of surgery.

Be strong . . . be strong. Keep it together, he told himself.

But when he walked into the room, he sucked in his breath. She was white with the loss of blood. The lower right side of Bergan's face was swollen, and a deep purple bruise circled a red gash with stitches near her jaw. She had dried blood on her face and arms and was hooked up to a gaggle of tubes and monitors. The nurses were bringing her out of sedation so she could see him.

As Bergan's eyelids started to flutter, Tom took her hand.

"It's okay, Berg. I'm here. I'm here now," he said in a voice that did not sound like his own. "It's going to be okay." Bergan's eyes blinked open as if she were waking from a nightmare. She locked eyes on her husband

and tried to speak, but with so many tubes in her mouth, it was nearly impossible.

"It's okay. It's okay," he said. It was obvious to Tom she was in immense pain. "Do you want them to give you something for the pain?" Tom asked.

Bergan winced, and Tom had the nurses put her back under sedation.

★

Bagram Airfield, Afghanistan

"Lieutenant Flannigan?" a nurse said. "Come on back with me."

Finally, thought Tom. While Bergan was undergoing another round of surgery, he had spent the five hours with Lieutenant Colonel Michael Yarman, the chaplain for the 16th Military Police Brigade. Tom knew whatever was to come was in God's hands.

At Kandahar, Tom had stayed by Bergan's side throughout the night, until at ten in the morning, a C-135 plane flew them both to Bagram Airfield, a large base north of Kabul. Bagram's Craig Joint Theater Hospital, marked with the iconic red cross, was the main combat hospital in the eastern region and treated thousands of soldiers each month, including about 750 trauma patients. In the trauma ward a starched American flag offered the only swatch of color against the monotonous gray walls, and staff dressed in blue medical scrubs moved through the room like whirling dervishes.

The operation had replaced the shunt in Bergan's femoral artery and the vein in her left leg. The good news was that Bergan's condition was more stable, and there was an 80 to 90 percent chance her left leg would be saved.

But Tom now had to tell Bergan what had happened.

Her eyes slowly opened. Oxygen streamed into her nostrils, and monitors and saline bag stands were all around. Her head felt like lead from the pain and medications, and her left leg was wrapped and swollen to three times its normal size.

Tom forced a smile.

"Berg," he said, looking into her eyes. "You lost your right leg. But your left leg will be fine. It has some damage, but it will be fine."

Tears streamed down her face. *You lost your right leg. . . .*

She felt like she already had known that, but hearing the words hurt as much as the pain.

"It's going to be okay," Tom said. "I'm here. I'm not going anywhere." He rubbed her hand some more. "And you're going to get the Purple Heart today."

Fewer than 1,000 military women have been awarded the Purple Heart for being wounded or killed in Iraq and Afghanistan. Surprisingly, the numbers of women wounded or killed has not renewed the public condemnation of military women in combat zones, an issue that had fueled the argument in the 1990s for keeping women off the battlefield. The focus has been on casualties rather than gender. More than 48,000 American troops—men and women—have been severely wounded in Iraq and Afghanistan, about 65 percent of them from IED blasts. Between 90 and 95 percent have survived, thanks mostly to advances in medical care and a quicker evacuation response.

Bergan was so thirsty. All she really wanted was a Diet Coke, but she had to settle for sucking ice cubes instead.

Later that day in the intensive care unit, with a crowd of doctors and nurses looking on, Colonel John Garrity, the 16th Military Police Brigade commander, stood next to Bergan, whose bed was slightly elevated to raise her head, and pinned the Purple Heart—a medal trimmed in gold and bearing the profile of George Washington—onto the right side of Bergan's blue bedsheet. The ward erupted in cheers.

Looking out of place amid the hospital hardware was Minnie Mouse. The toy, which had long been perched on Bergan's bunk, now sat on the bed near Bergan's shoulder. The soldier who had packed her assault bag after her injury had put the mouse in as well.

"You did a great job," Colonel Garrity assured Bergan. "No one else was injured, so you were doing the right thing as a platoon leader. I'm very proud of you. You relied on your training and discipline."

"I'm glad no one else was hurt, sir," said Bergan, who was still heavily medicated. "I'd rather it be me than one of my soldiers. I'm really thankful for my medic and all the doctors."

The colonel also presented her with the combat action badge and military combat coins from his brigade and the 82nd Airborne Division.

"You know, a lot of people will want to see you and talk to you," Colonel Garrity said. "Tom, you need to take care of her, and, if it gets to be too much at times, be her voice. Your wife's a real hero, and you're both going to have to get used to being rock stars for a while."

But Bergan felt like anything but.

Meanwhile at FOB Walton, the soldiers in Bergan's platoon were back out on patrol.

★

February 27, 2010. Landstuhl, Germany

Bergan's rook sister, First Lieutenant Meghan Kiser, waited outside Bergan's hospital room with a large gift bag until a doctor finished talking with Tom. She had no idea of what to expect, but she was intent on not showing any reaction. As she entered the room, she gave Tom a hug and started to tear up, but she didn't want Bergan to wake up and see her crying, so she blinked back her tears.

When she had heard Bergan was wounded, Meghan had lain awake all night, worried and anxious to know when her friend would arrive in Germany. Landstuhl Regional Medical Center is the largest American military hospital outside the United States and treats soldiers wounded in Iraq and Afghanistan before they head to the States. Meghan was stationed in an air defense battalion nearby. After graduation she had married a Norwich classmate, who was also posted to Germany.

"How're you both doing?" she asked Tom, as Bergan slept.

"She needs a couple more surgeries before we fly to the States," said Tom, who was unshaven and wearing the same uniform he'd had on when he'd heard Bergan was wounded. After seventy-two hours with no sleep, the nurses had made him take a sleeping pill and put him on a cot on the plane to Germany.

"Berg . . . Berg . . ." Tom said. "Look who's here." As Bergan woke up, Meghan started to speak, but Bergan opened her arms.

"Come here," she said, and the two friends hugged.

Bergan seemed alert, so Meghan showed her things she had brought from the PX—basic toiletries, a sports bra, underwear, and comfortable workout clothes, along with some stuffed animals. She also got her a small Vera Bradley cosmetics bag. Both were big fans of the colorful accessories, and she thought Bergan would enjoy having something feminine.

Before helping her get dressed, Meghan wiped the blood off Bergan's face and arms with cleansing wipes she'd also brought with her.

"Can you do something with my hair?" Bergan asked. "It's all messed up." Matted with hair spray, it hadn't been cared for in three days, and that bothered her greatly. Hair spray was a necessity for many women in uniform in order to maintain a polished appearance, but the cans were never in stock at the large base exchanges in theater. Bergan's mother sent her a steady supply, along with care packages of chocolate. Bergan had gone through at least eight bottles of the stuff since arriving in country seven months before.

"I can't get a comb through it with all this hair spray!" scolded Meghan. "It's flaking apart."

Meghan stayed late that night, then returned the next morning and helped pack Bergan's things for the flight to the States.

"You're coming with us, right?" Bergan kept asking.

"I'm not allowed to, Bergan," Meghan said, wondering whether, with all the medication, it had really sunk in to Bergan that she'd lost her leg. "But I've got a four-day in April, and I'll come to see you then. I promise."

Weather and Bergan's low oxygen level caused a day's delay, but finally she was approved to fly out.

On Monday, March 1, Meghan and Tom helped lift Bergan's stretcher through the back door of a white school bus, which was used as an ambulance to transport the wounded between Landstuhl and Ramstein Air Base.

"I love you," Bergan said to her rook sister.

"I love you, too, Berg. I'll see you in April." Then Meghan watched as the school bus pulled away.

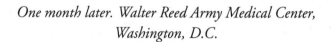

One month later. Walter Reed Army Medical Center, Washington, D.C.

Bergan sat in her wheelchair outside in the sunshine on Walter Reed's 113-acre campus, surrounded by spring's bounty. An unattached IV needle was inserted in her arm. The smell of freshly cut grass wafted through the air, as Bethany and her mother rolled her past rows of orange tulips that sat on sturdy stems in tidy rows that led to the hospital's main entrance. Azaleas just starting to bud in bursts of pink lined the perimeter of the campus, forming a boundary with a run-down section of D.C.

It was everything Afghanistan was not, and yet that was where Bergan longed to be, back with her soldiers in a godforsaken place, doing a job few would want to do, marking off the days on her calendar until their mission was complete. She'd been fitted for her prosthetic leg earlier that week and was already able to walk across the parallel bars during physical therapy.

Amy had been in Washington helping to care for Bergan in her fifth-floor room ever since Bergan arrived back in the States. Amy hadn't been sure if she'd be sick or scared when she saw her daughter for the first time. In fact, what struck her was how small Bergan looked, and she hadn't expected her daughter's face to be so battered. After a round of hugs and kisses, Bergan flung her blanket back.

"Mom, this is a damn Christmas ham," Bergan said as she kept hitting her stump. "It's a damn Christmas ham."

"Oh, Bergan," Amy said, though she had to admit it did resemble one.

From her hip down, Bergan had a ten-inch stump, and with each surgery she lost a little more bone.

As an official caregiver of a wounded soldier, Amy was "on orders" with the Army and had her travel, lodging, and meals covered; her husband, Billy, came down every few weeks. Each morning Amy took a bus from her hotel in Silver Spring, Maryland, to be with Bergan. And after Bergan started suffering from pain and was ringing for a nurse to bring medication throughout the night, Amy and Tom traded off sleepless nights on a chair in the room, relieved by Bethany when she was visiting.

It wasn't always smooth going. Tom, as her husband, wanted Bergan to be strong and independent, while Amy, as her mother, pacified Bergan. Meanwhile, Bethany was affected more deeply than her mother realized. She withdrew into herself, but one day she blurted out, "We'll never be the same again. We're not the same anymore."

"You'll always be the same," Amy assured her, even as she realized that a part of Bethany was missing, too.

The three continued to soak in the spring sunshine.

"What a gorgeous day," Amy said.

"Mom?" Bergan said. "Can we go back inside?"

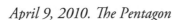

April 9, 2010. The Pentagon

"I'm going to stand," Bergan said. "I'm not sitting."

Amy looked at Bethany.

"How are we going to do this?" she asked. The first lady was going to be there any minute. The three had come with fifty other wounded warriors and their families for an unpublicized procession that takes place monthly through the Pentagon corridors. That morning hundreds of employees, military and civilian, from janitors to generals, lined both sides of the hallway as Amy pushed Bergan in her wheelchair amid a throng of other wheelchair-bound service members from Walter Reed. As they passed, cheers erupted.

Some of the patients struggled to walk. All had visible wounds; some had no limbs. But all held their heads high. Many employees reached out and shook Bergan's hand, offering a hug to Amy or a pat on the back and a thank-you. The clapping was deafening.

For Bergan, it was both humbling and nerve-racking. Humbling because people genuinely cared, nerve-racking because so many generals shook her hand and she wasn't able to jump to attention.

Bergan remembered what Colonel Garrity had said, but she still wasn't used to all the attention.

Now, during lunch in one of the Pentagon's private dining rooms, a guide had announced to the group, "We might have a special guest." It was Michelle Obama's first visit inside the Pentagon since her husband took office the previous January. She strode into the room wearing a white spring dress with bold blue, pink, yellow, and purple flowers, under a thin yellow cardigan. The first lady was prettier in person—and taller—Amy thought. In heels she was over six feet tall.

When it was Bergan's turn to meet her, Bergan rose so fast from her wheelchair that Amy and Bethany never got a good grasp on her, and Bergan fell toward the first lady, who helped catch her.

"What a strong young woman you are," the first lady said. "You make me want to work out. I'm very proud of you." Mrs. Obama gave each of them a hug and then moved on to the next family.

It wasn't the first time Bergan had exerted her independent streak. Despite the nurses' warning her not to attempt to stand in her room unassisted—the boot she had to wear was slippery on the bottom—Bergan was stubborn. She loved being up and around. And PT was her favorite part of the day. Talking with other amputees who understood what she was going through lifted her spirits. Bergan was the only woman in her rehabilitation program and the quickest on her artificial limb. She was so determined that the therapists and the relatives of other wounded soldiers told her that their guys always moved faster and worked harder when they saw her doing laps around the room with her walker.

Bergan had a reason to work so hard. She had promised herself she would stand, walk, and welcome her soldiers home when they returned to Fort Stewart that summer.

May 31, Memorial Day, 2010. Tupper Lake, New York

Kneeling on the floor, Amy tried and tried again to get Bergan's Army boot onto her artificial foot.

"Make it look right!" Bergan pleaded. She was staying in the downstairs bedroom, since there were too many steps to get up to her old room.

They had spent the last fifteen minutes trying to get Bergan's camouflage ACU pants on over the socket of her new prosthetic leg. Pants she'd normally wear didn't fit, and larger ones gaped around her waist. Bergan decided to wear a pair of altered ACU pants with a zipper along the leg that the occupational therapists at Walter Reed gave every amputee. But she thought the zipper made her look like she was out of regs. And that was the last thing Bergan wanted to be.

"It doesn't look right, Mama!" she said, as Amy tried to blouse Bergan's pant leg around the boot. "Make it look right."

Amy wasn't sure how that would happen, since Bergan had no shin or calf, and her artificial limb was made of metal rods, but she was trying her best. It was the first time Bergan had been in uniform since she'd been wounded three months earlier. Amy knew Bergan wanted to look perfect, always. Especially on a day like today.

She was the guest of honor for Tupper Lake's annual eleven a.m. Memorial Day ceremony, downtown at the war monument on Park Street, next to the old State Theater, whose marquee announced, "Welcome home, Bergan" above the movie offerings—*Shrek Forever* and *Prince of Persia*.

Bergan hadn't been back in Tupper Lake for almost a year. The doctors at Walter Reed had granted her a four-day weekend convalescent leave pass, but recurring infections had made the trip a touch-and-go proposition.

Tom couldn't be there because of his duties with the 3rd U.S. Infantry Regiment, "the Old Guard," in Arlington, Virginia. The Army had a signed him there as a platoon leader, which allowed him to be close to his wife as she rehabilitated.

Bergan was walking, but only at physical therapy, since she still had open wounds. Her therapists allowed her to take her prosthetic leg home to Tupper Lake as long as she promised she would put it on only for the ceremony. It wasn't a hard promise to keep, since it was still painful to wear.

She realized she probably wasn't ready to be out in public yet, shaking hands, making small talk, and getting interviewed by the local TV stations and newspapers, but Bergan was insistent about being there. She wanted everyone to see that she was all right, and she especially wanted to stand up and say how thankful she was for everyone's support.

Ten days after her injury, the town's veterans' organizations and business council had sponsored "Bergan's Day at Big Tupper," a ski event followed by a spaghetti dinner fund-raiser, with proceeds going toward the family's travel expenses.

"Bergan Flannigan, Our American Hero!" read a large poster outside the ski center, with a smiling photo of Tom and Bergan in uniform from happier days.

But "hero" was far from how Bergan saw herself. Though everyone said they were so proud of her, she couldn't help wondering, *For what?*

"I'm no hero," she told her mom. "I let my platoon down. It shouldn't have happened."

To her, the real heroes were the soldiers she'd left behind in Afghanistan. Platoon leaders are responsible for the health, welfare, morale, training, and leader development of their troops. *I let them down*, she thought. *I left them hanging there. . . .*

Six weeks ago, as Bergan was weaned off some of her medications, she had moved into Mologne House, a hotel for outpatients and their families on the Walter Reed campus. She found the place depressing and cramped during visits. And living outside the hospital meant she also had to start doing things for herself. Bergan grew bitter as the reality that her life had changed truly sank in. Mostly she was angry at herself for not noticing the IED. She knew she should be thanking God it didn't kill her, but she just couldn't do it. Instead she kept thinking, *How could this have happened to me?*

There was a lot of speculation about what had actually happened. The unit knew the attack had been planned, because it had been videotaped, while Bergan wondered if it was payback for her calling out the Afghan police officer for touching her the day before she was wounded. In any case, she believed she was targeted because she was a woman in charge. She didn't take any guff, and the enemy knew it.

If they wanted to eliminate women officers, however, they would be thwarted. The new platoon leader who replaced Bergan was Lieutenant Lisa Ernst.

After two months by Bergan's side, Amy knew her sick days had run out, and she had to return to New York. Bergan found that hard to accept. She didn't want anyone around her except her mom. Looking at Tom only reminded her of her life before she was injured.

"I don't want to live," she'd tell her mother over the phone as she battled infections and chronic pain. "Can you come down?"

Still, Bergan always managed to pull herself together when VIP tours and groups—everyone from Kathy Ireland to the pop rock band Train—came through Walter Reed. On those occasions she returned to platoon leader mode and told her story.

But now, on Memorial Day, half-dressed, with nothing fitting or looking right, Bergan was starting to crumble.

"I don't think I can do it, Mama," she said, bursting into tears.

"Yes, you can. You'll be fine," Amy said. "But if you don't want to, you don't have to."

"No, I want to," Bergan said, as she dried her eyes. "I don't want to disappoint anyone."

"Well, then we've got to get you dressed," Amy said. After five more minutes she paused and asked, "What do you think?"

Bergan looked at herself in the mirror, zeroing in on the zipper and the lack of fullness around her leg. Her boot and pant leg looked like they were cinched around a broomstick handle. Tears streamed down her face.

I'm not a soldier anymore. I'll never be one again, doing what I love.

"It's time to go," her mom said.

Bergan put on her black beret and sunglasses, despite an outdoor haze that was the result of Canadian forest fires. She didn't want anybody to see her reddened eyes.

She may have been Tupper Lake's hometown hero. But she was filled with uncertainty over all that had happened, as she wondered about what came next and tried to envision the road ahead.

CHAPTER 22
Stars

Angie: March 2010. Fort Myer Officers' Club, Fort Myer, Virginia

 The social hour was coming to an end. As the roomful of Marines moved to their tables for dinner, Angie's cell phone vibrated, and the word "Commandant" flashed onto the screen.

"Excuse me; I have to take this call," she told her colleagues as she hurried out into the hall.

Angie was sitting on a reserve policy board, which was part of a two-day conference at Fort Myer, Virginia, a historic Army post on the banks of the Potomac that shares a border with Arlington National Cemetery and offers panoramic views of Washington, D.C.'s national monuments.

She had been stationed at Quantico for seven months, and unlike her controversial arrival in San Diego, this time she walked into her job with instant acceptance. Traditionally, the director of manpower management, a two-star billet, has been an influential position filled by a combat arms general. In recent years, though, the job had become a revolving door, a holding place, of sorts, for generals about to move into postings in Iraq or Afghanistan. Even a colonel had once been at the helm for a year. Angie's predecessor had left in June, which left a three-month gap before her arrival.

Manpower management was Angie's occupational field, and she knew what the business was about. Once the corps named her director, people knew she was someone credible who could lead the organization, especially with the Marines going through challenging times with budgets and downsizing.

Angie spent a good chunk of her time at events and meetings in D.C., which was forty-five minutes north of Quantico. Rumor was that President Obama had already signed the list of Marine brigadier generals selected to rise to the rank of major general. The scuttlebutt had been confirmed earlier that week, when General James Conway, the Marine Corps commandant, started his round of calls to congratulate the selectees.

"Did you get the call yet?" a brigadier general had asked Angie excitedly. "I got mine."

"No . . . " Angie said.

"I'm sure you're gonna get the call soon, Ang."

Angie wasn't so sure about that.

Her peers had been receiving the congratulatory messages all week. But there were only eleven spots, and twelve Marine brigadier generals up for promotion. One would *not* get selected for a second star, and Angie thought there was a good chance she was "it." The others had all been to "the fight" in Iraq and Afghanistan.

Even though her current job was usually held by a major general, she knew you couldn't assume anything when it came to promotion boards. Nor would the Marine Corps bend to the pressures of promoting a woman or a Hispanic to fill a quota. The institution wanted the best-qualified Marine. At the general-officer level, promotions were not as much about what one has done but what one can still do. Angie thought she was too specialized.

This is it, she thought. *I'm going to be a one-trick pony. . . .*

She was trying to be a realist.

"Hello, sir. This is Brigadier General Salinas speaking," she said into her cell phone when she reached the hallway.

"Hey, Angie, you probably already know this," General Conway said. "I'm about ready to release the public announcement of the major general selects. Congratulations, you're on it."

The commandant assumed Angie had seen the promotion list, since she was the director of manpower management, but she'd had no idea.

"Thank you, sir, for the opportunity to serve," she said. "I'm honored and humbled by the selection, and I appreciate your support."

A few days later the list became public, and phone calls, e-mails, and cards quickly stacked up. So much so that Sergeant Major Bobby Woods had to leave a congratulatory voice mail until he was finally able to get through and actually speak to Angie.

Pending Senate confirmation, Angie would be promoted to major general in a few months. She would become only the fourth woman to achieve the rank of major general in the corps, and the only female general on active duty in the Marines. In 2011, Marine officer Lori Reynolds would be promoted to the rank of brigadier general and become the first woman Marine to command units in a war zone (Afghanistan). But in the near future the potential for other women Marine officers, who make up about 6 percent of the force, to reach flag rank isn't high. The number of female Marine generals is not expected to increase over the next four to five years, though as more opportunities open for women Marines, the figures could change.

To Angie, being chosen for a second star was validation. To the naysayers and doubters and all those who thought she'd been lucky the first time, she'd proved she could perform with the very best. She had passed the real test.

Three weeks later. Marine Corps Base Quantico, Virginia

As predictable as the setting sun in front of her, beltway traffic on a Friday was a mess as Angie made her way from Reagan National Airport some thirty miles down Interstate 95 to Quantico. She was returning from a two-day trip to Parris Island, where she briefed officers as part of their Professional Military Education (PME) on promotion statistics, selection boards, and commands. As a general officer, Angie was cognizant of not wanting her presence to be a burden on another command, so she kept her visit brief.

After three years of "making Marines" on the West Coast, Angie enjoyed the opportunity to talk with Parris Island officers about their careers and to demystify the process of how promotion and command boards work. But for her, the visit to the South Carolina depot was like opening a yellowed scrapbook. To be sure, except for the screaming of the drill instructors, much had changed since 1974, when recruit Salinas had gotten off the bus in the middle of the night and stepped onto the island.

Back then, since the draft had just ended, the Marines were looking for a few good women. Attractive women, though the Marine Corps would never admit to that publicly. Unlike male recruits, who could resemble Beavis or Butthead, women had to submit a photo with their paperwork. If they were accepted, the picture would be stamped "Approved" at higher headquarters. Female applicants also had to be high school graduates and score fifty or higher on the Armed Services Vocational Aptitude Battery, a multiple-choice test that "measures developed abilities and helps predict future academic and occupational success in the military." Guys could get by with a score of eleven and could enter boot camp if they had a GED or had gotten through the tenth grade.

Angie remembered Lieutenant Jill Berle and her drill instructors—Sergeant Hodson, Sergeant Exworthy, and Gunnery Sergeant Gonzales—as if it were yesterday. Their uniforms were free of wrinkles, not a hair was out of place, and, as far as she could tell, they never slept. But they were DIs in name only. Until women were admitted to Drill Instructor School three years in the future, their official titles would remain platoon sergeants and platoon leaders.

During Angie's second week at boot camp, the drill instructors informed the female recruits that they would attend a garden party on Sunday at 1400 hours, after services. Dressed in the uniform of the day—ugly blue culottes, baby blue shirts, and tennis shoes—Angie and the others rushed back to the squad bay to put on their lipstick before the party. (In those days the Marines actually issued the women makeup kits instead of rifles.) Then the women hurried back out to stand in formation. The women had classes on how to apply makeup, how to walk like a model, and how to sit like a lady, so it seemed logical they'd have a garden party. Angie was looking forward to it.

At 1400 on the nose, the drill instructors handed the women rakes, brooms, and clippers to police up the barracks grounds.

"Here's your garden party! Welcome to the Marine Corps!"

The female recruits did have a tea party, however, just before graduation. They not only got to practice their social graces by chatting up commanders and other officers over punch and coffee, but they also were graded on their mastery of etiquette.

In 2010 beauty school boot camp was unthinkable, and Angie remained good-humored at the memory of it. But other lessons she kept close to her heart, like her brief interaction with Gunnery Sergeant Gonzales, a Hispanic Marine who held a position of authority over the other DIs. Angie, who may have been the only Hispanic recruit in the platoon, never had a conversation with Gonzales until the day before graduation, when the stern gunny called Angie into the DI hut. The other recruits had selected Private A. Salinas for the Molly Marine Award, which is given to the person in the platoon who "best exemplifies the meaning of being a Marine." Angie received a foot-tall statue of a female Marine in a knee-length skirt and fitted jacket with tie and cap, holding a book with binoculars at the ready. The statue is a replica of the ten-foot original in New Orleans that was commissioned to help recruit women during World War II.

Angie imagined the gunny would tell her how proud she was, since they came from the same roots.

"Recruit Salinas reporting as ordered," Angie said, standing at attention before the seated drill instructor.

"Congratulations on becoming a Marine," Gonzales said. "Now go!"

Angie remembered thinking, *I'm a Marine. I'm not a Hispanic Marine. I'm a Marine.* Gonzales had clearly conveyed the message that whatever connection Angie was looking for was secondary to their bond of being in the corps.

By 1996, when Angie took command of the 4th Recruit Training Battalion, Parris Island's female drill instructors still lacked one sign of their status: There were no Smokey Bear hats on their heads. Instead women DIs wore a bucket hat and a scarlet shoulder cord. Thanks in part to some behind-the-scenes maneuvering by Angie, that was about to change.

A female corporal who was a combat engineer at Camp Lejeune sent the Marine commandant an e-mail, wanting to know why women DIs couldn't wear the campaign cover.

"They do now," the commandant replied, making the corporal the public face of a policy change that had already been in the works. It was a good story, the kind the Marines loved, despite the fact that male drill instructors weren't happy about it.

In truth, Angie had cut a deal with the commandant, ensuring that women would be able to wear "the hat" before she agreed to take charge of the all-women's training battalion. She was happy to have the young Marine receive the credit, though, as she didn't want the issue to be about Angie Salinas; nor did she want to be perceived as the commandant's girl.

Two months after Angie assumed command, on October 2, 1996, General Chuck Krulak flew down to Parris Island for the "cord retirement ceremony," as it was being billed, a huge event held at Tun Tavern, a large gym on the depot. Angie stood at attention in front of her battalion formation as General Krulak entered. He made a beeline for her.

"Here," he said, handing Angie a paperback book. She looked down. It was a Harlequin romance novel with Fabio on the cover.

Angie looked at the general, waiting for the other shoe to drop.

"Can we work on better PME reading?" Krulak asked. Professional Military Education reading is a rank-based recommended reading list in the Marine Corps.

A red tint crept across Angie's face. During visits, Krulak was known to go where people least expected him. In this case he had walked around 4th Battalion's squad bays and plucked the novel from a female recruit's gear.

Nevertheless, after the ceremony the scarlet shoulder cord had a new home: the depot's museum, where it remains on display today.

Angie had spearheaded other changes, too. She received approval to activate a fourth company, P Company, to more effectively train female recruits and manage the battalion. She also got the women's official battalion color—pastel "Carolina" blue—changed to burgundy. To Angie, the 4th Battalion's "baby blue," as she called it, seemed wimpy, unlike the male battalions' bold colors. (Ironically, in the Army, the shade is called "infantry blue" and is worn by the still-male-only infantry branch units.)

The new color put it in line with the men's hues: 1st Battalion's deep red, 2nd Battalion's deep yellow, and 3rd Battalion's navy blue. The first time the women drill instructors walked into a training meeting wearing their Smokey Bear hats and burgundy sweatshirts, their male counterparts just stared.

It was important to Angie that the 4th Battalion be an extension of the other battalions, not a separate women's entity. She was all about the message: Marines are Marines are Marines—just as Gunnery Sergeant Gonzales had gotten across to Angie years ago.

Angie had almost reached Quantico. The Marine base, nestled in the Virginia pines between I-95 and the Potomac River, is known as the "Crossroads of the Marine Corps," since most Marines pass through the base a number of times throughout their careers for schools and training. For Angie, it was her third time stationed there. She had traded Quarters One for another stately home, this one on Generals' Row, a cul-de-sac of white-clapboard, black-shuttered homes with portico columns and Potomac views. Ten days after she moved in, her car (which she'd shipped) arrived with all the farewell gifts she'd received during her final days in San Diego.

Angie carried the "memory box," the gift from Bobby Woods and RhodaAnn, up to her bedroom suite. *Open this at home*, she remembered the sergeant major saying. Finally she had a home, albeit one that was still buried under unpacked boxes.

She took a seat at her desk and unwrapped the jewelry box. She opened it and started reading a note: "Thank you and your family for sharing your life with us. Calamari and margaritas! Never thought I'd be chowing on that. We had an absolute wonderful ride together. I was always told as a sergeant major you take care of your boss, and keep them out of trouble. I think you took better care of me. I will always cherish your leadership and friendship. THANK YOU."

On another slip of paper the sergeant major had written, "Habitat for Humanity, one of the most rewarding things I've ever done."

Angie realized then that the sergeant major had made her a better person, a better commander, and a better Marine—and she had done the same for him. The memory box was "a feel-good little box" that became Angie's most treasured secret possession, something just for her, that she could go to for comfort after a tough day.

Angie slowed down as she approached Quantico's main gate, which consisted of a brick guardhouse and a steel canopy with lights that expanded over the road like a horseshoe. She rolled down her window and handed her military ID card to the guard.

"Attention on deck!" the Marine yelled. He saluted as all the guards came to attention.

The guard returned her ID card. "Have a nice day, ma'am."

"Ooorah. You, too, Marine." It was a source of frequent frustration when she drove onto the base, but she had learned to pick her battles carefully, and this wasn't one she was going to take on.

Despite the one-star decal on her windshield, indicating she was a brigadier general, the guard assumed Angie, who was dressed in civilian clothes, was a general's wife and asked to see her military ID card. Angie had often been a passenger in vehicles driven by male generals in civilian attire. Upon seeing the windshield sticker, the guards never bothered to ask for ID cards and immediately brought the sentries to attention.

Because she was a woman, she didn't always get that courtesy. She could have made a big deal out of it, but she didn't want to leave the sentry with a lasting impression of a female Marine as being "the Big B," as she called it.

Angie realized she had a reputation for being stubborn and hard to get along with. In some circles she had become known as "Sister No," thanks to people asking for money or resources that weren't within policies and directives. Only Angie could grant an exception to such rules, but she had no problem turning down requests. She could look herself in the mirror and know she was doing the best she could for the institution.

Angie's job required that she execute the commandant's guidance on how to use resources, which are people, not just assignments. Her office oversaw awards, records, promotions, separations, and retirements—everything that touches a Marine from beginning to end—and the impact of war on the corps can be seen in the thousands of Purple Hearts it has awarded since 2003. Her staff handled posthumous promotions for Marines who were already on a selection or promotion list, so they could be buried with their higher rank. And when asked to do so, they also snooped out fakers, such as public figures and others who lied about or embellished their war service records. Her office accessed all the 800,000 service documents and records dating back to 1775.

May 11, 2010. Marine Corps Base Quantico, Virginia

"I think I'm going to die today," said Angie's mother, Florita.

"You can't, Mom," Angie said. "I'm not married yet." Florita sat at the kitchen table as Angie prepared her two packs of oatmeal, which was her mother's daily breakfast.

"Who are you again?" Florita asked.

"Mom, it's Angie."

"But you're too old!" her mother insisted.

The ninety-six-year-old had done better than her daughters thought she would during their cross-country move to Quantico. But when they arrived at their new house, it was like the lights went off in their mother. She never managed to adjust and often asked, "When are we going home?"

The previous week Angie had hosted a Cinco de Mayo party in her backyard, and many of her siblings came in for the party and to celebrate Mother's Day. Angie hired a mariachi band, since her mother always loved to hear the music. But Florita had to be coaxed out onto the back porch, and it was evident she was there only in body.

"Can I go to bed now?" she had asked.

Every day Angie followed the same routine. After her daily run in the basement, and before heading to work, she woke her mother at six, changed her adult diaper, washed the linens if they were soiled, bathed, dressed, and fed her mother, and often put her back to bed. Janie took over caregiver duties for the rest of the day. Some at her office said Angie didn't know what it was like with kids, but in many ways she did.

On the West Coast Angie had been the queen bee in her own hive. At Quantico, however, Angie was one of eight generals on the base, each with his or her own area of responsibility, and the highest-ranking wore three stars. Unlike at Pendleton Hall, where Angie had her own headquarters building, she shared Quantico's Marsh Building with three other generals.

Later that morning the administrative assistant rushed into her office.

"The oh-eight list was approved, ma'am!" The Office of Legislative Affairs advised the General Officer Management Office that the Senate had approved the Marine Corps major general slate. There was no time to waste. Her promotion to one-star status had been planned in advance with programs and a reception, but this ceremony would go down more like a shotgun wedding. E-mails, phone calls, and word of mouth spread the word that the promotion would be tomorrow at 1500 at the Clubs, which housed the enlisted, senior NCO, and officers' club lounges on base.

That night, at home, Angie pulled out a small box that her mentor, Lieutenant General Walt Gaskin, had given to her the previous year. Gaskin had promoted Angie to brigadier general in 2006, and he evidently had been more optimistic about her selection than she had, because the box held the two-star rank insignia.

Angie stared at the stars.

This is it, she thought. *My last promotion.* She had been saying that ever since she pinned on the rank of lieutenant colonel.

But in truth, she never thought this would happen, to go from private to major general in thirty-six years of service.

She closed the box and set it aside for Wednesday's promotion. As a woman Angie had many firsts in the Marine Corps. She had satisfaction in knowing she would not be the last.

CHAPTER 23
The Afghan Trimester

Candice: June 18, 2010. Kansas City International Airport

⭐ "Mommy, your eyes are leaking!" four-year-old Kate proclaimed, as she blotted her mother's tears one by one with a tissue. Major Mike Hammerstrom's wife, Gala, came to the airport prepared with a box of tissues, which Candice borrowed liberally. Kate slid off her mother's lap and pulled another tissue from the box, while Tom, who had turned two just a couple of months earlier, in April, jumped on and off the other half of his mother's lap.

Gala was so strong, sitting there with her five-year-old twin boys, Candice thought. Joining them was another classmate, Major Juan Nava, and his wife. In recent years airports had allowed military families to stay together in terminals during deployment good-byes and reunions. The three officers were traveling in uniform, and the other passengers could tell this was no ordinary good-bye.

The men's eyes welled, too, but Candice's face streamed with tears as they waited to board their midmorning flight from Kansas City to Atlanta.

She tried every technique she could think of, from taking deep breaths to pointing her face upward in the hope that gravity would sink the tears back into her head. But then a stray one would slip out.

"Don't cry, Mommy! It's okay," Kate said. "See, smile."

Kate showed off an exaggerated smile, revealing a mouth full of mini-Chiclets teeth. Over and over she tried to tickle her mother under her chin, which only brought more tears.

The children, whose worlds revolved around Mr. Potato Head, Play-Doh, LEGOs, and Dora the Explorer, understood little about their mother's leaving the country for a year. The O'Briens had told Kate that her mother was going away for a long time. But at her age, five minutes seemed an eternity.

The night before, Candice had bathed the children together. When she took Tom out of the tub, she wrapped him tightly in a towel and used him as a weight for arm curls, while singing a made-up song called "Baby Burrito." It always made Tom laugh, and he begged his mother to do it every night. Later she read a book to each child. She had just finished singing "Danny Boy" and Kate's favorite, "You Are My Sunshine," when Kate asked, "Mommy, sing that song in Spanish."

"It's German, honey," Candice said. Candice studied German in high school and for two semesters at West Point. Ever since the children were babies, she'd sung a soothing German love song as a lullaby.

As she sang, she sat on the couch and stroked their faces until Kate and Tom fell asleep in her arms. That was what Candice would miss most. She loved having them fall asleep on her and feeling their breath on her skin. It was like the breath of little angels.

Regardless of that emotion, Candice's decision to volunteer for Afghanistan was based on the facts. She hadn't deployed in five years, and it was her turn to go. The previous September she had brought the SAMS assignment list home and showed Will.

"Here are the options, but the point is moot," she said. "We can fill in the top ten, but I'm going."

While no spouse is ever thrilled about a deployment, Will understood the rationale behind the decision and supported it. It was a matter of Candice's picking her own poison: Volunteer for a corps-level position and deploy in a job and place of her choosing with a known time line, or choose an assignment with one of the infantry divisions, which would likely still mean a deployment somewhere at some point. Candice saw volunteering as a way of having some control over her future. She always believed that if everyone in the Army took their fair share of the deployment pie, it was manageable. That Christmas, Candice submitted her choice to the Army.

More than ever, she grasped the meaning behind the motto that she and her classmates had voted on as seventeen- and eighteen-year-old plebes at West Point: Duty Will Not Wait.

Since Will's parents lived only forty-five minutes from Fort Leavenworth in Sugar Creek, Missouri, it made perfect sense to Candice that Will and the kids would move in with them and have some needed support in her absence. Will had never lived alone with the children, except during four days when Candice was on temporary duty in Key West for a SAMS assignment. And those four days proved to be a lot for Will to handle. During a "freak-out" phone call, with Kate screaming hysterically and Will shouting at the child over something minor, Candice had to get both of them on the phone to calm them down. *There is no way I can deploy for a year and have this happen over and over again*, Candice thought at the time.

But what made perfect sense to Candice did not to Will. While he welcomed the help, he wasn't eager to live with his parents again.

"Living with your parents is the right thing to do," Candice reassured her husband over and over. He would need a support system. If he wouldn't consider living in Iowa at the cabin, near her parents, that meant his folks. Will finally relented.

Now, at the airport, Will sat to Candice's left and pulled at his shirt collar. Yes, he knew it was hard for a mother to separate from her children, but there were easily 150 people in the waiting area, he was hot, and, as far as he was concerned, the kids were going ape shit. There was a point where you were just prolonging the suffering for everyone involved, and it was time to kiss good-bye and go, Will thought. They had already passed that threshold.

When it comes to deployment good-byes, military families fall into two categories: Will was a get-out-of-the-car-and-go, it's-okay-to-look-back, but-don't-draw-it-out kind of guy. Candice was a lingerer. She just wanted to hold on tighter to Kate and Tom.

"Delta flight twelve seventy-two nonstop to Atlanta . . . now boarding all rows. . . . "

The last moment together had arrived. Candice hugged the children as much as she could and gave Will a hug and a quick kiss. Then she picked up her duffel bag, which contained a box of Crayola-colored markers, so she could make the kids cards that night. As Candice walked down the Jetway with Juan and Mike, her private thoughts slipped out, "This sucks."

Candice had heard civilian women, including military wives, tell her they couldn't do it—leave their four- and two-year-olds for a year. That never occurred to Candice. It was her duty; she had to do it.

★

One month later. Kabul, Afghanistan

Candice always tried to give as many compliments as possible in the ladies' room. It was hard to be chipper so early in the morning, but she would rally a, "Your hair looks great," or, "Go rock it today," to the other women. Just thinking something positive seemed to help, since everyone was struggling with exhaustion or lack of sleep. Candice often worked from seven a.m. until midnight. The women's bathroom was the one place where servicewomen could congregate and have a conversation—maybe the only one all day—with another woman.

At six in the morning, Candice headed there now. It was Wednesday, hump day, although the days of the week didn't really matter. Weekends didn't exist in war zones. Saturdays felt like Mondays. Every day felt like Monday.

The United States and NATO now had 143,000 troops on the ground in Afghanistan, with another 7,000 arriving by August for a counterinsurgency effort against the Taliban and al-Qaeda. An average of two to three troops died each day. By the end of 2010, 499 U.S. troops would be killed, making it the greatest loss of American service members to date in Afghanistan.

Candice was under a different kind of stress than were officers in tactical line units. Working on a staff at the operational level of war meant that she was constantly handling multiple plans and projects within a condensed time line, always striving to ensure that what she planned was feasible and attainable. She knew that the orders that derived from her work would be executed by her peers and former subordinates.

On top of it all, at month's end WikiLeaks released tens of thousands of classified documents on the Afghan war effort, an act that Washington said would endanger informants' lives.

Candice had just finished her morning run along the camp's concrete-and-steel T-walled perimeter, which provided the camp with blast protection. Kabul was suffused almost completely in gray and brown, with the exception of sunrise and sunset, when the sky bled with brilliant hues. Candice always tried to be outside then, running in the morning and eating dinner as the sun set. She always enjoyed a good rain; it made everything look clean again.

On this morning, sweaty and dust covered, she was looking forward to a shower. Candice still marveled that the bathroom was just down the hall from her room. Merely having a bathroom and a room to sleep in was a change from her deployment in Afghanistan five years earlier, when she was constantly covered in dust, slept in a tent, used a portable toilet, and had to walk out a quarter mile to a shower trailer—assuming she happened to be at a base with showers. In those days, out on patrol, Candice and the other women had to use empty widemouthed Gatorade bottles as a substitute for a toilet, something that wasn't an issue for men.

Dressed in her gray PT shirt, black shorts, and sneakers, Candice made her way down the coed hall, laden with her standard brown towel, flip-flops, hair dryer, curling iron, and shower bucket. A big load for what Candice termed "the morning clean." As she approached the bathroom, she cracked her eyes open a bit wider.

"What the . . . ?"

Standing like a statue in front of the bathroom was a hairy Frenchman in his late forties, dressed in nothing but black Speedo-like underwear, with a sizable belly collapsed over it like a roof. Candice gripped her hair dryer tighter and stood face-to-face with the pudgy man, who was her height. The Frenchman didn't move, and the two played a game of *poulet*.

"Ahem . . . " Candice said finally, pointing with her shower bucket to the women's door behind him. The man turned to look at the door.

"Oh!" he said, inching aside.

Inside the women's room, Candice glanced at her reflection in the mirror.

"This is unbelievable," she said.

The walk to the showers in the morning was always interesting, since Greek, French, and Italian male NATO officers in their forties and fifties weren't used to wearing much. They'd saunter by in small towels or skimpy underwear.

It was all part of living in "Bizarro Land," the name Candice and Mike Hammerstrom coined when attempting to describe life at the International Security Assistance Force Joint Command (IJC) at the North Kabul International Airport. The IJC served as the operations center for much of the war effort and was responsible for operations throughout Afghanistan. While choreographing missions for frontline troops, the coalition members from armies around the world roomed and worked together, sometimes with noticeable friction. Each service branch in the U.S. military and the coalition partners had their own respective cultures, which compounded the complexity of planning at the operational level and added to an already pressure-filled environment. Candice's studies at Fort Leavenworth certainly hadn't covered this side of coalition war.

As if a harbinger of off-kilter things to come, news broke on June 23 that President Obama had fired General Stanley McChrystal, the top U.S. commander in Afghanistan, after a *Rolling Stone* article attributed insulting comments about administration officials to McChrystal and his staff.

It was a shocking moment for Candice and the other SAMS planners, who were at Fort Benning for a week of training before heading to Afghanistan. They knew that when the boss changes, so do the plans, which meant they would be walking into an environment where an operational plan might have to be redrafted based on a new commander's guidance. And they would be the ones to do it.

Within hours of arriving at IJC after three days of grueling nonstop travel, it was clear Candice wasn't in Kansas anymore. As Candice struggled to keep her eyes open, Major Mandi Bohrer, a West Point classmate (and fellow redhead) who had arrived in Afghanistan four months before, grabbed her and Mike and sat them in the back of the Future Plans room.

"Wait here," Mandi said to the two weary travelers. It was nice to see a familiar face, Candice thought. She'd last seen Mandi on SAMS graduation day. Mandi's entire house had been packed up, and the family had a trailer ready to go in the driveway. Military life is full of good-byes and reunions, such as this one, in unusual places.

Moments later, a tall, lanky officer swooped into the room, picked up a fly swatter next to a coffeepot, and started going mad with the thing.

Candice and Mike glanced at each other.

The officer continued to slash at the air, killing several flies.

"Add three to my total," he said. And with that the officer walked out.

The champion fly killer happened to be Brigadier General Michael Linnington, who would be promoted to major general in a week and would become the new coalition joint planner, Candice's boss.

The two majors, now fully alert, looked at each other again.

"I know I'm tired," Candice said, "but did I just see a general killing flies? What in the world goes on here?"

Three weeks after that initial descent into the NATO rabbit hole, following her shower, Candice trekked back to her room without further incident and was greeted by the familiar smell of perfume.

"Hallo, Kan-deeece!" said a tall young woman with olive skin dressed in a red bra and matching undies edged in black lace. Anree slipped into her khaki uniform. As usual she was doused in perfume. While it was a pleasant enough smell, it was odd for a combat zone. Ditto the lace lingerie. Unlike the loose American Army ACUs, which hid guts and girth, French uniforms were cut so tight you could see the outlines of underwear.

"Good morning," Candice said as she placed her shower bucket on the floor and her toiletries on the desk. The piece of furniture, with its three drawers, held all Candice's clothes, since her two French roommates had claimed the two available closets.

"You like some tea?" offered a second young woman, Renoir, whose English was much better than Anree's. Renoir pointed to the electric water boiler, which the women used as a kettle. Renoir had wrapped her stocky five-foot frame in a fluffy yellow-and-blue robe that she liked to wear down the hall to the shower. She, too, wore lacy undergarments under her uniform.

"Oh, *merci*," Candice said, which was about the extent of her French. "I don't have time today. I have to get to work."

"You work too hard," Renoir said as she nibbled on a biscuit, the European name for a shortbreadlike cookie. "Here, have a candy." Renoir always offered Candice candies. "How are you doing?" she asked.

Candice smiled. "I'm doing well."

There was no way she could explain to anyone the amount of stress she was under. *"Merci,"* Candice said again, as she took the hard candy. Between her roommates and her French boss, Candice joked she was glad she'd taken years of German.

The sound of planes taking off and landing filtered through the room. The base had the busiest airfield in the country, and military and political bigwigs—including President Obama, Vice President Biden, Secretary of State Clinton, and numerous lawmakers—frequently passed through.

As Candice changed clothes, her roommates chattered in French. While most American male officers on the base roomed with officers from Germany, Poland, or Italy, the American female officers often had foreign junior enlisted roommates, due to a shortage of rooms for women and the fact that NATO women made up only 7 to 8 percent of their countries' armies. That meant the three were stuffed into what should have been a two-person room, crammed with two sets of bunk beds. As the new arrival, Candice had one top bunk, and she used the other to store her four duffel bags of combat gear.

The Frenchwomen had little gear, but they slung their weapons over the bunks' metal posts as if they were overcoats. They worked eight-hour

290 ★ UNDAUNTED

shifts in the geographic intelligence cell, making overlays on maps for planning operations. Candice considered their deployments almost like summer jobs, since the Frenchwomen were there only four months before rotating out. Candice couldn't help but feel a twinge of anger at the fact that three different people would rotate through a job during her one year in theater. Their minimal investment in the blood, sweat, and tears of Afghanistan made it difficult for Candice to relate to them. Still, she was proud to meet women serving in other countries' armies, and her two young roommates were kind and polite and always asked about Candice's kids.

Renoir looked above Candice's desk at the ever-growing collage of photos and crayon drawings taped to the wall.

"How can you do it, leave your kids and support a family?" Renoir asked.

Sometimes people inquired out of pity or scorn, reactions many military mothers encountered, but Candice found that these two women genuinely couldn't fathom the American military, where women rose in rank through a meritorious system and could perform almost all of the same jobs as men. For Anree and Renoir, that didn't fit within their paradigm of possible career paths. The French had yet to recognize the contributions of its servicewomen in the way America had.

What the roommates didn't know was that it hadn't been easy. Candice recognized that she sometimes got brash unnecessarily because she'd had to swim against the current for so long. Will would tell her, "I'm not the one you have to fight against," when she pulled out what she called a "superfeminist" reaction to something.

Candice had been the "token" female in most of her jobs. She never took it as a token to fill a quota, but instead as a token for someone to point to and say, "See, we have strong women who can hang with the guys and do it better."

Later that night, after work, when her roommates were asleep, Candice Skyped with Will and the kids. Sometimes conversations were easy, other times not. The week before, Kate had had an especially tough day, and Candice had to sing all three verses of the German love song to calm her. She'd also sing on the phone if Will sent an e-mail asking her to call immediately. Like other deployed mothers she did whatever she could to remain involved in the daily lives of her children, while balancing the demands of the war mission. Along with holding Skype sessions, Candice mailed a card to Kate and Tom every day, dropping it into the paint-chipped and padlocked box outside her office.

"When are you coming home?" Kate asked as she bounced on Will's lap, wrestled with Tom, and peered at her mother on the computer screen.

"A really long time from now," Candice said as her heart started to break.

Candice had forty-eight weeks left in Afghanistan. Counting days was too depressing. Counting months was also depressing, but weeks made it seem like a long pregnancy.

Candice was in her first Afghan trimester.

★

One month later

After hours of long meetings in Future Plans, Candice scurried outside to coordinate with the guys in the Information Dominance Center, the fusion center for intelligence in Afghanistan. The Afghan parliamentary elections were just one month away, and Candice was assigned to the elections planning team as one of a special group that followed the process from the formation of the Independent Elections Commission through publication of the results. After the grossly contested Afghan presidential election in 2009, everyone was focused on corruption and fraud. But this was an Afghan election led by Afghans; the international community was there primarily in a supporting role or in case military assistance was needed.

The problem was Candice's French boss, team leader Lieutenant Colonel Anton Dubois. Smirking, arrogant, insular, and easily intimidated, Dubois barely made use of his team, never asking for feedback or else ignoring it. In the French Foreign Legion, Dubois had been a stellar performer, but in the context of the NATO big picture, with military planners from the United States, the U.K., and Australia who had experience in a number of war zones, Dubois was out of his depth.

Lieutenant Colonel Dubois's English wasn't strong, and when he spoke, the colonels and generals in attendance would roll their eyes. No one could understand what he was saying. At meetings where election experts were needed, Candice and Mandi would accompany the generals and make sure the job got done.

As she walked outside, Candice winced in the blinding light and replaced her glasses with her extra-dark prescription sunglasses. Kabul was always hot and exhaustingly bright. Yet the glare didn't seem to bother one certain military group.

In the half-size soccer field adjacent to the headquarters building, rows of Belgian guards with skin the shade of vanilla ice cream were lapping up the sun like raisins. They wore nothing but tight Speedos. As soon as these men finished their eight-hour shifts providing security to the camp, out to the soccer field they went. To Candice they looked like beached whales.

But she had more pressing matters. Candice's job was to attempt to predict the likely contentious areas of the upcoming elections. With more than a thousand polling centers, that task required the focused collection of intelligence, surveillance, and reconnaissance on the high-threat areas. And doing that depended on devising a plan to focus key assets in key areas.

Candice was assigned to work with Major David Zhang, a half-Chinese Canadian who had recently arrived in Afghanistan and was in charge of collection management (CM). A short, chubby artillery officer, Zhang had recently converted from the Canadian Navy to the Australian Army, which had a shortage of midgrade officers. However, in hiring Zhang, who lacked a background in intelligence work, the Aussies had made a mistake.

As September approached, it became apparent that intelligence gathering on contentious polling stations wasn't in motion.

"What collection plan?" became almost a running joke in the office.

Several times a day Candice tried to find Major Zhang, a task in itself, since the office area where he worked was under renovation. Zhang had no desk, and he hot-seated from place to place.

Candice was in her own cubicle in Future Plans when U.K. Army

Major Andy Williams stopped at her desk. "Candice, have you seen the revised collection plan?" he asked in a Scottish brogue.

Candice stood up. "It's all smoke and mirrors," she said, a little louder than she should have. "There is no specific dedicated collection plan for the elections."

"CM said it's done," Williams replied.

"Well, they're blowing smoke up your ass, because it doesn't exist," Candice said.

Like a bat swooping out of a cave, Major Zhang suddenly appeared between the two officers and faced Candice.

"I've had enough!" Zhang said, muttering incoherently. "There is a fucking collection plan! It is working, just because *you* . . . "

Zhang extended his left hand like a dagger and struck Candice on the right side of her chest, above her breast and below her collarbone. She lost her balance, stumbled, and fell backward. She looked at her chest and then into Major Zhang's black eyes.

"Back down, Captain!" Candice said pointedly, as if commanding a disobedient dog to sit. She had accidentally added insult to injury by demoting the major one rank. Before she could launch into a verbal ass chewing, though, Andy Williams and an American officer, Major Joel Vernetti, grabbed Zhang under his arms and moved him away. It looked as if he were being escorted out of a bar by two bouncers.

Candice stood there dumbfounded a moment; then she started to follow.

"No, don't go out there," said Major Vernetti, who had returned. "Andy's got it."

Candice stopped and looked around, as everyone else went back to work. Few American officers—and none of her chain of command—were present.

What the fuck? Candice thought. *I was just hit, and it's back to normal. This isn't right.*

Candice marched off to speak to a trusted friend, U.S. Navy Commander Seth Walters, who worked in the Information Dominance Center. She stood at his desk, white and shaking. He instantly knew something was wrong and grabbed his hat.

"Let's go for a walk," he said.

"I'm totally shocked," Candice said. "After thirteen years in the Army and seventeen in uniform, I've never, ever had anything like this happen."

"Write everything down," Seth advised, "but first you have to calm down." Candice was still seeing red.

"Why don't you go for a run?" he said.

She took his advice. But afterward she was still furious. By then she had missed dinner and returned to her office.

Lieutenant Colonel Dubois spotted her as she walked in. "Come with me," he said. Dubois rarely came back to work after dinner, which often prompted jokes about the French going to war only in daylight hours, but here he was. Candice followed him outside. The wind had picked up and swirled dust like the white flakes in a snow globe.

"I heard what happened," said Dubois, who, as usual, had his hands planted in his uniform pockets (not exactly military bearing in the U.S. Army). "I am very mad. I will kill him with my own hands."

Okay, thought Candice, *that's a bit extreme.*

"But you must still work with him," added Dubois in the next breath. He couldn't help but read the look on Candice's face.

"I demand you will work and finish the elections!" Dubois said.

Candice's bottom lip started to quiver, but she was damned if she was going to let him see her cry.

"Sir, I will not work with Major Zhang after he hit me."

"You must!" Dubois insisted. "We will get beyond it and work together."

"Sir, would you ask your wife or daughter to work with a man who just assaulted her?" Candice said. "Would you even respect a boss who told her to do so?"

Dubois stopped to take that in. "Do not file a complaint until tomorrow," he said. "You must sleep on it."

Candice walked away. This was just too much. But she was facing a mountain of work. As the IJC's main counternarcotics planner (in addition to her elections role), she was facing a briefing with Lieutenant General David Rodriguez in the morning, and the following day she would present the information to General Petraeus. She couldn't afford to lose more time.

Candice went back to her desk, furiously diving into data, statistics, and speculations on the upcoming year's poppy harvest. Afghanistan is the world's largest opium producer, supplying 90 percent of the world's heroin, and opium poppies finance the Taliban.

As she worked, she overheard Dubois talking with Major Zhang's boss, Colonel Murray, a U.S. Air Force officer.

"We are very sorry for the things Candice said," Dubois was saying. "She was wrong to accuse your shop of not doing the collection plan."

Candice slammed both her hands down. She stood up, took a sworn statement she had typed, and made two copies—one for Dubois and one for Colonel Timothy Russell, the British cavalry officer who was the deputy coalition plans officer. She dropped the papers on their desks and then went to find Mandi and another friend, Deb Phillips, an Australian intel officer.

Once outside, the women ran into Colonel Russell. Tall, skinny, and bald, Russell had an uncanny resemblance to the villainous Mr. Burns from the TV show *The Simpsons*. But he could tell something was wrong.

"Khan-dice," he pronounced in a proper British accent, "are you upset about your upcoming briefing to Lieutenant General Rodriguez? I know it was sprung on you—"

"No, sir," Candice said. "I'm upset because I was assaulted, and Lieutenant Colonel Dubois told me I had to work with the jerk."

"What?" Colonel Russell asked. Candice explained what happened, and Colonel Russell took the action she'd expected of a real commanding officer. He informed American and Australian leadership, and Major Zhang was immediately removed from working on the elections.

Later that night, Deb, Mandi, and Candice formed the "CWG," the Cigar Working Group, and for their inaugural meeting Deb pulled out some cigars that a friend had mailed to her. As passersby gawked, the women shared stogies on a bench out by the smoke pit. In front of the bench stood the Afghan Good Enough tree. It was little more than a leafless, four-foot stick protruding from the ground, covered like a rash with inch-long stubs instead of limbs. It was obviously dead, but the women held out hope.

Everyone called things "good enough" in Afghanistan. As in the country was "good enough" to stand on its own. This little tree was "good enough."

September 9, 2010

Candice woke up in a sour mood. A stomach virus was snaking through the base. A number of people were hospitalized and needed IV bags. She had already been to the care clinic but felt it was her duty to just suck it up and keep working. With the elections less than ten days away, meetings, briefings, and presentations jammed her days from early to late. On top of it all, Candice was applying for a doctorate program and working on a thesis overview. If accepted, she would start work on credit hours during the deployment.

It wasn't until later that she noticed the date on a calendar and realized it was her tenth wedding anniversary. She wished she could have started off the day snuggling with Will. Still, she thought that making it this far was an accomplishment for both of them.

"We've lived in four countries, five states, and ten houses or tents between the two of us," she wrote in her journal during a break that day. "We made two beautiful children and continue to grow old together."

But the satisfaction of being Mrs. Candice O'Brien took a hit that night when she called Will on her cell phone as she walked home after work at eleven.

"Happy anniversary!" Candice said.

"Happy anniversary," Will said. "Your parents are really pissed about an e-mail I sent."

"What e-mail? What did it say?" Candice hadn't checked her unclassified e-mail all day.

Will had sent a lengthy note to his in-laws and wife, setting boundaries and insisting, among other things, that taking Kate out of preschool for several weeks to visit Nana in Iowa was not okay with him. He wanted everyone to speak with one voice when it came to Kate.

"Really, on our anniversary?" Candice said.

"I wrote it; it's done. They'll get past it," Will said.

"I can't believe you just did this, Will," Candice went on. "I'm not feeling good, it's our anniversary, I'm busy at work, and now my parents are hurt. Thanks for this anniversary present."

Back in her room, Candice called her parents.

"I can't even talk about it. I'm so distraught," her mother said in tears. "Will accused me of wanting custody of the children during the deployment. All I had said was, 'We'd love to see the kids more. We miss them so much.' We tried calling him, and he's not returning our calls."

Even Candice's even-keeled father was distraught. "What possessed him to do this?" he said. "Why would he write this?"

From her bunk bed, still feeling sick, Candice took it all in—hurt parents and a continually raging husband. She remained determined, though. She would fix her marriage—sandbag it and save it, just like she helped save her cabin from the Mississippi River.

Meanwhile, she still had the stress of the upcoming Afghan elections to contend with. She knew she was only as good as her last plan or briefing. She never doubted her ability, though her confidence had been rattled several times. It was just that she'd been rowing the boat so hard without a break for so many days. She always reminded herself that no matter how hard she had it, the guys carrying out the operation plans had it even harder. She didn't feel sorry for herself—she just kept rowing.

CHAPTER 24
The Long Road Home

⭐

Bergan: July 21, 2010. Hunter Army Airfield, Georgia

⭐ Bergan and Tom stood on the flight line at the bottom of the plane's stairs, behind a row of higher-ranking officers and NCOs. The moment she'd been waiting for and working toward had finally arrived. She had been determined to be up and walking when her soldiers got home. She'd had seven surgeries and more recurring infections. But she was going to be there no matter what.

As for the 293rd Military Police Company, it took several days of flying with stops in Kyrgyzstan, Romania, Ireland, and Bangor, Maine, before the plane finally touched down on Georgia soil on July 21.

Bergan wore her ACUs for the first time since the uniform malfunction on Memorial Day. This time around, with Tom's help, it was a little easier getting dressed.

At the beginning of June, the Flannigans had moved out of Mologne House and into quarters at Fort Meade, Maryland. Every day Bergan took the shuttle bus from the Army post to Walter Reed. But the ride quickly got old, and one day in July, Bergan asked Tom, "Can you take me out driving tonight?"

She quickly got the hang of driving with her left foot. For the ten-hour drive to Fort Stewart, however, Tom drove, while Bergan napped.

Now she tried to harness her emotions; she was so nervous.

Inside the plane, Specialist Beebe—he'd been promoted after Bergan was injured—was nervous, too. Captain Thurman, the company commander, had told the soldiers before they left Afghanistan that the Flannigans would be there for their arrival. For some reason Beebe had never been so nervous in his life. All he could think about when he thought of Bergan was loading her onto the helicopter and watching it rise into the air.

What if she's different? he wondered.

Finally the aircraft door opened. Southern Georgia was just as they'd left it a year ago—a dripping ninety-six degrees. As Captain Thurman bounded down the steps, Bergan broke down in tears.

After a big hug, he told her, "I expect you to command an MP company someday, Bergan."

"Yes, sir," she said, quickly regaining her composure.

"We missed you so much, ma'am," said Sergeant Thomas, as he leaned over and gave Bergan his own huge hug. "There's not another LT like you. Thank you for your dedication to your platoon. You're walking really well," he added.

"I've been working on it," Bergan said.

"Ma'am, that new LT wouldn't make me noodles at seven in the morning," Sergeant Thomas went on.

Bergan laughed. "That's because she's not your ma." Bergan had had a hot-water boiler in her room in Afghanistan, and on the occasional morning off, Sergeant Thomas would wake her so he could eat ramen noodles for breakfast.

Specialist Torres was next. "Ma'am, I didn't tell you this before, but we love you. You've had a great impact on me. On all of us. Your leadership and your ability to drive us toward goals . . . the feeling of comfort you gave us, it's rare to find in the Army. Thank you."

On and on it went. When Specialist Beebe got off the plane, it was still hard for him to look his old lieutenant in the eye.

"Ma'am," he said, shaking Bergan's hand, so scared, happy, and nervous at the same time that he could barely talk.

"Beebe . . ." she replied, and the two hugged as best they could.

In no time Bergan had a crowd of soldiers around her, even though they were supposed to get into formation. She wasn't just their leader; she was family.

Finally, Doc Newman rambled off the plane. He and Bergan hugged but spoke few words. Then everyone piled into buses for the ride to Fort Stewart, where their families were assembled.

Bergan's parents sat in the back of the bleachers, surrounded by people overcome with happiness. The Arsenaults had flown in for the occasion, as had Tom's parents. Bittersweet as it was, their children had asked them to come. This was the way their homecoming was supposed to be.

When the buses arrived, the soldiers lined up in formation behind the field, with Bergan and Tom in the back row. Ten minutes later the company passed through a row of pine trees, formed back into ranks, and marched across Cottrell Field to their waiting loved ones.

"I'm having trouble," Bergan said. "I'm not going to be able to keep up."

"We'll get you across the field, ma'am," said Master Sergeant Shaul.

Tom took Bergan's crutches, and she leaned on him and Shaul as they crossed the enormous parade field. Captain Thurman's words played over in her head, kindling a new resolve.

I expect you to command an MP company someday. . . .

Bergan had already been back in the States for five months, but at that moment, she finally felt home.

CHAPTER 25
Diva in Boots

Amy: October 2010, Parris Island, South Carolina

Amy's recruits had no way of knowing October was the deadliest month so far in 2010 for the corps, which lost eighteen Marines and a Navy corpsman in Afghanistan. So far that year, 132 Marines and four corpsmen had died in combat as part of President Obama's counterinsurgency offensive in Afghanistan. Having returned fire when her convoy was fired upon and earned the combat action ribbon, Amy knew all too well the very real dangers her young charges would face.

But first, she had to make them into Marines.

The sixty female recruits in Platoon 4038, Oscar Company, stood at attention in a line at the center of the squad bay, stripped down to their bras and underwear.

"Start turning and don't stop!" Amy ordered. The former Marine Corps truck driver–turned–drill instructor was now on firm footing at Parris Island. Still sleep-deprived but no longer frazzled, she'd been tested, and the proof was in her swagger.

Sunburned and sweaty, the recruits obediently turned in tight circles, scruffy versions of plastic ballerinas swirling inside satin-lined jewelry boxes. The recruits, most of them just out of high school, pulled at their brassieres to show Amy and the other DIs, Staff Sergeant Tammy Wood and Staff Sergeant Theresa Estrella, that they weren't hiding any bullets there.

From the drab green-painted floor to the rifles slung over the rows of metal bunk rails above worn wooden footlockers, the squad bay looked like it came straight from a movie set, except that its occupants were all women.

"You *stink*!" said Staff Sergeant Estrella, the senior drill instructor. With a disgusted look on her face, she plugged her nose and sprayed air freshener around the women. The DIs had just finished searching for live rounds in the recruits' gear and cammies, which were behind them near the bunks. The bra inspection was actually the third ammo check that day.

The first had occurred out at the firing range, before the platoon hiked back to the squad bay. The young women had to shake out everything—canteens, cammies, magazine pouches, belts, and hats—in front of Amy and Staff Sergeant Woods. Each recruit then ran up individually to the senior DI, who wielded a metal detector.

"No brass! No trash! No saved rounds, ma'am!" each recruit screamed while spinning around.

During rifle qualification, the recruits had more pat-downs than prison inmates. The reason? With the exception of chow, the recruits took their rifles with them everywhere. And the drill instructors didn't want to end up like Gunnery Sergeant Hartman, the DI in the movie classic *Full Metal Jacket*, who was blown away by a wild-eyed recruit in the latrine.

Getting smoked by a recruit was a frequent topic of conversation among the drill instructors. Rifle range training occurs during phase two of boot camp, at the halfway mark. The mantra "Every marine a rifleman" means that the women, like the men, must qualify to graduate in one of three categories—marksman, sharpshooter, or expert (the top category). By this point in the training, any loony tunes recruits had been weeded out and sent home, and the remaining recruits had some loyalty to their drill instructors.

They may not like us, but they respect us, Amy thought.

But nobody wearing a Smokey Bear hat was willing to bet her life on it. Earlier that day, as the recruits, lying prone, fired their M16s at 500-yard distances, Amy and the other green belters kept their distance, out of sight of the firing line. Meanwhile, among the equipment that the recruit squad leader carried was an olive drab–colored ammo can, a metal-lidded box filled with tampons and pads. Many recruits don't get their periods during boot camp because of emotional and physical stress. But for those who do, just as in combat, it is an added stressor, because the women barely have time to use the bathroom at all. The tampons apparently had other uses as well.

"Whitaker, are you serious?" asked Staff Sergeant Estrella, as the platoon was about to start drill practice on the parade deck the previous week. "What is that?"

Staff Sergeant Wood turned her back to the recruits and covered her face with her hat to hide the fact that she was laughing. The DIs took a few breaths to regain their composure.

Everyone in the platoon looked at Recruit Alexis Whitaker, who tried to explain why she had a tampon stuffed up her nose.

"Ma'am, this recruit gets nosebleeds all the time, ma'am!" Whitaker had been frantic to do something fast, and Recruit Gina Castro had pulled the tampon out of her pocket.

Amy smiled and nodded her head. "Adapt and overcome," she said. "And get that thing out of your nose!"

Now Amy wanted them to hurry before chow.

"All right, get dressed!" Amy said. "Now! *Moooove!*" The recruits scrambled like ants back to their bunks and put on their damp uniforms in a specific order: trousers, T-shirt, blouse, then boots, left boot first, with laces left over right, then the right boot. In the Marine Corps, everything was left, then right.

"Did you hear me?" Amy shouted. "I know what I said, 'cause I was there when I said it!"

After her six platoon cycles as a drill instructor, Amy's voice was as raspy as an autumn night's wind rolling in from the Atlantic. But her scream was always pitch-perfect. She was no longer a "new hat," which was evident by her stance. She walked and talked like it was her business to make Marines. The recruits considered her a "badass," the highest compliment one could receive at Parris Island. And after three platoon cycles as a fourth and third hat, she'd been promoted to the position of "heavy hat," which was the heartbeat of the platoon, responsible for teaching drill and getting the recruits to the right place at the right time, with the right gear. Since graduating from DI School, Amy, who was already a black belt, had graduated from the Martial Arts Instructors Course. She had long ago moved out of Saleem's apartment and gotten her own place. It was time to cut ties. She was married to the corps now.

"I hear voices," Amy said. "And they're not in my head!" Under her fringe of false black lashes, she eyed the recruits. Amy stood akimbo, her acrylic French-tip nails contrasting like pearls against her camouflage uniform.

Beauty wasn't bashful at Parris Island; it was bold and badass. The message Amy wanted to get across to her impressionable recruits was, "Yes, we are Marines, and, yes, we are drill instructors, but first we are women—not men."

To prove that point, Amy, like all tiny-waisted DIs, accentuated hers by cinching her green web belt so tight that she had to take it off when seated in the DI hut so she could breathe.

The drill instructors made sure they were looking good. The DI bathroom could have been in a sorority house. Tubes of hair gel, hair spray bottles, flatirons, blow-dryers, vent brushes, and makeup compacts battled for counter space, with bobby pin casualties scattered on the floor. An Oscar the Grouch garbage can was the only indication that this was no ordinary girls' primping room.

To a woman, the DIs wore their hair long and pinned up in "sock buns," a Marine Corps specialty 'do that required snipping off the toe line of a sock, rolling the fabric into a doughnut shape, and wrapping and winding a ponytail's worth of hair around it. The result was a perfect, plump bun. Amy had to forgo the sock, though, because her hair was too long and thick and would have stuck out farther than the Marine Corps' three-inch bun limit.

The process of looking good could be painful. On some Sundays, the gunnery sergeant—despite protests—made her DIs wear skirts, so the recruits had the opportunity to see how they were worn. But modeling the outfit made for an excruciatingly long and uncomfortable workday.

The smooth tucked-in shirt the Marines are known for required undercover theatrics. Both male and female DIs used two shirt stays, an inverted Y-shaped garterlike contraption that clipped to the bottom of the front and back of the shirt hem, ran down each leg, and clipped onto the top part of each sock. On Sunday skirt days, however, the women DIs had to cross the shirt stays between their legs and cinch them tight to ensure the shirt remained in place. For a painful eighteen hours the DIs ran after recruits in skirts and panty hose and uncool flat shoes. And if there was one thing a DI didn't want to be, it was uncool.

Meanwhile, the gunnery sergeants, who didn't wear the DI belt, got to have comfortable untucked shirts with their skirts and fashionable pumps. Amy wondered why skirts were even part of the DI uniform to begin with, since they were impractical for drill field duty.

In contrast to the DIs, the recruits weren't allowed to wear makeup, except before graduation, when their individual photos in their dress blues were taken. Those with short hair all sported the same shaggy style that looked like the barber had used a pair of orange Fiskar scissors. Those who wore glasses (no contacts allowed) had their last names typed on white paper and taped to the left arm of their glasses. Some of the recruits had tape along the bridge holding broken glasses together.

The recruits hadn't expected their drill instructors to be so pretty. They also looked harmless—like jellyfish. It gave them the false impression that boot camp wouldn't be painful. Staff Sergeant Wood sported a Winnie the Pooh tattoo on her ankle; how bad could *she* be? The recruits in Platoon '38 had their answer soon after they arrived in September, when the DI team came into the squad bay like storm troopers and circled the women like sharks.

One day at the beginning of the cycle, Amy and Staff Sergeant Wood had the platoon's flag carrier, a twenty-three-year-old recruit named Castro, against the wall crying. She had messed up at something, and they were laying into her so hard that the recruit was losing her voice from yelling and crying. Staff Sergeant Estrella saved her by calling off her drill instructors. But the episode made a lasting impression on the new recruits. If it could happen to Castro, who was the oldest, a college girl, and a track star, what would it mean for them?

Amy tried to instill lessons with her discipline. One evening when the platoon was at chow, she caught a recruit on fire watch sitting down on duty. A few other recruits were also in the squad bay, designing a flag for the platoon guidon. Amy made those recruits eat an orange slice with mustard on it from a boxed dinner.

"You should have said something," Amy said. "And here's why . . ."

She told a story about a driver on a convoy in Iraq. The passenger wasn't sitting all the way back in her seat and was hanging her arm out of the window.

"They hit an IED," Amy said, as the recruits listened intently. "The driver was fine; the passenger wasn't so lucky. That driver always has the guilt of not telling her passenger to sit back in her seat, because she didn't want to sound uncool, when she could have saved a life."

The recruits' eyes grew wide. "It might not look like a big deal that fire watch was sitting on duty, but anything can happen," Amy said. "The lesson is, you should always do the right thing no matter what."

Amy didn't tell the recruits *she* was that driver, and she had changed a detail to make her point. Six years earlier, when Amy was a lance corporal just two years out of high school, she was a driver in a convoy, and her passenger was a corporal who outranked her, a female Marine from the supply detachment whom Amy admired. It was the corporal's first convoy, and she was seated forward, manning her weapon out the window and exposing her upper body and face above the truck's L-shaped armor on the windows.

Man, I have to tell her to sit back, Amy thought. But she didn't want to say anything, because she was afraid she'd come off as a "belligerent Marine" and a know-it-all to someone higher-ranking. As the corporal chatted about missing her daughter back home, and Amy wondered whether she should say something, the truck struck an IED, and Amy and the other Marines were soon firing their weapons after being fired upon. Because the IED hit on Amy's side of the truck, the truck's armor protected her, and she was unhurt. Had it hit on the passenger side, the corporal would have been killed. Amy believed God was sending her a message, and she passed it along to her recruits.

There were lighter moments, too. One night during mail call, Recruit Samantha Evers, who at six feet tall was the tallest recruit and not as girlie as some of the others, went up to get her mail. "Recruit Evers, all mail received . . ."

"No," said Amy. "You have to say, 'Recruit Ogre, all mail received.'"

Trying not to laugh, Evers gathered her military bearing and what she hoped was a serious look on her face. "Recruit Ogre, all mail received! Aye, ma'am! Good evening, ladies!"

As she made her way back to her rack, the other recruits bit their lips and stifled their smiles. Amy had nicknames for several of the women. Recruit Williams was Recruit Snotty, because she was always looking up during drill. Recruit Wright was Recruit Wrong, since she didn't do anything right and was always pissing off the drill instructors. Then there were Marshmallow, Chicken Little, Olive Oyl, and SpongeBob.

That evening, at eight, with the recruits in their racks, Amy yelled, *"Lighttsssss!"*

"Lights! Aye, ma'am, good evening, ladies!"

Amy closed the DI door, known as the "hatch," and in the darkness the recruits screamed, "Good evening, Drill Instructor Sergeant Stokley!"

Amy reopened the hatch. "I hate you, 'Thirty-eight!" Then she slammed it shut.

It was her parting shot whenever she was on night duty, and the recruits would have been sad if she didn't say it.

Four a.m. the next morning

Dressed and ready to rumble, Amy woke up Platoon '38 with the usual, *"Lightssssss!"*

The recruits, who slept in their racks in an alternating head-to-foot pattern (to reduce spreading illnesses), sprang to a seated position of attention, like mummies rising from their sarcophagi.

"Lights! Aye, ma'am! Good morning, ladies!"

The recruits had gone to bed wearing "green-on-green" PT clothes and white socks, but had to wake up wearing brown boot socks. That meant quietly changing footwear after lights-out. A recruit was not to question but to do.

Once fully dressed, the women made head (toilet) and water calls.

"Port side!" Amy said.

"*Port side!*" screamed the recruits on the left side of the squad bay.

"Starboard side!" Amy said.

"*Starboard side!*" screamed the recruits on the right.

Port side screamed louder, so they got to use the head first, while the starboard side recruits made water calls, which meant filling up their canteens. The recruits had to always have two full canteens and were supposed to drink twelve canteens' worth a day.

"Eighty . . . seventy-nine . . . seventy-eight . . . " Amy counted down. When she got to "two," the recruits were to be online at the position of attention. At "one" the recruits had better be as stiff as Popsicles on sticks. Then, after making their racks with eighteen inches of white sheet folded over green wool blankets with hospital corners, the recruits knew what was coming next.

"When I say, 'Move,' you will grab your scuzz brushes and return online," Staff Sergeant Wood said. "Ready . . . *move!*"

The recruits ran and grabbed their "scuzz brushes," six-inch wooden-handled hard-bristled brushes, and returned online, holding the tiny brushes in their right hands, arms parallel to the deck.

"When I say, 'Move,' you will run to the back of the squad bay," Wood said. "*Move!* Five . . . four . . . three . . . two . . . one!"

"Done, ma'am!" the recruits yelled from behind their racks. "*Scuzz!*" Wood yelled. "Sixty . . . fifty-nine . . . fifty-eight . . . "

And with that, the recruits assumed the low squat of a duck position and waddled with one hand behind their back, palm outward, fingers extended and joined, toward the center of the squad bay, brushing under their racks and in between them. It was like trying to sweep the floor with a hairbrush, but with sixty people the job got done.

In the center of the squad bay, the recruits made multiple piles of refuse. Then a few recruits used dustpans to finish the job.

Finally it was time for chow. The recruits lined up in formation outside, trying not to scratch, as pinging sand fleas, known as "flying teeth" in some circles, bit into their flesh like razor-blade nicks.

"Let them eat!" Amy yelled, in her usual power stance of hands on hips, with her DI cover tipped ever so slightly forward. "They have to eat, too!"

It was still two and a half hours before sunrise, but Amy wasn't happy that the platoon was running a few minutes late for five a.m. chow. The male recruits from Hotel Company, 2nd Recruit Training Battalion, were already marching, which meant the females would have to march double-time to beat them to the front of the line.

The males took forever to eat and were allowed larger food allocations than the females. Since chow out at the rifle range—where the recruits were spending their days for two weeks—was first-come, first-served, getting behind the men meant a limited food selection.

The rifle range was the first place that the males and females actually were near one another. Since the two companies were on the same training schedule, they would also do the rappel tower, gas chamber, basic warrior training, and the crucible (a simulated combat exercise) together.

"Take them shoes off yer teeth and quit runnin' yer mouth!" Amy warned.

"Double tiiime!" she shouted. "Forward! Stand tall . . . lean back . . . maaarch!"

The recruits were supposed to keep "forty inches back to chest" from one another, while maintaining "cover" (staying directly behind the person in front) and "alignment" (staying even with the person on the left and right). But on this morning double time turned into a high-spirited schoolgirl race to beat the boys.

Recruit Kara Ann Kessey almost broke her neck stumbling over rocks, and Recruit Mariah McClain somehow managed to keep up on her short legs while carrying the water cooler. The food wasn't the greatest, but at this point in the cycle, it was starting to taste really good.

The women hated eating with the men at the range, the only time they shared a chow hall. It was hard to watch the guys wolf down cake, cookies, and brownies. Recruit Sarah Wilson, who, at four feet, eleven inches, was the shortest in the platoon, was tempted to grab a cookie, but she knew she'd get chewed out. The best she could hope for was a banana. And those always ran out early. As the women ran by in formation, laughing, Hotel Company's recruits looked at them as if they were crazy. To the males, the 4th Battalion was more like the fourth dimension.

Once in line and out of breath—and ahead of the males—the women, with their cheeks flushed and shoulders heaving, stared at the wall in silence.

"Fucking Fourth Battalion, so disgusting . . . " a male drill instructor said, as he walked by, out of earshot of the female drill instructors. The women continued to stare at the wall. Their DIs did not allow them to look at the males.

"Boys . . . don't do it," Staff Sergeant Wood warned the women. "You look at them, and you're pregnant."

Even at Sunday services the male and female recruits were segregated, sitting on separate sides. But church was the one place and one hour each week where the DIs didn't have their eyeballs lasered on the recruits. So sideways glances and looks were exchanged, and the occasional note was passed between the pews. Still, the females were too scared to try to talk to the males. They were suspicious of the Navy chaplains' assistants. Someone was always watching.

Later that morning, at the range, despite the warnings of Sergeant Marco Martinez and the other male drill instructors, Hotel Company's recruits couldn't help but sneak peeks at that creature known as the female DI.

"We've never seen one of those before," was the usual reaction.

Amy was checking target scores. But like a cat stalking prey, she was ready to pounce when she walked by and male recruits didn't issue the proper greeting.

"Did you get a good enough look? Are you done?" she asked two male recruits who were several inches taller than she was. "Keep your eyes ahead and to the front. You're representing your platoon, and you're embarrassing your senior DI."

"Aye, sir!"

That sent her from zero to a hundred. "Oh, do I look like a man to you? *Do I sound like one, too?*" Amy said, with her face tilted upward, her jaws ready to chew off the recruit's chin. "I guess it's 'cause I'm female, you don't show the proper respect?"

"No, sir!" It was a hard habit to break and an unfortunate mistake for the recruit.

"Really? How 'bout you say something! Get out of my face, you disgusting piece of crap!"

"Aye . . . ma'am."

"Scream! Scream, 'Aye, ma'am!'"

"Aye, ma'am!"

"Get back!"

All recruits were fair game, even if Amy couldn't "incentive train" the ones that weren't hers. All she could do with the males was blast them and correct them. Getting yelled at by a female DI was embarrassing, in any case.

Amy went back to checking scores, but not before she overheard a male DI rubbing it into his recruit.

"You had to let a Fourth Battalion Marine correct you?"

Amy didn't care. She knew she was the real deal, and she was training Platoon '38 to carry themselves the same way. Her cockiness had rubbed off on them. As far as her recruits were concerned, the "O" in Oscar Company stood for "Outstanding."

They were the best company in 4th Battalion, known for their drill skills and taking good care of their uniforms. Papa Company was known for their hair and looking pretty. That was why they were called Pretty Papa or Pussy Papa. And November Company, well, they weren't good at anything; they were just Nasty November.

By this point in the cycle, Amy's platoon was marching better, and she wanted to show them off. And the recruits wanted to make her look good.

Drill is at the heart of the Marine Corps, and through practice and repetition it instills discipline, bearing, confidence, and proficiency, important things that resonate beyond the parade deck.

Drill was always about more than a "left, right, left" thing for Amy. It was about life. She taught the recruits not only how to be good Marines but also how to be good women. Every day at the range she marched the platoon back and forth, back and forth, always in front of the male drill instructors.

Amy: "Lean back!"

Recruits: "At the waist!"

Amy: "Lean on back!"

Recruits: "And strut!"

Which they definitely did with Sergeant Stokley.

Later, as the recruits sat on the bench behind the firing line, waiting for their turns to shoot, Amy walked down the line helping them record their shots in their data books.

First Sergeant Toshia Sundermier, who sported a blond bob under her campaign cover, pulled up in her car.

"Sergeant Stokley, I need to see you."

Ah, shit, Amy thought. *What happened now?* She made her way over to her company first sergeant.

"The regimental sergeant major approved your package," Sundermier said. "Congratulations. You'll be a senior DI for the next cycle."

Most senior drill instructors were staff sergeants. Since Amy was still a sergeant, it meant her chain of command had confidence in her ability to lead at that level despite her rank. Amy maintained her military bearing in front of her first sergeant, but inside she was bursting with excitement.

Four weeks later

On a rainy evening in late November, Platoon '38 sat in the squad bay, cleaning their rifles. The recruits were preparing for Final Drill, and for inspiration they were watching video performances of the Marine Corps Silent Drill Platoon, a twenty-four-member all-male team that performs with spinning rifles and fixed bayonets.

During the Final Drill competition on the parade deck, one platoon competes against another, and a drillmaster grades both the platoon and the senior drill instructor. For their Initial Drill during the fifth week of boot camp, the platoon had performed terribly. As the heavy hat, Amy had taught the recruits drill, but they had tested with Staff Sergeant Wood, and since her cadence and pace were so different from Amy's, the platoon failed.

Whatever the reason, they had embarrassed their drill instructors and would pay for it.

"Don't worry, 'Thirty-eight," Amy told them, as the platoon marched back to the squad bay that day. "I got you. I got you. No, really, 'Thirty-eight, I got you."

The recruits knew what was in store. Outside the squad bay, they took off their blouses and got in the pit for push-ups.

"You've ruined my reputation!" said Amy, who was known for high drill scores on the island.

Recruit Wilson and a few others who had failed miserably put in extra push-ups in the pit, then joined the other recruits in the squad bay.

But on this November night all was calm. Although they weren't Marines yet, the recruits could feel that goal within their grasp, like the promise of summer during the last week of school.

"Who knows how to spin a rifle?" Amy asked as the silent drill video continued to play. A few recruits got up and tried.

"Do you want to see me drill?" Amy asked.

"Yes, ma'am!"

Amy grabbed a rifle and started performing some of the same moves as the video drill platoon. The recruits were as giddy as little girls.

They clapped loudly, and Amy turned around so they wouldn't see the smile spreading across her face. But in classic Sergeant Stokley style, she turned back around and went into the DI hut, slammed the door shut, and screamed, *"Shut up, 'Thirty-eight!"*

The next morning before Final Drill, the platoon was nervous and excited.

"Remember who you are," Amy said, to calm everyone down. The recruits ironed their cammies, tightly rolled up their sleeves, and made sure their hair was perfect.

Amy took out her perfume and sprayed each recruit on the back of her neck.

Now they were ready.

December 3, Graduation Day

"Wilson, can you hear me, Wilson?" Amy whispered as Platoon '38 waited to march onto Peatross Parade Deck for the graduation ceremony. It was fifteen minutes before nine on a bright, chilly Friday morning.

Amy continued to joke with the newly minted Private Wilson, kicking her in the back of the knees to try to make her fall. Wilson was in the fourth squad, directly in front of Amy.

"Wilson, can you hear me, Wilson?" she whispered in her ear.

"Yes, Sergeant," Wilson said, barely keeping her military bearing.

"Hit Saucedo's bun!" Amy whispered. Private Saucedo stood in front of Wilson, and Wilson gave Saucedo's hair bun a good whack. Soon they were all issuing "bun checks," whopping one another.

The previous week, members of Platoon '38 had officially earned the title of U.S. Marine after the grueling fifty-four-hour crucible, a test of courage at boot camp that starts at two a.m. and involves forty miles of marching with forty-five pounds of gear, eight hours of sleep, three MRE meals, and twenty-nine problem-solving situations that test teamwork and leadership.

Afterward, exhausted, dirty, and blistered, the women stood on the yellow footprints outside the Receiving Building, where their journey had begun three months ago. While the Emblem Ceremony was usually held at the depot's replica of the Iwo Jima statue, that spot was taken by another unit's graduation ceremony, which had been moved up because of the Thanksgiving holiday.

"Congratulations," Amy said, shaking Andrea Castillo's hand and placing in her palm the EGA (Eagle, Globe, and Anchor) emblem. "Welcome to the Corps, Marine."

Tears rolled down Castillo's cheeks. It was the first time any of the women had shaken Amy's hand or looked her in the eyes.

Now it was graduation day. It was forty-four degrees, cold for the island, but the women were so pumped they barely noticed. Plus they were dressed in their wool service Alpha uniforms topped off with their bucket hats. That morning, Amy had helped the women with their hair and uniforms. Then she offered up one last piece of advice.

"Hold yourself high. Remember who you are," she said, with hands, as always, planted on her hips. "Don't forget what you've learned. When you get out to the fleet, observe for the first couple of weeks before you pick your friends. Be careful who you follow, so you don't get caught up in the wrong crowd. And don't get pregnant or be a slut."

"Aye, ma'am!"

It was important to Amy that they hold themselves high, not only as Marines but also as women. Women with courage, confidence, and character.

"Forward! March!" And with that, Platoon 4038 quick-timed onto the parade deck.

Nine days later

Through the walls of the DI hut, Amy could hear her company and series commanders giving their speeches to the latest cycle of recruits, Platoon 4009. Recruits who attended boot camp in the winter months had a reputation on the island for being lazy, since they'd been sitting around since high school graduation the previous summer.

Around her tightly cinched waist, Amy wore a black leather sword belt with a gold buckle that set her apart as a senior drill instructor. She'd made sure that her black watchband, a Baby-G, was a perfect match.

Amy was filled with nerves, as she and her two drill instructors waited to be announced.

As senior DI, she was the first in the recruits' chain of command, responsible for their well-being. She also knew that the drill instructors who worked for her would put in a lot more heart and be effective if she took care of them.

But as she stepped out on the deck, her nervousness receded like Parris Island's evening tide. With all the recruits sitting on the deck, legs folded, the three drill instructors recited the DI pledge after the company commander. Then Platoon 4009 was turned over to Amy for her "pickup speech."

"My name is Sergeant Stokley, and I am your senior drill instructor. I am assisted in my duties by Drill Instructor Sergeant Melendez and Drill Instructor Sergeant Cerda. Our mission is to train each one of you to become a United States Marine. A Marine is characterized as one who possesses the highest in military virtues. She obeys all orders, respects her seniors, and strives constantly to be the best at everything that she does. Discipline and spirit are the hallmarks of a Marine. Each one of you can become a Marine if you develop discipline and spirit. We will give every effort to train you, even after you have given up on yourself. Starting now you will treat me and all other Marines with the highest respect, for we have earned our place as Marines and will accept nothing less than that from you. We will treat you as we do our fellow Marines, with firmness, fairness, and dignity.

"Now that I have told you what my drill instructors and I will do, from you we demand the following: You must give one hundred percent of yourself at all times, obey all orders quickly, willingly, and without question. You will not physically abuse or verbally threaten another Marine or recruit. Be completely honest in everything that you do. A Marine never lies or cheats. Respect the rights and properties of all others. A Marine never steals. You must work hard to strengthen your body, your spirit, and your mind. Be proud of yourself and the uniform you now wear. Above all else, never quit or give up. For we offer you the challenge of recruit training and the opportunity to earn the title *United States Marine.*"

2011

The Arab Spring, a wave of revolution marked with protests and demonstrations across several Arab nations, includes the fall of corrupt regimes in Tunisia, Egypt, and Libya.

On May 2, Navy SEALs kill Osama bin Laden during a raid in Pakistan.

In September, the repeal of "Don't Ask, Don't Tell" goes into effect.

By the end of 2011, after eight years in Iraq, the war draws to a close.

A decade of war in Afghanistan continues.

CHAPTER 26
The Iron Major

Candice: March 2011. Kabul, Afghanistan

Candice often toiled until midnight, since she didn't want to go back to the quiet of her room to sit and think. Luckily there was plenty of work to be done on the AfPak border plan, a NATO initiative to neutralize the troublesome regions that straddled the borders of Afghanistan and Pakistan, where terrorists trained and insurgents incubated violent plots. With the elections over, the political aspects of the border issues, as well as how to get the Afghan and Pakistan militaries to work together, were Candice's latest focus as the lead planner for future operations. Nine months into her deployment, Candice continued to perform at 100 percent go time. These were days of action and decisiveness, and Candice pushed herself, as always, to exceed standards.

Turnout for the parliamentary elections, which had consumed Candice's time over the summer and early fall, was lighter than hoped. But then, pulling off a democratic-style election in a country once controlled by the Taliban, and now at war, was no simple task. Defining any kind of success in Afghanistan was always complex, but the parliamentary elections had gone off with no sensational or high-profile incidents, despite threats from the Taliban and 610 enemy-initiated attacks that killed fourteen people. Of the 10 million eligible to vote, 4.3 million did so, including 1.4 million women.

With the exception of Lieutenant Colonel Dubois, Candice had a great elections crew. Working on a plan and seeing it through was rewarding. She found great humor in the fact that three of the lead planners and executors tracking the elections were female. If only the Afghans knew who put together the military side of support for the elections!

Working on border crossing points and the legitimization of illicit trade in those regions was Candice's latest challenge, as evidenced by her presence in the empty plans room at the late hour.

The silence was interrupted by the appearance of Major Felix Anderson, a Brit who had been working alongside Candice for about a month. "How was your leave?" he asked. Candice had returned three days earlier from two weeks of leave, which is authorized to soldiers who serve in combat zones for twelve months or more.

"The kids were great," Candice said, sipping Diet Coke. Large quantities of the soda could be hard to come by, and as a Diet Coke addict, Candice always stashed a row of them under her desk for late-night pick-me-ups.

"And you finally got to see your husband," Felix said with a wink and a raised eyebrow.

"Yeah, it was okay," Candice said, ignoring his implication.

"Okay? That's it? You're deployed a year, and you're not at each other like rabbits? What's wrong with you?"

Candice narrowed her eyes. "Don't go there."

Felix took that in. "So, admit it," he said. "Admit the problems. Admit your marriage is falling apart."

"My life is complicated, and it's not your business," Candice said.

"Fair enough, but you never smile," Felix said. "You spend so much time studying transparency and countercorruption, and I can see right through you. You're on the receiving end of constant insults, aren't you? You don't even recognize the neglect."

"Fuck you," Candice said. "You don't have the right to pry."

Candice couldn't believe she was having such a conversation. She got up to walk away.

"Just sit and listen," Felix said. "Calm down."

"Maybe my marriage isn't working," Candice said, "but how the hell can you figure out everything that's wrong in my life?"

Felix chose his words carefully. "Because I know about abuse," he said. "I can see it. I'm just saying that you're an amazing woman. You give so much to everyone around you but yourself."

Candice fell silent.

Later, as she walked back to her room, she replayed the conversation over and over in her head. His observations chilled her. No one had ever considered her a victim, least of all herself. Candice hadn't really shared her personal life with anyone, but she had known for a long time that something wasn't right. She'd seen men who missed their wives so much they almost pined for them. She could recognize the love her friends had for their spouses. Candice didn't have that, and now a too-perceptive colleague was calling her out on it.

The next morning, after a run and a shower, Candice had a few minutes to Skype with Will and the kids. Skyping had been a wonderful way to keep in contact. Technology allowed Candice to witness the kids opening their presents on Christmas morning. When Kate saw her package of eight fairy dolls, she said, "Doesn't Santa know I like Scooby-Doo?" Then she looked at the dolls and wondered, "Where's the boy one?"

Tom did a little dance when he opened his red-framed, gray-screened Etch A Sketch and called it a "sketch-a-sketch." Candice felt blessed to spend forty-five minutes with them on what is normally a somber holiday for deployed soldiers.

But this morning's Skype session did not go as well.

Kate immediately started to cry, which was happening more frequently. If Kate wasn't crying, she was sullen and quiet.

"It's okay, Kate. What's wrong?" Candice said, trying to stroke her daughter with her voice. But Kate just kept crying.

We're Frost women, Candice thought, referring to her maiden name. *We're not quiet.*

But she knew something wasn't right. She feared that her daughter's tears and sullenness were signs of depression. She urged Will to take Kate to a family therapist on post.

But Will's response was always the same: Kate was a smart little girl. She was manipulative. She was putting on an act.

Candice never believed that. She saw a little girl aching to be held by her mother. For the first time, Candice understood the deployment through Kate's eyes, and it was a crushing sight.

So Candice e-mailed often and called home at the same time every day to keep in touch. Will, though, interpreted this as Candice checking up on him and trying to control the home front from far away. He was tired of taking her constant written guidance and having to issue a verbal report every day at thirteen hundred, regardless of his convenience.

Before deploying, Candice had asked Will to send her a photo each day of the kids, as she had done for him when he was in Iraq. Will resented the pressure—if he didn't send a picture every day, he was a bad dad and a bad husband. If he sent a picture and Kate wasn't smiling, Candice would suggest that Kate should go to therapy or live with Candice's parents. In the end, she was lucky to get a picture once a week.

At the moment, though, she had a Skype image of a crying daughter in front of her. "Kate, it's going to be okay, honey."

Kate responded by crying harder. "Maa-meee!"

Several minutes into Kate's meltdown, Will rolled his eyes.

"She's putting on a show, Candice." Then he disappeared from the computer screen and walked out of the room.

The professional, efficient side of Candice—bam, bam, bam, execute—which had served her so well in the Army and in Afghanistan, did not apply to a miserable child seven thousand miles away. Candice couldn't do anything to make it better; she felt completely helpless.

Seeing Will walk away set something off in Candice.

I can take it. I'm callous, she thought. *But here's a four-year-old. . . .* Candice had had enough.

★

April 18, 2011

As she walked along a brick path on the base, Candice called Will several hours earlier than usual. It was eight p.m., and as she waited for the call to go through, it felt like her heart was beating outside of her chest.

With Candice returning home in two months, Will had let her know a few days earlier that he'd scheduled a consultation for a vasectomy. Candice had been pushing him to make the appointment ever since Tom was born. Although it was a common enough procedure among military men with established families, Will was understandably reluctant. But Candice kept telling him she didn't want any more children, and it was time for her to get off birth control.

"Hello?" Will said, answering the phone.

"Don't get the vasectomy," she blurted out. "Will, this is really hard. This isn't working. Our marriage is broken. I want a divorce."

"What? How can you say that?" Will said.

"It's been a death by a thousand cuts, and I'm bled dry," Candice said. "I can no longer go on trying to fix something that is inexorably broken."

She could hear Will's voice break. "What do you mean?" he said.

"This isn't easy for me to say, but I'm not going to just spring it on you when I return," Candice said. "I wanted you to know now that I'm going to file for divorce when I get back."

"Can't we go to counseling?" Will said. "Can't you wait until you get back?"

Candice knew they'd tried that before. It always came around to Will's talking about *his* problems and *his* life, "him and he" instead of "us and we."

"Are you a hundred percent sure?" Will asked.

"I am ninety-nine percent sure that this is what I really want," Candice said.

"Then I will hold on to that one percent. I'll change."

"You can't change the past, Will. Your PTSD just overtook our lives," Candice said. "I cannot live the life of a victim anymore."

"But I'm better now," Will said. "I've gone to counseling; I'm taking medication. What more can you ask?"

"I want a husband who loves me and cares about me and is part of a team with me," Candice said. "It's such a heavy load that I've got to give this up. I want a divorce. I wanted you to hear it from me."

After hanging up, Candice realized she was shaking. She knew she had a long road ahead, yet she finally felt a sense of lightness.

I am done having to worry about every little thing, she told herself as she walked back to her office. *I am done hiding so much of my life. I am making decisions about what I want. I love myself more than I do our marriage. I love my children enough to know that some things are not going right with my daughter right now.*

Back in Missouri, Will felt as if he were going to throw up. Candice had sounded serious about the divorce. He realized they'd been through some really hard times the last five or six years, most of them his fault. *But I refuse to allow my family to become another statistic,* he told himself. He would fight to save his marriage. *We've given so much to this nation and this war, but I refuse to sacrifice my family and the woman I truly love to its effects.*

Will was going to hang on to that 1 percent.

The following day he e-mailed Candice with a plea for one more chance. His message was heartfelt, but Candice had heard it all before. She had had enough to last a lifetime and was ready to start savoring life again. The year alone helped her see that. She felt immensely sad, but still she couldn't give way to the emotions that threatened to overwhelm her. She was, after all, one of the Army's Iron Majors.

"When do I get to cry?" Candice whispered to herself. "When am I allowed to cry?"

June 18, 2011

The sunflowers that lined the farmers' fields just beyond the base's T-walls were in full, fiery bloom, and dusk brought the trill of crickets to Kabul. It was as if nature were beckoning Candice home.

Dressed in a fresh set of ACUs, Candice finished packing her duffel bag. The wall above the desk, which had always been dressed with crayon drawings and smiling faces, now looked threadbare. It was difficult for Candice to face her departure. Her final day in Afghanistan lacked the elation it held for others, who were aching to reunite with their families. Candice was bursting to hold her children, to become a mother again, but she knew that she'd no longer be a wife.

"I have a huge mountain to climb as soon as I get home," she told her dad earlier that day.

"You already climbed the mountain, and now it's time to come down," he said.

Candice thought about that as she looked around her room. The irony, as any climber knows, is that the descent is often significantly harder, because you're tired and it's a killer on the knees. And Candice was coming down much faster than she or anyone expected.

She'd be home in a matter of days. Traveling military style meant it could take a few days or a week to reach the golden ground of the United States. The route ahead: Kabul to Kuwait, then Germany for aircraft refueling. Next Shannon, Ireland, for a change of crew. Then Atlanta and a bus ride to Fort Benning for an overnight stop to out-process at the Combat Readiness Center, and finally on to Kansas City, where Kate, Tom, and Will's mother would greet her at the airport.

Will was in Arizona, signing for quarters and unpacking their household goods. Candice had received orders in March to be a battalion executive officer at Fort Huachuca, a historic Army post that dates back to the Indian Wars of the 1870s. Will had volunteered to go ahead and get the house settled. He still clung to a hope of reconciliation, though Candice had every intention of filing for divorce in Arizona.

Facing Will weighed heaviest on her mind. Candice knew he was a good father who truly loved his children. He was devoted to ensuring that his family was protected and safe. Despite his shortcomings, he was always trustworthy and honest and could provide Candice with great comic relief from the daily grind.

But those attributes weren't enough to save her marriage. Candice wanted to live life, not just endure it.

For her work in Afghanistan the military awarded Candice the Defense Meritorious Service Medal and two one-blocks—the Army's equivalent to A-pluses—on her Officer Efficiency Report, for a job well-done.

Candice was sure of her place in the Army and her life ahead, her choices weighed and decisions made. She was on her way.

She zipped her duffel bag, hoisted it over her shoulder, grabbed her backpack, and took one final look at the room that had served as a home away from home. Then she walked out the door.

EPILOGUE

★ As I write this, I've just learned of the recent deaths of six MPs from the 978th Military Police Company in Afghanistan when their armored vehicle struck an IED. Except for their squad leader, who was thirty-one, none of the soldiers was older than twenty-one. And none of the headlines or stories highlighted the fact that one of the six killed was a woman. Her name was simply listed with the others—a tragic example that reflects the changes in social attitudes on gender and the military that often come with—and are accelerated by—war.

The wars in Iraq and Afghanistan over the last dozen years have been the backdrop for the stories of the four women profiled in this book, shaping many of the events that touched them and coloring their decisions. But those conflicts are not the whole story. The women's broader experiences in their military careers, and the issues they raise, will only continue to grow in importance in the years ahead, long after U.S. troops have returned home.

Of course, the wounds, both visible and invisible, are paramount. Bergan's combat injuries are representative of what the Department of Veterans Affairs 2012 Women Veterans Task Force Report found: Women are sustaining similar injuries and wounds to male troops in both their "severity and complexity." This is a tangible reminder of the dangers today's women face in modern wars that have no front lines.

VA secretary Eric Shinseki formed the Women Veterans Task Force because of the "rapid growth" of the female veteran population. Women make up 1.8 million (8 percent) of the 22.2 million U.S. veterans. And while the male veteran population is expected to decrease by 4 million by 2020, women veterans are projected to grow by 2.7 percent, making them 10.7 percent of the veteran population by 2020.

Meanwhile, VA medical centers and clinics across the country, long known for treating an aging male population, are scrambling to improve care and services for a changing demographic in the areas of health care, rehabilitation, outreach, benefits, and compensation claims. Some 56 percent of female Iraq and Afghanistan veterans have used the VA for health care, and almost half are younger than thirty.

The problems these women face can be different from those men face. One in five seen at the VA respond "yes" when screened for military sexual trauma, which now has its own acronym at the VA (MST) and covers sexual harassment and assault during military service. PTSD is one of the top medical reasons women veterans seek care at the VA, yet how PTSD affects women and can best be treated is still being studied.

With women now making up 14.5 percent of the 1.4 million active-duty forces, the issues of marriage and motherhood for service members loom ever larger. About half of all service members are married, and half of the married servicewomen are married to a fellow service member. In contrast, only 10 percent of servicemen are married to servicewomen. If the question "Can women have it all?" commands attention in the civilian world today, it resonates even more for those who have to balance personal goals and childbearing opportunities with a career where duty and the mission must come first. Success in the military and success on the home front may mean two very different things.

Candice O'Brien was one who took on marriage, motherhood, and the military; when her marriage ended in divorce, she was not alone. Servicewomen are more than twice as likely to end up divorced as are married servicemen, and enlisted women are three times as likely to divorce, according to a research study that made headlines in 2011. Almost 8 percent of married servicewomen divorce, compared to 3 percent of servicemen, who are below the national divorce rate of 3.5 percent.

Why the disparity in divorce rates? I can only surmise, but military women are outside the norm for traditional gender roles, and the societal pressures placed on them as mothers and wives could be a factor, along with demanding jobs and the stress of deployments and other separations.

Sergeant Amy Stokley's story raises an important issue most service-women don't talk about openly: Can one be feminine and still maintain a military bearing? What are the unspoken rules? Is there a proper balance? Does womanliness interfere with respect and professionalism? These are questions outside the realm of military regulations that govern lipstick shades and nail length. Examples are plentiful throughout the book. Candice deploys with her curling iron, Amy sprays perfume on the necks of her recruits before final drill, Bergan wears a dress instead of a uniform to Norwich's ball, and Angie is known for her "hair-dryer taskers." And while these may seem like casual details, they have to do with deeper issues of identity.

Amy put it bluntly: "We are Marines and we are women—not men." The takeaway lesson? Being a strong woman is not a masculine trait.

No military woman—or man—wants to be labeled as "weak," a general term in the military used to describe one's overall performance, whether in PT, leadership, military bearing, or the ability to accomplish tasks. Successful servicewomen, who are very conscious about how they are perceived, are more likely to persevere through pain, underemphasize the severity of their medical issues, and delay treatment because they are task- and mission-focused and don't want to appear weak.

Major General Angela Salinas's story of living with debilitating pain and keeping it to herself is representative of servicewomen of her caliber. We see it in the other subjects of this book as well: Bergan insists she would be standing and walking by the time her troops came home, Amy lets her guard down only behind a bathroom stall door, and Candice pushes herself to the point of physical exhaustion, fully committed to being a wife, mother, and officer.

These women are the best of the best, which begs a different question: How likely are other women, like Major General Salinas, to achieve flag rank? Today women make up only about 7 percent of the general and flag officer ranks and close to 11 percent of the senior enlisted ranks, according to Pentagon statistics. The vast majority of generals—80 percent—come from the combat arms, where women are still banned from serving.

Yet, as the first woman to hold a number of key positions in the Marine Corps, a branch that prides itself on its warrior culture, Angie has spent her career in places she was not always wanted. If women are eventually allowed to serve in the combat arms, they will likely face similar challenges that come with being "the first." This makes the bond between her and Sergeant Major Bobby Woods all the more remarkable—and hopeful—for up-and-coming female commanders in predominantly male units.

★

Doing and achieving brings the one constant in military lives: change. Each of the four servicewomen I followed in this book has continued on her personal and professional journey.

Major General Angela Salinas still serves as the director of the Manpower Management Division, Manpower and Reserve Affairs, at Marine headquarters in Quantico, Virginia. She continues to receive invitations to speak at events ranging from women's leadership conferences to diversity celebrations, including those at the National Character and Leadership Symposium at the Air Force Academy, the Department of Veterans Affairs, and the Ronald Reagan Library. Angie was also the recipient of the 2012 Soldiers, Sailors, Marines, Coast Guard, and Airmen's Club Distinguished Military Leadership Award.

First Lieutenant Bergan Flannigan, after welcoming her soldiers home from Afghanistan in July 2010, endured a number of medical setbacks, which resulted in a total of twenty surgeries and delayed her release from Walter Reed until December 2011. During her rehabilitation, Bergan was promoted to the rank of captain on July 1, 2011, and was able to compete in the hand-cycle category in the 2010 Army Ten-Miler; despite little training, she was the second woman to finish. From January through June 2012, Bergan and her husband, Tom, attended the Military Police Captains' Career Course at Fort Leonard Wood, Missouri, and in August they reported for duty in Hawaii, where she serves with headquarters, U.S. Pacific Command. Bergan hopes to deploy again.

Sergeant Amy Stokley served ten cycles as a drill instructor, including three as a senior drill instructor at Parris Island. She was meritoriously promoted to the rank of staff sergeant in July 2011, an achievement bestowed on less than 1 percent of sergeants. She graduated her last platoon in October 2011. At Parris Island, Amy began dating a fellow drill instructor, and they were subsequently both assigned to Camp Lejeune, North Carolina, but he died prematurely in 2012. Amy currently serves with the 2nd Marine Division as a section leader in a truck company, and her ultimate goal is to serve as a sergeant major.

One month after her return from Afghanistan in June 2011, Major Candice O'Brien filed for marital separation. Her divorce was final eight months later, and she was granted primary physical custody of her two children. Candice—who has since resumed her maiden name, Frost—served as the operations officer in the 304th Military Intelligence Battalion at Fort Huachuca, Arizona, for one year and was selected for promotion below the zone to lieutenant colonel in July 2012. She started her new job at the Army Human Resources Command, Fort Knox, Kentucky, in August 2012.

And for women in the armed forces generally, change is definitely coming—possibly faster that one might have thought.

Who could have imagined, for example, the rapid developments due to the repeal in 2011 of the "Don't Ask, Don't Tell" policy, which prohibited gays and lesbians from serving openly in the military? By 2012 the Pentagon had announced June as gay pride month.

The biggest question is: Can women reach their full potential in the military? At the moment, in the Air Force, 99 percent of jobs are open to women, 88 percent in the Navy, 68 percent in the Marine Corps, and 66 percent in the Army. In 2011, Congress directed the Pentagon to review policies that restrict military women from career opportunities and advancement. And in February 2012, the Defense Department stated in a report that it is "committed to removing all barriers that would prevent service members from rising to the highest level of responsibility that their talents and capabilities warrant."

As part of that report, the Pentagon eased some of its assignment policies, officially allowing women to be closer to combat. More than 14,000 positions, mostly Army jobs and assignments, were opened to women. In doing so, the Pentagon did away with an outdated 1994 combat exclusion policy that had barred servicewomen from certain jobs, such as tank mechanic and field artillery radar operator, because of their close proximity to combat units. In any case, the old policy did not fit the realities of asymmetric fighting in Iraq and Afghanistan, where women assigned to transportation, military police, and other "support" units found themselves at the front in a new kind of warfare.

The changes also allowed women already serving as intelligence, signal, or logistics officers to be formally assigned to combat battalions, places they had successfully been all along in Iraq and Afghanistan, due to a policy loophole that "attached" the women to the units. Female soldiers had even started deploying with Special Forces and Ranger units to Afghanistan on "cultural support teams" to engage women and children. Throughout more than a decade of war these servicewomen had not only been needed but, in the case of female officers in infantry divisions, also wanted by battalion commanders who wanted to be able to choose from the best pool of officers, regardless of gender.

Critics see these policy revisions and adjustments as not going far enough, but the 2012 policy will likely pave the way for more in the future.

The first group of women lieutenants began attending the Marine Infantry Officer Course at Quantico in September of 2012 as part of a larger study examining the practicability of women serving in broader roles in the corps. Meanwhile, the Army's top leadership is looking at allowing women to go to Ranger School and at the feasibility of allowing women to join the infantry and armor branches. After a decade of war, the Army is designing body armor for women.

What the future truly holds for women in uniform is yet to be determined. What is certain is that women in the military will continue to grab headlines for some time to come.

When I began this project, I set out to write about a few good women and their place in military life. I came away with a deeper admiration and respect for them—not least for how they, undaunted, are paving the way for the thousands of others who will come after them.

GLOSSARY

ACU—Advanced Combat Uniform

A-DRIVER—assistant driver

ANP—Afghan National Police

BELOW THE ZONE—selected for promotion one year ahead of an Army officer's year group

BEQ—Bachelor Enlisted Quarters

BERTHING—sleeping quarters on a ship

BLASTING—yelling

BLOCK LEAVE—a specific time period when service members in a unit take vacation over the same general dates

BLOUSE—top to the combat uniform

BOQ—Bachelor Officers Quarters

CAMMIES—Marine digital camouflage uniform

CG—commanding general

CGSC—Command and General Staff College

CIVVIES—civilian dress

CLASS A—the Army green service uniform, replaced in 2008 by the blue Army Service Uniform (ASU), with full implementation by 2015

COMBAT ACTION RIBBON—awarded by the Navy, Marine Corps, and Coast Guard for active engagement in ground combat with the enemy

COVER—military hat

DEEP SELECTION—when a below-the-promotion-zone Marine Corps officer is selected for promotion ahead of peers

DI—drill instructor

DOC—familiar term for a medic

DUAL MILITARY—both husband and wife are active-duty military

EGA—Eagle, Globe, and Anchor: emblem and insignia of the Marine Corps

FLEET, THE—Fleet Marine Force

FOB—Forward Operating Base

G2—division intelligence officer

HEAD—Marine Corps and Navy slang for toilet

HOSPITAL CORPSMAN 2ND CLASS—an enlisted Navy medical specialist (E-5)

IED—Improvised Explosive Device

IJC—International Security Assistance Force Joint Command

ILE—Intermediate Level Education

INCENTIVE TRAINING—physical exercise punishment, considered a physical training tool used by Marine Corps drill instructors at boot camp to instill discipline

IRON MAJOR—Army expression for officers in the rank of major who carry the workload

JEDI KNIGHT—nickname for SAMS graduates

KAF—Kandahar Airfield, Afghanistan

KILL ZONE—an area of terrain where direct and indirect fires are concentrated in order to kill troops

LANCE CORPORAL—E-3 in the Marine Corps; above the rank of private first class and below corporal

LCAC—Landing Craft Air Cushion; an armored ship-to-shore Navy hovercraft

MCRD—Marine Corps Recruit Depot

MEDEVAC—medical evacuation

MEU—Marine Expeditionary Force

MIRPS—Modified Improved Reserve Parachute System

MOTOR POOL—a designated area to secure and perform maintenance on military vehicles

MRAP—Mine Resistant Ambush Protected; armored fighting vehicle

MRE—Meals Ready-to-Eat

MTVR—Medium Tactical Vehicle Replacement

O-CLUB—officers' club

OSCAR MIKE—radio shorthand for "on the move"

PITS, THE—Sand pits, used for "Incentive Training"

PLF—Parachute Landing Fall

PME—Professional Military Education

POV—Privately Owned Vehicle

PT—physical training

PURPLE HEART—heart-shaped medal awarded to service members wounded or killed in action

PX—Post Exchange, a store on a military installation

RACK—bed

REAR-D—rear detachment

ROOK—name for first-year cadets at Norwich University

SAMS—School of Advanced Military Studies

SAW—Squad Automatic Weapon

SERVICE BRAVOS—a khaki Marine service uniform, long sleeves

SERVICE CHARLIES—a khaki Marine service uniform, short sleeves

SHOP—unit section office

SMOKING SPONSON—a balconylike projection on the side of a ship designated as a smoking area; also referred to as the smoke pit

SOI—School of Infantry

TOC—Tactical Operation Command

UP—pronounced U.P., Upper Parade Ground at Norwich University

USDB—U.S. Disciplinary Barracks

XO—executive officer

YEAR GROUP—year Army officers enter active-duty service

ACKNOWLEDGMENTS

In the military, where a game face is standard issue, I have a tremendous amount of gratitude to the four active-duty servicewomen who shared their personal lives with me.

Telling their stories on a deadline came with challenges—deployments, surgeries, booked calendars, and hectic work schedules often left them little time for a writer with too many questions. I thank each of them for their commitment to this project.

Special thanks to my agent, Rafe Sagalyn, for his guidance, vision, and support. Thanks, also, to his assistant, Shannon O'Neill.

I'm grateful to Mark Chait, my editor at NAL Caliber for his interest in the project, support, and patience. Mark's careful and thoughtful review of the manuscript encouraged and challenged me to think in ways that strengthened the book. Many thanks, too, to my editor at NAL Caliber, Brent Howard, for his enthusiasm in seeing the project through.

Book writing can be a lonely and difficult road. I'm glad to have shared the journey with my editor, friend, and confidante Joan Tapper, whose skills as an editor are evident throughout the pages of this book.

The careful copyedit by Tiffany Yates is much appreciated.

Many thanks to the following people from the military community who gave me their time as I researched this book: Andy Masslofsky, Jason

Schwarzkopf, Daniel Bennett, CJ Summers, Dina Williams, Meghan Kiser, Bobby Woods, Rick Huenefeld, Sarah Wilson, and Chad Craven.

A special thank-you to Bergan Flannigan's soldiers, especially, Jacob Beebe, Paul Torres, Aaron Thomas, and Jeremy Newman.

The important role parents play in the lives of their servicewomen daughters was evident as I wrote this book. Thank you to each of them, especially Amy Arsenault and Diana Neeley Henry, who filled in many gaps.

Finally, I thank my family. Writing a book is often compared to birthing a baby. In my case it took on a literal meaning. I found out I was pregnant a month after receiving a book contract and deadline. Throw in two military moves and it was quite a year. A big thank-you to my dedicated parents, Sam and Pat, for traveling many miles on many occasions to babysit their grandchildren, Jack and Violet. Most of all, thank you to my husband, Michael, who took care of the home front while I wrote.

INDEX